# Domestic Architecture and Power

## The Historical Archaeology of Colonial Ecuador

# CONTRIBUTIONS TO GLOBAL HISTORICAL ARCHAEOLOGY

Series Editor:
**Charles E. Orser, Jr.**, *Illinois State University, Normal, Illinois*

A HISTORICAL ARCHAEOLOGY OF THE MODERN WORLD
Charles E. Orser, Jr.

AN ARCHAEOLOGY OF MANNERS: The Polite World of the Merchant
Elite of Colonial Massachusetts
Lorinda B. R. Goodwin

AN ARCHAEOLOGY OF SOCIAL SPACE: Analyzing Coffee Plantations
in Jamaica's Blue Mountains
James A. Delle

BETWEEN ARTIFACTS AND TEXTS: Historical Archaeology in Global
Perspective
Anders Andrén

DOMESTIC ARCHITECTURE AND POWER: The Historical Archaeology
of Colonial Ecuador
Ross W. Jamieson

HISTORICAL ARCHAEOLOGIES OF CAPITALISM
Edited by Mark P. Leone and Parker B. Potter, Jr.

THE HISTORICAL ARCHAEOLOGY OF BUENOS AIRES: A City
at the End of the World
Daniel Schávelzon

LANDSCAPE TRANSFORMATIONS AND THE ARCHAEOLOGY OF
IMPACT: Social Disruption and State Formation in Southern Africa
Warren R. Perry

MEANING AND IDEOLOGY IN HISTORICAL ARCHAEOLOGY: Style,
Social Identity, and Capitalism in an Australian Town
Heather Burke

RACE AND AFFLUENCE: An Archaeology of African America and
Consumer Culture
Paul R. Mullins

A Continuation Order Plan is available for this series. A continuation order will bring delivery of each new volume immediately upon publication. Volumes are billed only upon actual shipment. For further information please contact the publisher.

# Domestic Architecture and Power

## The Historical Archaeology of Colonial Ecuador

### Ross W. Jamieson

*Trent University*
*Peterborough, Ontario, Canada*

Kluwer Academic/Plenum Publishers
New York, Boston, Dordrecht, London, Moscow

**Library of Congress Cataloging-in-Publication Data**

Jamieson Ross W. (Ross William), 1966–
    Domestic architecture and power: the historical archaeology of colonial Ecuador/Ross
W. Jamieson
    p.   cm. — (Contributions to global historical archaeology)
Includes bibliographical references and index.
ISBN 0-306-46176-5
    1. Cuenca (Ecuador)—History.   2. Architecture, Domestic—Ecuador—Cuenca.   3.
Excavations (Archaeology)—Ecuador—Cuenca.   4. Cuenca (Ecuador)—Social life and
customs.   5. Material culture—Ecuador—Cuenca.   I. Title.   II. Series.

P3791.C9 J36 1999
986.6'24—dc21                                                                          99-406707

ISBN: 0-306-46176-5

©2000 Kluwer Academic/Plenum Publishers
233 Spring Street, New York, N.Y. 10013

http://www.wkap.nl/

10  9  8  7  6  5  4  3  2  1

A C.I.P. record for this book is available from the Library of Congress

Printed in the United States of America

For Laurie, who makes it all worth doing

# Foreword $\square$

Historical archaeology, one of the fastest growing of archaeology's sub-fields in North America, has developed more slowly in Central and particularly South America. Happily, this circumstance is ending as a growing number of recent projects are successfully integrating textual and material culture data in studies of the events and processes of the last 500 years. This interval and this region—often called Ibero-America—have been studied for a century or more by historians with traditional perspectives and emphases focusing on colonial elites and large-scale politico-economic events. Such inclinations fit well into world-system and other core-periphery models that have had a major impact on historical thought since the 1970s. Over the past 20 years or so, however, world-system models have come under fire from historians, anthropologists, and others, in part because the emphasis on global trends and the growth of capitalism denies the importance of understanding variability in local histories and circumstances. Historians have increasingly turned their attention to local, rural, and domestic contexts, thereby illuminating the great diversity of responses to colonial domination that were played out in the vast arena of the Americas.

It is not coincidental that this is the intellectual climate in which historical archaeology is establishing itself in Central and South America. Nor is it coincidental that these themes of rural diversity and exercise of social power are emphasized in Ross Jamieson's pioneering archaeological study of the architecture and material culture of colonial-period Cuenca, in the southern highlands of Ecuador. As he points out (p.157), there are no other published analyses of colonial urban domestic sites in Ecuador; what is known of the archaeology and material culture of the period has come from work at religious sites.

In his study, Jamieson follows the well-known model of "backyard archaeology" proposed by the late Charles Fairbanks and commonly practiced by historical archaeologists in the southeastern United States. This approach focuses on domestic adaptations to the colonial situation in both rural and urban contexts, and facilitates research questions involving household economies, social and gender relations, ethnicity, and many other issues. Here, Jamieson is particularly interested in the ways houses and artifacts (including clothing, furniture, and pottery) participate in the negotiation of relations of social power and in the creation and subsequent reification of categories such as urban/rural, elite/poor, men/women, and Andean/Spanish.

Jamieson's investigation underscores the many ways in which architecture and domestic objects reproduced the institutions of Spanish colonialism and control. With respect to architecture, a prime example is the gridiron town plan with its open plaza surrounded by public buildings, and the urban house plan with its inner courtyard and exterior balconies. These patterns, with their structured dialectic between visibility and privacy, allowed elites to monitor others' activities while maintaining their own domestic insularity. Material culture, particularly that associated with formal meals, such as individual chairs, silver serving items, and eating utensils, provides insight into the complex dualities of urban and rural, elite and commoner, and Andean and Spanish. In particular, Jamieson argues that the presence of these items points to a re-negotiation of power relationships within the household as well as a growing emphasis on "an ideology of individualism" in the mercantile capitalist economy.

This is a fascinating study, illuminating details of domestic life in a small corner of Ibero-America and firmly establishing their relevance within the broader context of discourse on power relations in the colonial experience. Jamieson has made an important contribution to historical archaeology in the Americas.

PRUDENCE M. RICE
*Southern Illinois University*
*Carbondale, Illinois*

# Preface

The city of Cuenca, in the southern highlands of Ecuador, was succes-
sively a Cañari and an Inka center before it officially became a Spanish
town in 1557. In 1821 the town and its surrounding countryside became
part of the newly formed Republic of New Granada, and eventually a part
of the nation of Ecuador. Thus, for almost three hundred years, from the
sixteenth to the early nineteenth centuries, the town was a part of the
Spanish empire, a medium-sized center far from the imperial centers of
power. During that time the city and its surrounding countryside changed
and grew, and more important, the relationships among the people of the
region changed. The colonial history of the region has left an indelible
mark on its people and on the landscape itself.

*Domestic Architecture and Power* focuses on the houses and domestic
objects of the colonial period in Cuenca. It is not an attempt to outline the
patterned regularity of a monolithic Spanish colonial culture (Deagan
1983). Instead, the book examines how the negotiation of power in colonial Cuenca was carried out by the people who lived there, through the
multiple meanings that people gave to the houses they lived in and to the
objects they used every day (Beaudry et al. 1991).

From June 1993 to May 1994 I lived in Cuenca. During that time I
sought out, measured, and photographed standing houses that maintained
colonial architectural features. I also undertook a series of archaeological
excavations in house yards to recover archaeological remains related to
colonial domestic occupations in the region. Finally, I undertook a survey
of colonial notarial documents in the Cuenca archives in order to place
the architectural and archaeological data into a social historical context.

Since the early 1970s, archaeological research focused on Spanish
colonialism in the New World has expanded rapidly in the southern United
States, the Caribbean, and Mesoamerica. Overviews of the current state
of this research are readily available for the southwestern United States
(Dobyns 1982; Farnsworth 1986; Hurst Thomas 1989), the southeastern
United States (Deagan 1983; Hurst Thomas 1990; Maüsen, 1985), and the
Caribbean (Deagan 1983, 1988, 1995b; Hurst Thomas 1990; Marrinan
1985). Among the many research projects already carried out, two must
be mentioned because of their influence on my work in Cuenca, as well as
the work carried out by many other Spanish colonial archaeologists. The

first is the archaeology at the town of St. Augustine, Florida, which began in the early 1970s when Charles Fairbanks instituted a program of "problem-oriented backyard archaeology" (Deagan 1983; Fairbanks 1975). This work has been continued by Kathleen Deagan and represents the first serious research into Spanish colonial domestic habitations from an anthropological perspective. St. Augustine was founded by the Spanish on their far northern frontier in 1565, in response to French settlement further up the eastern coast of North America. The military, the Franciscan missionaries, and the people who supported these two groups largely made up the town's population. St. Augustine was taken over by the British in 1763 but had a second period of Spanish occupation from 1783 to 1821, after which Florida became a U.S. territory (Deagan 1983:22–27).

Deagan (1983) has also led a second major research project, consisting of large-scale excavations undertaken from 1979 to 1985 on the site of Puerto Real, now in Haiti. Puerto Real was occupied from 1503 until 1579, when the population was relocated by the Spanish Crown in order to reduce piracy on the north coast of Hispaniola (Hodges and Lyon 1995). Research there has involved large-scale excavations of several habitation sites, the results of which are comparable to the research at St. Augustine (Deagan 1995b). The St. Augustine and Puerto Real projects have greatly expanded our knowledge of Spanish colonial domestic adaptations in the New World and were a major inspiration for my excavations in Cuenca.

There has been an expanding research interest in the history of domestic architecture in North America since the publication of Henry Glassie's seminal book *Folk Housing in Middle Virginia* in 1975 brought vernacular architecture to the attention of historical archaeologists and many other scholars (Deetz 1977a; Upton and Vlach 1986). This era has also seen the publication of many important studies of the role of all types of material culture in both the colonial and post-Independence periods (Leone and Potter 1988; McGuire and Paynter 1991). In contrast, the study of historical archaeology and the study of colonial domestic architecture are still very new disciplines in the Andes. Studies of Latin American domestic architecture have only just begun to look at their role in the development of Spanish colonialism. Works focusing on Spanish colonial domestic architecture are still quite rare in comparison to a more art-historical approach to architecture focusing on churches and other public buildings (Corradine Angulo 1981; Gutiérrez et al. 1981, 1986; Manucy 1978; Téllez and Moure 1982; cf. Kubler 1948; Kubler and Soria 1959; Markman 1966, 1984).

I employed an explicitly anthropological focus in examining the architecture of Cuenca. In many ways Cuenca resembled other towns in the Spanish New World, but in others it was a unique embodiment of the urban ideals that were of such great importance to Spanish colonization. There were many cultural influences that went into the formation of the colonial domestic architecture of Andean South America, and particularly of the southern highlands of Ecuador. Through the description and analysis of standing houses within and just outside the city, I attempt to bring forward the role that these houses played in colonial social relations. The economic value of the houses, the changing role of construction materials, and the variety of social groups who lived in particular neighborhoods are all important sources of information; the mapping of the spaces within the houses themselves is, however, the most important goal of my architectural analysis. All of this information contributes to our view of the colonial Cuenca house as architecture that facilitated the surveillance and disciplinary power of the colonial elite, but also facilitated the community solidarity of the urban poor.

Research focusing on the archaeology of Spanish colonial sites in Mesoamerica has taken great strides in the past ten years (Fournier Garcia and Miranda Flores 1992; Hurst Thomas 1991), but in South America colonial period archaeology is still very much in the "developmental stage" as a discipline. Archaeological test-pitting in Cuenca was undertaken at two rural and two urban houses in an attempt to make some contribution to redressing this balance. The excavations provided a broad range of material culture, including Inka ceramics and a variety of colonial and Republican period artifacts. The National Archive in Cuenca houses a large collection of household inventories from the colonial period and these historical resources were compared to the excavated colonial materials. The similarities and contrasts between these two sources of information have allowed me to explore several issues. These included the role of domestic materials in the growth of the ideology of individualism associated with merchant capitalism, the use of tablewares in expressions of social relationships, and the expressions of ethnicity in domestic material culture.

The overall goal of this book is to use Cuenca as an example in order to examine the role of domestic architecture and domestic material culture in the Spanish colonial world. The research of Kathleen Deagan has led to the formulation of a model based on archaeological excavations in St. Augustine that masterfully combined the roles of gender, ethnicity, and status in the colonial household and their relationship to material culture. Deagan has proposed that Spanish colonists in the New World incorporated "Native" elements into their lives but largely in "socially invisible" areas, whereas "Spanish" material culture was preserved in more "socially visible" areas. For Deagan it is the incorporation of Native American and African women into "Spanish" households, and the dominance of

ethnically Spanish men in more public areas, that is the key dichotomy in
Spanish colonial material culture (Dillehay and Deagan 1992:118).

In Cuenca my goal has been to examine the relationship of particular social categories such as gender, ethnicity, and status, and how these
categories relate to the use of material culture. I do not want to characterize this relationship as a single "crystallized Hispanic colonial adaptive
pattern" (Deagan 1990:233). Instead, we need to look at the variation over
space and through time in Cuenca as a factor of the "dynamic, highly
varied, and influential roles of individuals and their ideologies" in shaping
the archaeological record (Deagan 1995a:2). Spanish colonialism, as with
colonial efforts in other parts of the world, involved struggles over power
that were not just at the level of state intervention but permeated all
aspects of colonial life, including the role of objects in the colonial home
and the architecture of houses themselves. Not all Native Andean "elements" incorporated into colonial Andean society were in "socially invisible" areas, but many aspects of colonial life in the Andes did not incorporate any such Native Andean elements. Colonization in Cuenca was, rather,
a very heterogeneous process in which many people resisted Spanish
control of their lives through material culture, and many others used
material culture in their attempts to gain social power in the new colonial
regime.

# Acknowledgments

There are many people in Ecuador to whom I owe a debt of gratitude. In Quito, Jozef Buys of the Cooperación Técnica de Belgica provided valuable advice. At the Instituto Nacional del Patrimonio Cultural offices in Quito, the director, Monica Bolaños, was instrumental in granting permission for my excavations.

I had never been to Cuenca before beginning my research there, and as a stranger I was delighted with the warm welcome I received. At the Centro Interamericano de Artesanías y Artes Populares, Juan Martínez Borrero provided valuable information on the mural paintings of the chapel at Cachaulo. As head of the Instituto Nacional del Patrimonio Cultural offices in Cuenca, Licenciado Alfonso Peña Andrade provided assistance with permits for my work. The head of archaeology, Antonio Carillo, was also instrumental in permit-granting and in providing information on the archaeology of the Cuenca region. Architect Edmundo Iturralde shared with me his love of the old houses of Cuenca, his knowledge of their construction, and his friendship.

At the Municipal Museum the new director, Esperanza Cordova, generously allowed me to view and photograph the collection of historic ceramics. At the Manuel Augustin Landívar Museum I thank the director, Nancy Arpi, who allowed me to examine the archaeological collections from the Todos Santos excavations. Leonardo Aguirre, archaeologist at the Central Bank Museum in Cuenca, offered me the opportunity to excavate at the Pumapungo ruins as a very small part of his ongoing archaeological project there. I am grateful to him for this opportunity and for his documentary references and conversations on the Colonial period at Pumapungo.

At the Fundación Paul Rivet, Alexandra Kennedy Troya broke it to me gently that most of the "old" houses in Cuenca were not colonial. She was instrumental as a liaison who understands the role of foreign researchers who land on her doorstep. Her help, along with that of the rest of the staff at the Fundación, will not soon be forgotten.

At the Archivo Nacional de Historia in Cuenca, Luz-Maria Guapisaca provided an atmosphere of friendly collaboration unequaled anywhere. To both Luz-Maria and her assistant, Carmen Ortiz, go my heartfelt thanks for helping me in my documentary research, and most of all for making me feel welcome.

Deborah Truhan, of the City University of New York, made the archival sections of this research possible. Over many lunches Deborah provided me with friendship, research help, and the advice of a *Norteamericano* whose commitment to the people and history of Cuenca is obvious.

José-Luis Espinosa, formerly of the Banco Central Museum in Cuenca, gave endlessly of his enthusiasm for Cuenca's past. There is no way to repay the many times he found important leads, helped me to understand the people of Cuenca, and was simply a friend to someone far from home. For sharing his life in Cuenca with me, and for the endless conversations over ice cream at the Holanda, I will always be grateful.

In Canada my parents, Robert and Patricia Jamieson, have always been there to support me and have given to me the love of travel and of other cultures that has stayed with me throughout my life.

At Calgary there are many people who helped along the way. Scott Raymond was instrumental through all the stages of this research. There are many other faculty members who gave generously of their time, and I must mention Chris Archer, Jane Kelley, Peter Mathews, and Gerry Oetelaar, all of whom read and commented on this research.

The Social Sciences and Humanities Research Council of Canada provided both doctoral (Award # 752-92-2402) and postdoctoral (Award # 756-98-0272) fellowships for the completion of this research. Financial assistance was also provided by the Department of Archaeology at the University of Calgary and by a University of Calgary Thesis Research Grant.

For the initial faunal analysis I thank Patrick Gay, of the Salango Museum and the Fundación Presley Norton in Ecuador. Thanks also to Nancy Saxberg at the University of Calgary for the analysis of the rest of the faunal collection.

Finally, to my wife, Laurie Beckwith, no words can be enough. This work could not have been completed without the unwavering support that she has provided. I thank her for the love and understanding through it all.

# Contents

# Power, Colonialism, and Domestic Life

1

In Cuenca, as in other colonial centers around the world, colonialism was a history of attempts to assert Western ideals of rationality and order. In real colonial situations such "pieties of progress" were, however, quickly sacrificed on the grounds of expediency. Colonial oppositions became hybridized, and the divide between colonized and colonizer was constantly reordered (Prakash 1995).

My goal is to examine the exercise of colonial power through the architecture of the houses that the people of Cuenca lived in, and the material culture that was used in those houses. Domestic material culture provides evidence of the relationships between different groups in colonial Cuenca and the role that objects played in these relationships. It is an arena that is rich in meaning, and many of these meanings have not yet been explored by Spanish colonial archaeologists. There is a need for a new synthesis, in which architecture and excavated objects are both seen as material culture. Material culture should be treated as an inherent part of the "transaction and translation between incommensurable cultures and positions" (Prakash 1995:3) that occurred in Cuenca throughout the colonial period just as much as in other colonial contexts around the world.

## ANDEAN COLONIAL ARCHAEOLOGY

In contrast to a long tradition of research in the United States, and a growing tradition in Mesoamerica and the Caribbean, historical archaeology with an anthropological perspective is only just beginning in South America. This is due both to the severe funding limitations that South American researchers face and the lack of interest in historic period archaeological remains by foreign researchers. Much of the historical archaeology that has been carried out in South America has been the result of archaeological testing of monuments slated for restoration. This work is not often published and is accessible only as limited-circulation reports submitted to national cultural agencies. This situation is changing rapidly in the 1990s, and I hope that in the near future both the scope of research and the publication of results from South American historic period excavations will be greatly expanded. Although Richard Schaedel's (1992) summary of the contribution of archaeology to our understanding of colonialism in South America mentions almost no archaeological projects, his general conclusion that colonial archaeology does not exist in South America is an overstatement. The publication of the results of projects focusing on the South American colonial period is still variable, but more sources are becoming available, and the number of archaeologists focusing on this period is increasing.

The summary of Andean historical archaeology that follows focuses more strongly on the nations of Ecuador and Peru, as I am more familiar with the research that has been undertaken there. I do not claim to have a comprehensive grasp of the scope of previous archaeological research on the Spanish colonies in Andean nations, since much of the literature is in national journals not easily available to North American researchers, but what follows is a step in that direction.

In Argentina a large two-volume edited work (Morresi and Gutiérrez 1983) provides a detailed summary of colonial archaeology carried out in that country from the 1940s up until the early 1980s. Various types of protohistoric, Spanish colonial, and Republican period archaeological sites have been excavated by Argentinean archaeologists. These include two studies of trade beads and other items found in protohistoric Native sites (Lagiglia 1983b). Two settlements on the north side of the Magellan Strait in extreme southern Argentina, founded by Pedro Sarmiento de Gamboa in 1584 but abandoned soon after, have been excavated (Fernández 1983).

Excavations of larger urban colonial sites have also been undertaken in Argentina. Santa Fe la Vieja, a town in northeastern Argentina occupied from 1573 to 1670, has been the subject of ongoing excavations since the 1950s, and the town has been partially restored as a historic site. The archaeological research was not conducted using the methodological standards that would now be considered necessary, as artifact proveniences were recorded only to the nearest *solar*, or quarter of a city block, but the entire collection has been curated in the local museum (Ceruti 1983b). A detailed analysis of the ceramics has apparently not been published.

Two military installations have been excavated in Argentina. The first is a fortress, occupied from the late seventeenth to late eighteenth centuries (Cáceres Freyre 1983). The other military installation was a Republican period frontier fort in Mendoza, occupied from 1805 to 1879 (Lagiglia 1983a). In both cases very little attention has been given to archaeological context or artifact analysis.

Sites of Native *reducción* (colonial resettlement) villages have also received attention in Argentina. One of the earliest projects that could be classified as historical archaeology in Argentina was the 1948 expedition to relocate the site of a late-eighteenth-century missionary reducción in the Chaco region. This work was undertaken with the specific intent of recovering the remains of one of the missionaries, known from historical documents to have been buried under the main altar of the church. The ruin was located, the burial unearthed, and then reburied in the parish church at Castelli after great ceremony (Goicoechea 1983). This same reducción has recently been excavated by a professional archaeologist (Morresi 1983b). Work at another Native reducción village consisted of one week of rescue excavation in 1977 in San Javier, Argentina, which unearthed materials from the late eighteenth century. This report lists the artifacts recovered and gives a brief history of the village, but the artifacts are not illustrated, and no real research design was given for the excavations (Ceruti 1983a).

The main focus of historical archaeology in Argentina up until the 1980s was the commemoration of sites of national historic significance. Nationalism is an important part of the development of colonial archaeology in Argentina, an idea embodied by an Argentinean archaeologist's feeling that an archaeological site is "a location where each community experiences its heritage, and is the location of the roots of our national being" (Morresi 1983a:19, my translation). The theoretical focus of Argentinean historical archaeologists in the 1980s portrayed the conquest period as a time of "transculturation," with the mixing of Spanish and Native cultures. The results of this process were seen as the prevalence of "Spanish norms" and the "impoverishment" of the Native cultures of Argentina (Morresi 1983a:22). It was hoped that historical archaeology in Argentina would soon lead to the founding of a society and an academic journal devoted to the discipline, but as of 1983 this had not been accomplished (Morresi 1983a:26).

The situation of historical archaeology in Bolivia is largely unknown to me. One of the earliest excavations of a colonial period site in South America was Stig Rydén's (1947) excavation of two abandoned village sites in the Jesús de Machaca region of Bolivia, in the Desaguadero River basin south of Lake Titicaca, in 1938–39. One of the villages had only Inkaic period occupation, while the other, at a lower elevation in the same valley, was a very early colonial period Native village, with several preserved house foundations and the foundation of a church. The presence of iron artifacts initially alerted Rydén that this was a historic period site, but most of the ceramic collection was identical to the late prehistoric ceramics, with the sole exception of a single Spanish olive jar sherd (Rydén 1947:182–338). Mary Van Buren has recently begun a project of historical archaeology in Bolivia. Her first season of excavation included testing of sites in the urban core of the mining town of Potosí, and excavation at the colonial period hot springs site of nearby Tarapaya, at a lower elevation than Potosí itself. The results of this work have not yet been published (Van Buren 1996).

Most of the early efforts at historical archaeology in Peru were undertaken as small parts of much larger research projects whose main focus was on prehistoric archaeology. The earliest excavation of a colonial site in Peru may have been that of Marion Tschopik, at the village of Chucuito on the western shore of Lake Titicaca. Her excavations were part of her work with her husband, Harry Tschopik (1950). The focus of the work was the persistence of Aymara pottery traditions throughout the historic period. A single excavation unit provided her with the sample of early historic midden she needed.

Another small-scale 1950s project associated with prehistoric excavations was the early colonial church excavation at the site of Tambo Viejo in the Acari Valley, dug by Dorothy Menzel and Francis Riddell (1986). In the early 1970s Hermann Trimborn (1981) excavated the church at Sama, in extreme southern Peru, a project that was also part of a larger prehistoric research program and that concentrated on the construction phases of the church. The Chan Chan Moche Valley project encountered a colonial roadside rest station on the north coast of Peru in 1974, and this was excavated as a small side project to the overall goals of prehistoric research (Beck et al. 1983:54). All of these early efforts at historical archaeology in Peru were associated with foreign research projects, the larger goals of which were to deal with prehistoric archaeology. For Peruvian archaeologists, therefore, the true beginnings of historical archaeology are dated to the late 1970s, with the beginnings of a national program of excavations by trained archaeologists at colonial churches and houses that were undergoing restoration (Flores Espinoza et al. 1981:v). Work by Peruvian archaeologists on the colonial period has been ongoing since the 1970s in many locations throughout the country, but such work has rarely been published beyond the obligatory reports filed with the Instituto Naciónal de Cultura (National Institute of Culture) in Lima (Schaedel 1992:224). A partial and outdated list of these reports includes Bonnet Medina (1983), Cornejo Garcia (1983), Gonzales Carre and Cahuas Massa (1983), Oberti R. (1983), and Paz Flores (1983). This work by national scholars resulted in the founding of a Peruvian Society for Historical Archaeology in 1983, with widespread participation from within Peru (Deagan 1984). I am not aware of the current activities of the society.

Published excavation reports on Peruvian historic period research are rare, but include a study by Jaime Miasta Gutierrez carried out as part of the "Seminar on Rural Andean History" under the supervision of the historian Pablo Macera (Miasta Gutierrez 1985). This was an archaeological study of three villages in the southern portion of the province of Huarochiri, Peru, just southeast of Lima, with the objective of outlining the prehistoric to historic period transitions of the ceramic styles in the region, based on comparative stratigraphic sequences. The team chose to study these villages because they were probably supplying coarse earthenware ceramics to Lima throughout the colonial period. The villages have a long history of ceramic production and have not yet had large-scale metropolitan construction on top of the middens, as is the case in villages that have been subsumed by the growth of Lima (Miasta Gutierrez 1985:11).

All three villages are small, largely native, villages, which still export ceramics to Lima, and midden excavations provided a good-sized sample of ceramics from each (Miasta Gutierrez 1985). Miasta Gutierrez's research was hampered by both a lack of knowledge of imported ceramic types and an incorrect approach to stratigraphic chronology, but the study was otherwise carefully done and well illustrated and provides a useful guide to colonial coarse earthenware production for Lima.

Excavations at the Casa de Osambela (Osambela House) in the center of Lima itself in the late 1970s were intended to help restoration architects to do accurate reconstruction of this large colonial mansion. The small amount of camelid and guinea pig bone recovered was taken as important evidence of mestizaje in colonial Lima by the researchers (Flores Espinoza et al. 1981:vii). The ceramic analysis separated out coarse earthenwares, majolicas, refined white earthenwares, and porcelains (Flores Espinoza et al. 1981:35–46), but the lack of knowledge of European historic period ceramics on the part of the researchers meant that the ceramic analysis was not as detailed as it might have been.

Thomas Myers (1990) carried out an entirely different type of research on the eastern slopes of the Andes in the early 1960s. His eight days of excavation in 1964 on the Sarayacu Mission, in the Upper Ucayali River valley of Peru, was part of an overall survey of prehistoric archaeology in the area. This Franciscan mission was occupied from 1791 to 1862, with several priests, a blacksmith and carpenter, and 500 to 1,000 Setebo people occupying the village. About 8,000 artifacts were recovered from the excavations, only 10 of which were imported, all the rest being locally produced ceramics and faunal material (Myers 1990:70). Europeans did not heavily impact native material culture in the Upper Ucayali until the 1850s, although European crop introductions, diseases, and missionary activities had profound effects (Myers 1990:145). It is only at the end of the mission period, in the 1850s, that large quantities of European trade items tied to industrial capitalism began to enter the region. Myers's research is therefore very closely related to prehistoric and ethnohistoric studies, focusing on the prehistoric and historic chronologies and traditions of Amazonian native groups, using ceramic styles (Myers 1990:vii).

The Moquegua Bodegas project, under the direction of Prudence Rice from the University of Florida, was the first large-scale historical archaeology project undertaken by North Americans in Peru. Rice's participation in the Osmore Drainage project of the Programa Contisuyu, a large prehistory project with joint participation by Peruvian and foreign archaeologists (Stanish and Rice 1989), resulted in the identification of colonial period bodegas, or wineries, throughout the Moquegua River valley. From 1985 to 1990 the project undertook survey and test pitting at a series of wineries, with extensive excavations at four sites (Rice and Ruhl 1989; Rice and Smith 1989; Smith 1991). Associated with this work 26 colonial period kiln sites were surveyed and 2 were excavated. These kilns were used to manufacture the large ceramic vessels used in the wine industry and were presumably located throughout the valley in order to minimize the transportation costs for these very large ceramic vessels (Rice 1994).

The test excavations at 28 different winery sites, and subsequent extensive excavation by Greg Smith (1991) at four of these sites, provide very useful data for comparison to the Cuenca materials. The wineries represented agricultural extraction facilities with some parallels to the rural sites excavated in Cuenca. Smith's theoretical perspective is different from what I have proposed for Cuenca. He has framed his research within a "transculturation" model, looking at the Spanish and Andean cultures and how the colonial experience blended the more "adaptive" traits of each (Smith 1991:67–81).

The research carried out by Mary Van Buren (1993), also under the umbrella of the Programa Contisuyu, consisted of the excavation of several domestic contexts in the village of Torata Alta, in the Moquegua River valley. Torata Alta was a "colony" of the highland Lupaqa people, and such colonies figured prominently in Murra's (1972) original formulation of the concept of the "vertical archipelago" as a distinctly Andean system of social organization that allowed highland groups vital access to lowland crops without the necessity of trade. Van Buren's research has focused on the political and power relationships that led to the pre-Hispanic founding of the village of Torata Alta and to the maintenance of this Lupaqa village in the colonial period. Van Buren proposes that the prehistoric Lupaqa lowland sites were controlled by highland elites, and the crops brought from them were used in the negotiation of political power within highland Lupaqa society. The village survived into the colonial period not because the pre-Hispanic Andean economic systems endured, but rather because

the colonial villagers avoided forced labor in the Potosí mines. Their unusual position as a highland ethnic enclave on the coast allowed them to
participate in the market economy by supplying basic foodstuffs for sale
(deFrance 1996; Van Buren 1993, 1996; Van Buren et al. 1993). Van
Buren's research is an important step forward in the sophistication of
studies looking at early colonial Andean Native villages and their role in
the socioeconomic and political structure of the colonial Andes.

In summary, the current state of historical archaeology in Peru falls
into two separate categories. The first category includes the largely Peruvian efforts to gain information from archaeological data recovered at
urban sites where restoration projects are under way. The second category is the international effort of the late 1980s in looking at colonial
sites concentrated in the Osmore drainage. I hope that in the future such
efforts on the part of both Peruvian and foreign researchers can be expanded to create more co-operative efforts and particularly greater access
to avenues of publication for Peruvian archaeologists.

In Ecuador the historical archaeology that has been undertaken so
far has been related to rescue excavation during the restoration of colonial monuments (Buys and Camino 1991). Since 1988 the Instituto Naciónal
de Patrimonio Cultural (National Cultural Heritage Institute) has had an
active program in "rescue archaeology" in Quito (Bolaños and Manosalvas
1989), a system that has resulted in considerable activity in the area of
historical archaeology. The Instituto Ecuatoriano de Obras Sanitarias
(Ecuadorian Sanitary Works Institute) has also sponsored excavations in
a Quito hospital that dates to the colonial period (Rousseau 1989), and the
municipality of Quito sponsored excavations in the plaza in front of the
Dominican monastery (Rousseau 1990). I was unable to locate publications relating to these excavations, and I am not aware of their findings.

The main focus of historical archaeology in Quito has been on religious institutions. Work during restoration of the El Robo chapel in Quito
resulted in the recovery of several colonial period subfloor burials (Bolaños
and Manosalvas 1989:8–9). The Mercedarian monastery in Quito underwent excavation in the main church and a side chapel, which resulted in
the recovery of a burial chamber (Díaz 1991:15–19). In the mid-1980s the
San Francisco monastery in Quito had several excavation units placed
throughout the building complex. These revealed two brick-vaulted ossuaries
under side chapels of the church and several prehistoric burials (Terán
1989). Unfortunately, there has been no publication of any detailed ceramic description for any of these excavations.

From 1987 to 1991 the Belgian development organization Ecuabel
and the Instituto Naciónal de Patrimonio Cultural undertook excavations
in the Dominican monastery in Quito (Buys and Camino 1991). This work

took place prior to the restoration of the monastery, in order to "resolve architectural and structural questions" for the restoration. It resulted in the recovery of a selection of local majolicas and coarse earthenwares, and the discovery of a large late prehistoric cemetery under the monastery.

One Republican period site has been excavated in Quito. The Astronomical Observatory, built in 1873, had several test units excavated around it when the building was going to be restored in the 1980s. No cultural materials were recovered apart from subsurface architectural features, suggesting that no domestic occupation has ever occurred on the site (Bolaños and Camino 1991).

In the city of Cuenca the only historical archaeology undertaken prior to my research was the 1973 to 1980 project at the Todos Santos site. This site was discovered in 1973 when Incaic stonework was uncovered during house construction on the riverside, and further excavation in 1974 revealed two mills and a house from the early colonial period at this site. Large quantities of historic period ceramics and other artifacts were recovered, and in 1980 a public park was laid out on the site for display of the ruins. The analysis and publication of a site monograph has never taken place (Agustín Landívar 1974; Almeida n.d.).

Historical archaeology in the Andes is still very much in the developmental stage. Committed individuals, most of them government archaeologists charged with the impossible task of mitigating damage to colonial monuments on almost nonexistent budgets, have made very serious strides forward in rescue archaeology in several Andean countries. This research has not been able to coalesce into the development of a truly Latin American colonial archaeology. This is due to the lack of training in the specifics of historical archaeology, the lack of access to published resources, and the lack of venues in which to publish the results of their own work. The Moquegua Valley project in Peru is an entirely different matter, consisting of trained foreign scholars with specific research designs and comparatively large budgets. Considerable useful data have been recovered and published from this project, and I hope that in the future other projects by both domestic and foreign scholars in Andean countries can continue to build on the work already completed in this emerging discipline.

My work is an attempt to make a small contribution to this effort, but with a perspective that is somewhat different from previous research in Andean colonial archaeology. Mine is the first Andean colonial archaeology that I am aware of with a focus on comparing the archaeology and architecture of a series of domestic sites in a Spanish urban area. In the remainder of this chapter I will outline the theoretical perspective that has shaped this research.

## HOUSE AND SOCIAL RELATIONS

The study of the house has been a part of anthropology almost since the inception of the discipline itself. Lewis H. Morgan's (1965 [1881]) book *Houses and House-Life of the American Aborigines* was one of the first books to look at houses as something other than expressions of the artistry of architects. Instead Morgan realized that the house and other buildings were direct expressions of the social organization of the people who occupied them. This meant that there was the possibility of looking at houses, and from their organization, to reconstruct the organization of the kin group that lived in them. In the 1950s, research by Jack Goody and others refined this basic anthropological concept, in pointing out that household composition varied throughout the "life cycle" of a house, as the kin group that occupied the house changed. This cycle is reflected in domestic architecture, although houses built of more ephemeral materials are much more likely to change drastically throughout a family's history than are houses built of durable materials, which are more difficult to alter (Goody 1971 [1958]).

Anthropologists are not the only ones who study domestic architecture and household material culture. Domestic life has been a topic of research by Latin American social historians since at least the 1920s (Carbia 1926; Torre Revello 1945). The topic remained on the fringes of historical research until the 1960s, when publications such as Jean Descola's (1962) *La vie quotidienne au Pérou au temps des espagnols, 1710–1820* brought a new focus within social history on the study of the household in colonial Latin America. Domestic architecture and material culture are still important topics for social historical researchers (Porro et al. 1982; Porro Girardi 1995:82–83).

It was also in the 1960s that Latin American architectural historians began to focus on the colonial house (Harth-Terré and Abanto 1962). Prior to this period the architectural history of Latin America was written largely on its churches and public buildings (Kubler 1948; Kubler and Soria 1959). Unfortunately, this overwhelming interest in the architecture of the churches is still evident among many architectural historians. They believe that "It is in church architecture that we should expect to find the true expression of the conqueror's beliefs about style: the church was the spiritual, cultural and geographical focus of both Spanish and Indian communities" (Fraser 1990:121). The focus of architectural historians in Latin America on the more highly decorated, and thus more easily analyzed, architecture of the church and state is also reflected in the treatment of houses. In current regional architectural histories it is standard practice to put in a section on domestic architecture, but the focus of the section is usually on the largest urban houses. There is a particular emphasis on facades, as "the ornamentation of the entrance" is felt to be "the main and in most cases the only important architectural feature" of colonial domestic architecture for architectural historians (Fraser 1990:136; cf. Markman 1984:153–157; Early 1994:129–162).

This lack of focus on the house is not the case for all architectural historians. Ramón Gutiérrez, professor of architecture at the Universidad Nacional del Nordeste in Argentina, has shown an ongoing commitment to the interdisciplinary study of Andean architecture in cooperation with historians and art historians. Although showing little interest in the more anthropological aspects of rural Andean architecture, Gutiérrez and the teams of researchers that work with him have produced numerous masterful studies of both domestic and church architecture in the Andes. These include treatments of the growth of urbanism, Native Andean influences on the art and architecture of the region, and the architecture of the Native reducción (resettlement) towns (Gutiérrez et al. 1981, 1986a, 1986b). Another example of architectural history that has focused on the colonial house is Germán Téllez and Ernesto Moure's (1982) study of the colonial household architecture of Cartagena, Colombia. Téllez and Moure reject the traditional "formalist" studies of Cartagena houses, which gave value only to houses with "typical" decorative elements, or houses identified with particular historical personages. Instead they attempt to move the level of analysis forward by looking at the intrinsic formal characteristics of anonymous domestic architecture. They reject the impenetrable jargon of semiotics, and decide instead to concentrate on a simple typology of houses, which they present with detailed diagrams of floor plans, building materials, and the many architectural details of doors, balconies, balustrades, and so forth.

## WHAT DO COLONIAL HOUSES MEAN?

In an attempt to go beyond studies of household decorative motifs and beyond typological studies of house forms, we must find the theoretical perspective to analyze domestic architecture that Téllez and Moure are missing. Some of the earliest work that addresses the role of domestic architecture in society was that of the French sociologist Émile Durkheim. In the early twentieth century Durkheim first drew attention to the fact that architecture is not only the product of representation based on social forms, but was also a model for reproducing those social forms (Durkheim and Mauss 1963 [1903]; Durkheim 1965 [1915]). Durkheim's work was extremely influential to the development of the British structural-function-alist school of anthropology, within which architecture was seen as integral to both the social and symbolic orders.

Durkheim was not alone in developing a new view of architecture. His contemporary, the German architect Paul Frankl, had attempted to integrate architectural history with cultural history as early as 1914. Frankl defined the building as a "theatre of human activity" (1969 [1914]:159). Throughout his work Frankl developed the idea that function, meaning, and spatial composition were all interwoven in architecture.

After World War I, Americanist anthropology emphasized "salvage ethnography" and avoided the whole issue of the role of architecture in society through the use of simple diffusionist explanations of architectural "style." This was a theoretical orientation that survived in the study of North American vernacular architecture into the 1960s (Kniffen 1965). In North America it was the work of Edward Hall (1959, 1966) that finally brought the relationship between architecture and social relations to the fore. Although best known for his work on proxemics, Hall also proposed that spatial relationships between individuals structured social relationships, and that architecture and material culture were important in helping shape these relationships.

Hall's contemporary, the sociologist Erving Goffman, proposed a "dramaturgical" model of human behavior. Goffman used the analogy of theater to portray individuals as "actors" in everyday life, and architectural space as divided between "front stage" areas, where people were "acting" their social roles, and "back stage" private spaces, where people could drop their social personae (Goffman 1959, 1963).

It is at this point in Americanist anthropology that one of the most important influences on the anthropology of the period began to take hold. This was structuralism, the anthropological theory that explained patterned cultural behavior as the result of a shared group unconscious (Lévi-Strauss 1963). Structuralism was a theoretical school with roots in Durkheim's work. Claude Lévi-Strauss in particular was fascinated with the rules and conventions that different cultures adhered to in the design of architecture (Lévi-Strauss 1963:132–163). The basic concepts of structuralism took hold in American anthropology in various ways. In Amos Rapoport's (1969) book *House Form and Culture,* the house was portrayed in an anthropologically "holistic" way, as part of economic relations, social relations, and as part of the cosmology of the group who inhabited it. Rapoport's volume was an important influence on many anthropologists (Lawrence and Low 1990:458). In Latin American research, Evon Vogt's (1969) study of village life in Zinacantan, Mexico, and Christine Hugh-Jones's (1977) study of Amazonian ethnography were both very good examples of the structuralist approach to architecture. Both studies looked at the use of space on various levels as a structured pattern and particularly as a metaphor for the structure of the universe.

Among archaeologists ideas from structural anthropology were accepted quite early by James Deetz (1967), who was instrumental in bringing these ideas to the discipline of historical archaeology (Deetz 1977a, 1977b; Fitting 1977).

One of the most innovative studies to use an explicitly structural approach to colonial material culture was Henry Glassie's influential (1975) study of *Folk Housing in Middle Virginia*. Glassie created a "syntax" akin to grammatical rules for the combination of geometric spaces in the colonial Virginia house. He concluded that it was rules of syntax, or formal geometry, rather than environmental or behavioral needs, that guided the design of the colonial Virginia house. Glassie emphasized the roles that both structural anthropology (Glassie 1975:215–218) and Noam Chomsky's concept of generative grammar (Glassie 1975:215–216) played in his work on colonial architecture.

Another closely related current of anthropology in the late 1960s and early 1970s was semiotics and symbolism (Barthes 1967 [1964]; Turner 1974), one of the major contributions of which was to examine the transmission of meaning through objects as a form of "nonverbal communication." To semioticians objects, including architecture, are invested with meaning by a culture and they function within a culture as signs used in a dynamic relationship to articulate cognitive information.

The major critique that has been leveled at structural and semiotic approaches is that the formulation of a "shared mental template" within an entire culture, or examining material culture as a "text" whose meaning can be read, creates a static view of the relationship of material culture to society. For many anthropologists a structural or semiotic approach denies the multiple meanings that an object may have as it is used in different contexts by different individuals, and also denies the historical aspect of material culture. In other words, the "meaning" of objects in any culture should never be considered static or immutable (Lefebvre 1991:7; Roseberry 1989:24–25).

The structural approach to material culture, in denying the possibility of change, created a profound theoretical gap between the disciplines of anthropology and history in the 1960s. It is Clifford Geertz (1973) who is attributed with breaking down this barrier between anthropology and history. Instead of the "general laws" that positivist anthropologists like Leslie White and Marvin Harris were searching for, Geertz advocated a search for the creative capacity of human activity in looking at the meanings humans attach to symbols. He is in basic agreement with the structuralists and semioticians up until this point, but Geertz goes beyond the structuralists in his insistence that these meanings are "historically derived," and thus the "history" and the "culture" of any human group are indivisible (Geertz 1973).

This is not the way that Spanish colonial archaeologists in North America have looked at material culture since the 1970s. The influential University of Florida program in colonial archaeology, and Kathleen Deagan's St. Augustine excavations in particular, began from an explicitly "processualist" premise of hypothesis testing. This premise was that "patterned regularity and variability in cultures, as well as changes in these patterns through time, are ultimately in response to techno-environmental adaptive factors" (Deagan 1983:5). This theoretical perspective has continued to be influential in Spanish colonial archaeology for a surprisingly long time (Ewen 1991:102). There is an implication in the very classification systems that Spanish colonial archaeologists have used, based on Stanley South's (1977) "functionally specific groups" and John Goggin's (1968) majolica typology. The implication is that the archaeologist has an a priori knowledge of the social role of all artifacts, and that the meanings of such objects did not vary through space or time. There is some evidence that this theoretical stance on Deagan's part may be changing. Recently, she has written that the theoretical orientation of her research "has been, for the most part, materialist and empirical," recognizing the "archaeological record as an expression of community phenomena." At the same time she acknowledges "the dynamic, highly varied, and influential roles of individuals and their ideologies" in shaping the archaeological record (Deagan 1995a:2).

Many social scientists have realized for some time now that in order to understand the meaning of material culture, whether in the form of the built environment or of more portable artifacts, such objects must be viewed within the context of their particular place and time. Anthropologists such as Michael Parker Pearson and Colin Richards have advocated the use of symbolic analysis to go beyond the formal properties or "syntax" of architecture. Instead, architecture must be studied with reference to the historical and social context it was built and used in. It is essential to understand the symbolic meanings that were given to architectural configurations in a given place at a certain time period, so that unique cultural strategies embodied in the architecture can be understood (Parker Pearson and Richards 1994:30).

We must conclude that there is no "general code" for applying meaning to spatial configurations or objects, but instead these meanings can be read by understanding the context in which the objects or space were used (Lefebvre 1991:17; Parker Pearson and Richards 1994:5). We must always keep in mind that these meanings resulted from complex struggles within the society and involved relationships of power (Foucault 1980; Hobsbawm and Ranger 1983).

## POWER AND PRACTICE

If the meaning of objects and buildings is contingent on their context, and not inherent in some "shared mental template," then how did the inhabitants of colonial Cuenca acquire knowledge of these meanings? Two social theorists provide us with possible answers. Pierre Bourdieu, whose (1977 [1972]) book *Outline of a Theory of Practice* was an explicit criticism of structuralism, portrayed structuralism as static and synchronic and as a theoretical perspective that ignored historical change and human action. As a counterpoint to structuralism Bourdieu proposed a theory of the "habitus." Bourdieu's habitus is the "way of being" or inclination in people generated by their daily practices. For Bourdieu people learn not by assimilating mental structures, but instead by imitating the actions of others. An important aspect of this is the spatial dimension of action, and for this reason Bourdieu looked at the house as a principal mechanism for inculcating "habitus" as people move through the space of household architecture and use the objects in the house (Bourdieu 1977 [1972]).

Another important theoretical challenge to structuralism was that of Anthony Giddens (1979, 1984). In a perspective remarkably similar to that of Bourdieu, Giddens proposed that "structures" are the rules and resources that are in people's memories and are embodied in social practices. It is daily life and its routines that both constrain people within these structures and enable them to either reproduce the existing structure or change it through new behaviors (Giddens 1984:25, 50). People are always aware when they are being watched by other people, and Giddens proposes that when we are subjected to this observation by others in society we reflexively monitor our own actions, thus ensuring that the structures of society are reproduced in our own behavior (Giddens 1984:68). This is a process that he called "structuration" (Giddens 1984:19). Time and space are seen by Giddens as crucial in providing contexts for these encounters and contributing to the "fixity" of particular institutions in influencing which encounters occur (Giddens 1984:118–119). In this way Giddens provides a crucial theoretical link among architecture, material culture, and social relations. His most important point for the examination of colonial societies, however, is the idea of "surveillance." In any modern state an elite supervises the activities of subordinates and collates information on their activities. Particularly in institutions such as schools

and factories, the arrangement of built forms provides physical boundaries that encourage people to move through their routines in specific
ways. Physical barriers combine with rules about time schedules and body
positions in helping to control social situations (Giddens 1984:127-136).
In this way discipline can be achieved through surveillance of subordinates, a relationship that is achieved through the attitudes of both parties.
Giddens makes another important point in specifying that "structuration"
theory is not just about the constraint of behaviors. Any structure can
either constrain or enable particular behaviors depending on the attitudes
of the individuals involved (Giddens 1984:25).

Giddens's ideas provide a useful tool in analyzing the material culture of colonialism, especially in his concern with the control that is re-
created daily in a society. These concepts seem closely related with those
of Antonio Gramsci, who reformulated Marxist theory in the 1920s and
1930s. Gramsci felt that specific historical conditions were what called
particular human actions, symbols, and ideas into being. Gramsci's idea
of hegemony explained how a particular system of meanings and values is
held by a given social class and is reciprocally confirmed by their daily
practices. Because the people involved have never experienced another
reality, these meanings and symbols are thus "reified" for those people
(McGuire 1992:35-36). An emphasis on this primacy of relations of power
is also evident in the influential work of Michel Foucault (1975, 1984),
whose analysis of Jeremy Bentham's eighteenth-century "panopticon" prison
architecture (Foucault 1975) was a key example of Foucault's realization
that space is fundamental to any exercise of power. Foucault's work was
an important influence on much of the postmodern movement in archaeology, architectural history, and other disciplines.

Power is exercised through the reproduction of the material world
and through social relations between people. In colonial situations the
meeting of European forms of power with indigenous forms of power
resulted in a complex series of encounters and many unintentional "para-
doxes and ironies" (Prakash 1995:3). Ideology and power have been studied for a long time by archaeologists, but usually using Max Weber's idea
of power as "the probability that one actor within a social relationship will
be in a position to carry out his own will despite resistance" (Weber
1964:152). Archaeologists (e.g., Service 1975) have traditionally made the
error of restricting their discussion of power to formal institutions and
particularly to "the state" (Paynter and McGuire 1991:6-7). This charac-
terization is particularly evident in the work of Spanish colonial archaeologists, in their assumption that Spanish colonial ideology was necessarily tied to things that were associated with Spain (Deagan 1983:266).

Kathleen Deagan's research in St. Augustine (1973, 1983) led her to the conclusion that the material culture of the houses of colonial St. Augustine was related to a relationship between Native American women and "low visibility" activities, such as food acquisition and preparation. High-visibility objects, such as tablewares and the architecture of the houses themselves, were associated with males and with Spanish cultural influences. To Deagan "Conservatism in certain areas—most notably, those that were socially visible and associated with male activities—was coupled with Spanish-Indian acculturation and syncretism in other areas, especially those that were less socially visible and female dominated" (Deagan 1983:271). Deagan has continued to expand her application of this model (Dillehay and Deagan 1992:118), and it has been extremely influential in Spanish colonial archaeology and is frequently invoked (Ewen 1991:102; McEwan 1995: 221–225; Deagan 1995c: 452). Bonnie McEwan recently expanded the application of this model to the roles of gender and ethnicity. She has argued that women of Spanish descent in the New World colonies "appear to have worked in the home and maintained traditional standards," and therefore, "the archaeological correlates of Spanish women are associated mostly with their domestic responsibilities" (McEwan 1991:34).

The assumption of the universality of Deagan's model is largely based on the work of anthropologist George Foster. Foster outlined a process of colonization in Mexico that involved the "screening" of aspects of culture by the "donor culture." For Foster it is this screening that determined what was presented to the "recipient culture," and then the "recipient culture" either willingly accepted or was forced to accept certain aspects of the "donor culture" (Foster 1960:10). In Foster's view this process led to the eventual "crystallization" of the two cultures into a new cultural whole, which did not allow for later variation (Foster 1960:227–234). Foster's perspective has profoundly influenced Spanish colonial archaeologists ever since Deagan proposed in her research at St. Augustine that Foster's "crystallized Hispanic colonial adaptive pattern" was evident in the domestic material culture of St. Augustine's houses. Foster's "crystallized pattern" is still invoked by many Spanish colonial archaeologists (Deagan 1989:233, 1995c:450; Ewen 1991:112).

Intimately related to Foster's conception of Latin American colonialism is the anthropological concept of "acculturation" (Foster 1960:7). Associated with Robert Redfield, the concept gained prominence in Americanist anthropology in the 1930s, particularly in relation to the anthropological study of Latin America (Beals 1953; Parsons 1933; Redfield 1929; Redfield et al. 1936). Redfield's attitude toward Spanish colonization is typified in an article he wrote with M. S. Singer in which he characterized colonial Latin American urban centers as "the mixed cities on the periphery of an empire which carried the core culture to other peoples." For them this was the venue in which "local cultures are disintegrated and new integrations of mind and society are developed" (Redfield and Singer 1954). The concept of acculturation is an important one to Spanish colonial archaeologists, who see acculturation as the process that resulted in the "crystallized pattern" of Spanish New World colonialism (Deagan 1995:452; Ewen 1991:1; McEwan 1995:202; Smith 1991:69–74).

Spanish colonial archaeologists have accepted a model of colonialism in which the Spanish, with inherently more power, forced cultural changes on local populations whenever possible, incorporating Native American elements into their lives only in dire circumstances, or in areas such as the kitchen, which were "socially invisible." In this model the pattern is quickly set and the acculturation is largely one way, although some Native American elements are accepted into colonial culture. This model is very similar to the economic "world system" model of Immanuel Wallerstein (1979), in which non-European societies were portrayed as peripheral and passive victims of the European search for markets. Eric Wolf (1982) challenged this view in defining non-European groups as an integral part of the growth of early modern European mercantile capitalism.

Rather than a crystallized pattern, I prefer to look at Spanish colonialism as a continuous and dynamic negotiation of power between the many groups that made up the Spanish colonial population. This is not to deny that particular processes were occurring in the colonial world. As was the case in Europe, the relation between urban elites and a rural peasantry in the Spanish colonies fueled the surplus production that led to merchant capitalism. Urban houses and plazas and the representation of such "abstract" spaces were tied to the growth of agriculture, crafts, and early industries in extracting surpluses from the countryside (Lefebvre 1991:78–79). Henri Lefebvre has accurately characterized the Renaissance as a period when "abstract space" took over from "historical space," historical space that was based on kinship, geography, and language, and was replaced by abstract space based on formal relationships of building materials and geometric shapes (Lefebvre 1991:48–49). This process, intimately related to the exercise of Spanish power, was evident in the Spanish colonies of Latin America.

This imposition of symmetrical geometry has been intimately linked to the grid pattern of Spanish colonial town plans (Lefebvre 1991:151–152). This architectural expression of the transition to mercantile capitalism has also been noted in worldwide changes in domestic architecture, in which open, nonsymmetrical houses with large multifunctional spaces were replaced by closed, symmetrical forms with barriers restricting access to small interior compartments for separate activities. The new symmetrical mask of the facade associated with mercantile capitalism has been associated with a change from egalitarian co-operative work based on sacred commandment to a hierarchical and competitive society founded on secular law and rules of decorous behavior (Glassie 1975, 1990; Parker Pearson and Richards 1994:61). These are just two examples of how colonial elites exercised hegemonic power through material culture.

The acceptance of the idea that colonial elites exercised power through material culture does not, however, necessarily imply that other members of colonial society were powerless. We can take Clifford Geertz's stance that colonized cultures each have their own structure and history, or Eric Wolf's view that it is impossible to disentangle the history of the colonizer from that of the colonized. In either case it is incumbent on us to accept that Spanish colonialism in the New World cannot be subsumed under any single "pattern." The "dynamic, highly varied, and influential roles of individuals and their ideologies" (Deagan 1995:2) are evident throughout the Spanish colonial world in the many contexts in which colonial material culture took on new meanings for different groups.

If the crystallized pattern does not exist, and instead of searching for it we turn to the multivocal meanings that different groups brought to colonial domestic material culture (Beaudry et al. 1991:175), then certain assumptions prevalent in Spanish colonial archaeology must be dropped. The economy of the Spanish colonial Andes, based on a mixture of slave, coerced, and free labor, was neither completely feudal nor completely capitalist (Stern 1988). As in other early modern societies, the domestic, private world of the family and the public world of the formal colonial economy were not as clearly separated as is the case in industrial capitalism (Yentsch 1991:198; Moore 1988). The role of the family, and of women within it, was of essential importance to political and economic power in colonial Latin America. In many regions a small number of families gained great power. It was these families, rather than formal business organizations or political parties, that were some of the most stable bases of the Latin American colonial power structure (Balmori et al. 1984:17). As Lavrin and Couturier warned historians of Spanish colonialism almost twenty years ago, "The assumption that colonial women were mostly occupied in familial household activities should be altered" (1979:300). "Women" were far from a single undifferentiated group in the Spanish colonies, and they participated in a variety of ways in the formal economy (Borchart de Moreno 1992; Wilson 1984).

Ethnicity was another area of contested power in the colonial world. It is only recently that archaeologists have begun to come to terms with the fluidity of "racial" terminology in the Spanish colonies (Deagan 1997:7). The naming of ethnic groups was all part of colonial power negotiation.

Becoming "Indian" in the colonial Andes, or for that matter becoming a *mitayo* (forced laborer), *forastero* (Native Andean who had left their original community), or any one of many other colonial social categories, brought with it both the social and economic burden of a particular role. It also brought the inherent ability to resist the limitations of that role in myriad ways, whether through migration, the *Taqi Onqoy* ("Dancing Sickness") and other "nativist" religious revivals, through endless litigation in the court system, or through outright violence. Rather than looking at ethnic categorization as a stable classification system within the colonial world, it is much more realistic to see the fluid categories of ethnicity as an important part of how people negotiated power relationships within the Spanish colonies (Powers 1995; Silverblatt 1995; Stern 1982).

By redefining some of the questions asked of Spanish colonial material culture, I want to avoid looking at the "weight of tradition" studied by many Spanish colonial archaeologists. Instead I want to use the example of colonial Cuenca to begin to explore struggles over the exercise of social power (Paynter and McGuire 1991:1). The houses of colonial Cuenca, the material excavated from the ground, and the documents of the notarial archive will all be used in the upcoming chapters to examine how several different categories of Cuenca residents used material culture in their daily lives. I also want to examine how the meaning they invested these objects with was related to relationships of ethnicity, gender, and political economy.

# The History | 2
of Cuenca

## A HISTORY OF INKA TUMIPAMPA

The modern provinces of Azuay and Cañar, located in the southern high-lands of Ecuador, are thought to form the general fifteenth-century bound-aries of the territory of an ethnic group known as the Cañari (Alcina Franch 1986:142). John Murra (1963 [1944]:799) placed the limits of the Cañari "confederation" from Chunchi and Alausí in the north to the Jubones River in the south (Figure 1), and from the Gulf of Guayaquil on the west to the *ceja de la montaña* on the east. The nature and extent of this Cañari "confederation" is very poorly understood. Hatun Cañar (now Ingapirca) has been identified as the village where the most powerful chief in the "confederation" resided (Gallegos 1965 [1582]:275). There were several *señorios*, or smaller chiefdoms, within the Cañari federation, but the federation is seen as based on a single language and cultural tradition (Idrovo Urigüen 1986:53). The area now occupied by the city of Cuenca includes archaeological remains dating to before the Inka period (Agustín Landívar 1974: 6), demonstrating that Cuenca itself was a Cañari settle-ment with a history of over five hundred years of occupation.

What we know about the Cañari territory comes from the oral histo-ries of their conquerors, the Inka. The history of the Inka was a vibrant oral tradition when the Spaniards arrived, and sixteenth-century Spanish chroniclers recorded various aspects of that history. As with any oral history (Vansina 1985), Inkaic traditions were deeply entwined in the ideological and political identities of the various peoples who transmitted their history to the Spanish chroniclers, and to the political intentions of the chroniclers themselves (Rosworowski 1988:11-14). Even the assigna-tion of absolute dates for the reigns of the Inka rulers is a difficult task (Rowe 1945).

It is difficult to date the Inka expansion into southern highland Ecuador, which was a part of the rapid expansion of the empire from the imperial center at Cuzco. It would seem to have occurred under the ninth Inka, Thupa Yupanki, in the 1480s or 1490s, although much of the consoli-

21

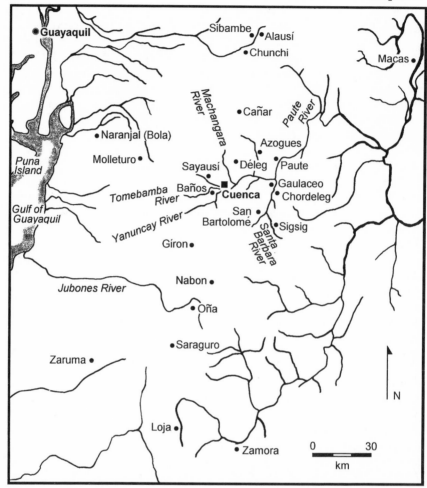

**Figure 1.** The Southern Highlands of Ecuador.

dation of Inka imperial settlements probably did not occur until later (Cobo 1964 [1653]:144; Oberem 1983:144; Salomon 1986b:144–145, 189).

   The Inka subjugation of Cañari territory was not easy, and the region was said to have been "totally destroyed," with thousands of captives sent to Cuzco as *mitmaq* (laborers for the state). Thupa Yupanki's conquest of the Cañari included at least the valley of Cuenca and the Jubones River drainage (Cobo 1964 [1653]:144; Idrovo Urigüen 1986:61). He is said to have imposed Inka religion and administration on the region, an important part of which was the construction of an Inkaic religious and administrative center at Tumipampa, or modern Cuenca. The Cañari at Tumipampa, under Inka tutelage, "built a temple and a house of the chosen women, as well as many palaces for the kings." They also built storehouses, irrigation canals, road systems, and expanded the local agricultural fields (Pablos 1965 [1582]:267; Vega 1966 [1609]:486).

It has been suggested that the Inka invasion had a lot to do with cementing local alliances into the Cañari federation, in a process of ethnogenesis (Idrovo Urigüen 1986:53). Garcilaso de la Vega stated that Thupa Yupanki "established order among the various tribes that are included under the title of Cañari" (Vega 1966 [1609]:486). Whatever their origins, the Cañari were an enduring ethnic group throughout the Inka period, serving as Inka troops in many regions (Salomon 1986b:160–161). The importance of Tumipampa as an imperial center is clear in that Thupa Yupanki's son and heir, Wayna Qhapaq, was said to have been born at Tumipampa around 1493 (Cabello Valboa 1951 [1586]:364; Cobo 1964 [1653]:155; Oberem 1983:145; Sarmiento de Gamboa 1947 [1572]:242). The building and maintenance of Tumipampa as an imperial cult and administrative center was greatly enhanced during the reign of Wayna Qhapaq. Garcilaso de la Vega (1966 [1609]:487) gives credit to both Thupa Yupanki and Wayna Qhapaq for the construction at Tumipampa of "royal buildings and palaces" with gold and silver, emerald and turquoise decorations, and specifically a "famous temple of the sun." Miguel Cabello de Valboa was the only sixteenth-century chronicler to actually interview the Inka nobility in Quito after the Spanish conquest of the region. His history of the empire suggests that Thupa Yupanki conquered regions as far north as the modern city of Quito, but was only able to consolidate the area as far north as Tumipampa into the imperial system. It was Wayna Qhapaq who is given credit for consolidating Inka rule north of Tumipampa, and Tumipampa may have been an Inka center well before any significant Inka presence occurred in Quito (Idrovo Urigüen 1986:61; Salomon 1986a:91, 94). Wayna Qhapaq's devotion to Tumipampa is clear. "He resided most of the time in Tumibamba, which is where the city of Cuenca is located now" (Cobo 1964 [1653]:159–160). He ordered the construction at Tumipampa of a temple for himself and one for his gods, and put a golden statue of his mother, Mama Ocllo, in the temple. Tumipampa was the place he was born, and he is reputed to have wanted to make Tumipampa the capital of "a kingdom in Quito similar to the one in Cuzco" (Cobo 1964 [1653]:155). Tumipampa was built to resemble Cuzco, and it had a temple of the Sun, a Huanacauri shrine, and other sacred spaces imitating those at Cuzco. It was even claimed that the stones used to build Tumipampa came from Cuzco itself (Borregán 1948 [1597]:84; Cabello Valboa 1951 [1586]:365; Cieza de León 1965 [1553]:144; Vega 1966 [1609]:486). Wayna Qhapaq is reputed to have taken the Huanacauri stone from Huanacauri Hill in Cuzco and placed it in Quito during his lifetime. The stone then returned with his mummy to Cuzco after his death (Anonymous 1979 [before 1571]:47). The temple of the sun was very subtly constructed of traditional Incaic masonry and was said to have been brought from Cuzco, with gold, silver, and precious stones as decorations. There were storehouses filled with cloth, more than 200 *aqlla* (women chosen for state/religious service) living in the temple, and "a great number of dwellings where the soldiers were garrisoned" (Cieza de León 1965 [1553]:144).

The gold statue of Mama Ocllo figures prominently in the sixteenth-century chronicles as a symbol of Wayna Qhapaq's matrilineal ties to Tumipampa. He was always accompanied in battle by the gold image, which contained the womb of his mother. When not in battle this image "lived" in its temple at Tumipampa (Cabello Valboa 1951 [1586]:364–365; Cobo 1964 [1653]:155; Sarmiento de Gamboa 1947 [1572]:242). In one particular battle the Carangui defeated Wayna Qhapaq on the northern frontier, which he blamed on nobles of Cuzco who had let him fall from his litter. The Cuzco nobles abandoned him when he refused to distribute gifts and supplies to them, but he sent the image of Mama Ocllo after them, with a Cañari woman who spoke for the dead Mama Ocllo. She persuaded the nobles to return to Wayna Qhapaq's side and continue the northern imperial conquests (Cabello Valboa 1951 [1586]:370, 374–375).

Wayna Qhapaq died along with thousands of his subjects in Quito in 1527 of a disease that may have been smallpox (Cook 1982:70; Newson 1991:88–91, 1995:145–146). He had not chosen an heir from among the sons of his consorts. He had reputedly just heard of Francisco Pizarro's initial contact with the Inca empire at Túmbez on the coast (Cieza de León 1965 [1553]:146; 1985 [before 1554]: 200–201; Cobo 1964[1653]:159–160). Before death he named his son Ninan Cuyoche as his successor, but the *calpa* (divination ceremony) said Ninan Cuyoche was a bad choice; Wayna Qhapaq then chose his son Waskar, but the calpa also showed Waskar to be a bad choice (Sarmiento de Gamboa 1947 [1572]:250–251). Wayna Qhapaq then died, before a decision about his successor had been made. His death created a crisis, and a delegation from Quito was sent to Tumipampa to give the fringe of the Inca to Ninan Cuyoche, who was in Tumipampa. The epidemic in the Cañar region at this time is said to have killed innumerable people, and when the nobles arrived at Tumipampa Ninan Cuyoche had also died (Cabello Valboa 1951:393–394; Cobo 1964 [1653]:161; Guaman Poma 1956 [1615]:86; Pablos 1965 [1582]:267; Sarmiento de Gamboa 1947 [1572]:251).

After Wayna Qhapaq's death, the lineage of Atawalpa in Quito attempted to put him forward as Wayna Qhapaq's successor and created two effigies of Wayna Qhapaq, one of which stayed in Quito and one that accompanied Atawalpa in battle on the northern frontier. Wayna Qhapaq's remains were transferred to Cuzco, where Waskar, his son by another lineage, took part in trampling on Wayna Qhapaq's "spoils and prisoners," thus legitimating Waskar as the successor. Waskar sent emissaries north to Quito to enforce his claim, and when these emissaries passed through Tumipampa one of the images of Wayna Qhapaq created by Atawalpa's lineage was installed in a temple there. The emissaries of Waskar offered the image sacrifices, but removed its Inka insignia to lessen Atawalpa's claim to rule (Sarmiento de Gamboa 1947 [1572]:254–257). Atawalpa won the war of succession between the two factions just before the Spanish arrived at Cajamarca in 1532. Pedro Pizarro stated that had Wayna Qhapaq lived it would have been impossible to conquer the Inka, as he was much loved by all (MacCormack 1991:130; Pizarro 1986 [1571]:49–50).

The 60 or 70 years of Inka rule in the Cañar region had caused massive changes in local populations. The Inka civil war and the arrival of smallpox had been the cause of the deaths of large numbers of people in the region of Tumipampa (Pablos 1965 [1582]:267). Inka imperial policy had moved at least 15,000 Cañari as mitmaq to other parts of the empire. These had in turn been replaced by mitmaq from other regions, such as the 4,000 families that Francisco Pizarro saw in 1534 being moved through Cajamarca on their way to settle in Cañar territory (Newson 1995:130).

The city of Tumipampa itself was destroyed in the Inka war of succession just before the arrival of the Spanish. Pedro de Cieza de León is the first European chronicler to describe Tumipampa, as he passed through it in 1547. He stated that "all is cast down and in ruins, but still it can be seen how great they were" (Cieza de León 1965 [1553]:142–147).

The location of Tumipampa was lost to historians at some point, and there was an ongoing debate from the 1870s up until 1923 as to which Inka ruins in southern Ecuador were the site of the regional capital known as Tumipampa (León 1983:1:95–197). The 1919 excavations of Max Uhle on the Hacienda Pumapungo, just to the southeast of the colonial core of Cuenca (Figure 2), revealed clear evidence of a major Inka administrative and religious center in that location, conclusively proving that the city of Cuenca was the location of Inkaic Tumipampa. Jesús Arriaga also points out that in 1922 several names still used in Cuenca for parts of the city, such as Huanacaure, Huatana, Cashapata, Monay, and others, were toponyms for locations in Cuzco. This is further proof of Wayna Qhapaq's determination to make the city an imperial capital (Uhle 1983 [1923]:158). Uhle's 1919 excavations reveal several palaces surrounding a central plaza (Uhle 1983 [1923]:159). To the south of the plaza was the aqllawasi (house of the chosen women) surrounding a square patio.

The identification of the building as an aqllawasi is based on the large
numbers of spindle whorls found in the excavations and the remains of
female burials found in the compound (Hyslop 1990:296; Uhle 1983
[1923]:192). East of the plaza Uhle describes a probable ushnu (ritual
stone/platform) located on the eastern side of the modern Huaina Cápac
Avenue. The sun temple at Tumipampa was one of the most famous in the
empire according to the chroniclers, but was not located in Uhle's excavations. He proposes that the sun temple was to the east of the ushnu (the
ushnu is always central to an Inka site, and thus this was probably the
central plaza of Inkaic Tumipampa) (Hyslop 1990:96–99; Uhle 1983
[1923]:164). Uhle also proposes that the modern Huaina Cápac Avenue,
which borders the colonial core of Cuenca on its eastern side, was the
main Inka road through Tumipampa, passing through the large plaza that
Uhle discovered and south past a bridge over the Tomebamba River. One
abutment of this bridge, built in Incaic style, was still visible in 1919 (Uhle
1983 [1923]:170). Excavations of Inka Tumipampa have continued in the
1980s under the sponsorship of the Central Bank Museum, and the work
of the archaeologist Jaime Idrovo has revealed fine masonry agricultural
terraces to the south of the Pumapungo temple complex. These are no
doubt related to crops grown for the ceremonial and administrative center, and their full extent is still unknown (Hyslop 1990:287).

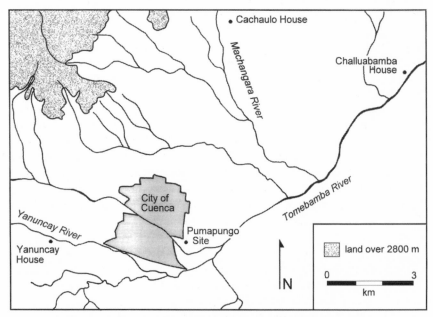

**Figure 2.** Tomebamba Valley, with sites mentioned in the text.

Excavations were also undertaken in the early 1970s at the site of Todos Santos, on the river terrace west of Pumapungo and in the southern portion of the colonial city core (Figure 3). These revealed finished Inka masonry and polychrome Inka ceramics consistent with Inka imperial styles (Agustín Landívar 1974: 6-7). Inka masonry blocks are visible as cornerstones in many standing buildings in the colonial core of the city, including the old cathedral on the east side of the central square. All of this indicates that there are extensive Inka ruins in many areas of modern Cuenca, perhaps largely focused on the riverside south of the colonial core of the city.

## FROM THE SPANISH FOUNDATION OF CUENCA TO THE TOLEDAN REFORMS

In 1519 the city of Panama, now known as Panama la Vieja, was founded by Pedrarias Davila on the south coast of what is now the nation of Panama (Figure 4). By 1522 contact with native boats on the Pacific had led to some Spanish knowledge that a rich land lay south along the coast. In 1524 Francisco Pizarro and Diego de Almagro, both citizens of Panama, formed a partnership to explore the Pacific coast south of Panama la

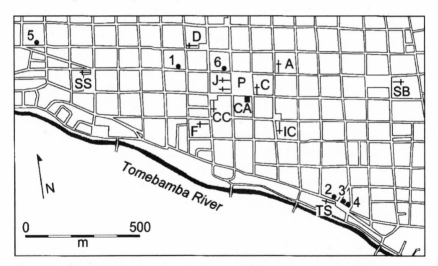

**Figure 3.** The colonial urban core of Cuenca. A: Augustinian church. C: colonial cathedral. CA: colonial *cabildo* (municipal council), CC: Carmelite convent. D: Dominican church. F. Franciscan church. IC: Immaculate Conception convent. J: Jesuit church. P: the main plaza. SB: parish church of San Blas. SS: parish church of San Sebastian. TS: parish church of *Todos Santos*. 1: *Tres Patios* house. 2: *Todas Sandos* house#2. 3: *Todos Santos* house #3. 4: *Todos Santos* house #4. 5: *Posadas* house. 6: Calle Bolívar excavations.

Vieja. They reached the coast of what is now Ecuador on their 1526-27 expedition, and at Túmbez they had their first contact with the Inka empire. They continued south along the coast and got as far as the Santa Valley, in what is now southern Peru. They captured Inka subjects, llamas, and gold and silver and returned to Panama (Montes de Oca 1983:72-78). With this evidence Francisco Pizarro returned to Spain and received the *capitulación,* or right of conquest, from Charles I. In 1531 he and his brother Gonzalo returned south along the Pacific coast and landed in what is now the Ecuadorian province of Manabí to start their travel overland. They moved south along the shoreline and eventually reached the island of Puna in the gulf of Guayaquil, where they waged war on the inhabitants for six months. They then moved on to Túmbez, where they learned that the Inka Atawalpa was in the city of Cajamarca. Moving farther south, the Spanish founded the town of San Miguel (now called Piura) in the location of a native settlement and used this base to move inland to Cajamarca in November 1532. It was in Cajamarca that the definitive actions occurred that allowed the Spanish to gain control of the Inka empire. Atawalpa was captured and killed, and with this action the Inka empire essentially fell (Montes de Oca 1983:79-84).

Sebastián de Benalcázar had been a part of Pizarro's expedition and had been left in San Miguel de Piura as the lieutenant governor. In Piura they heard news that Pedro de Alvarado, governor of Guatemala, had landed at Bahía de Caráquez on the Ecuadorian coast and was approaching the city of Quito to claim that part of the Inka empire. Benalcázar and Diego de Almagro, with two hundred men, moved north to attempt to take Quito for themselves before Alvarado could claim it (Montes de Oca 1983:85; Parry and Keith 1984:442). Benalcázar used the Inka road to move his troops north, and they stayed in the ruins of Tumipampa for eight days in February 1534 while gathering local Cañari forces to attack Quito (González Aguirre 1989:214; Parry and Keith 1984:442). The Cañari had become military specialists within the Inka empire and were resentful of the power of the city of Quito within the Inka imperial system. The Cañari, under their "generals" Vilcachumlay and Oyañe, joined Benalcázar and Almagro, hoping to overthrow their hated enemy the Inka general Rumiñahui, who was based in the city of Quito (Montes de Oca 1983:85; Salomon 1986a:103).

Rumiñahui destroyed the city of Quito as the Cañari and Spanish forces approached, and Benalcázar and his troops ended up roaming the northern part of the empire, killing and looking for treasure. When Pedro de Alvarado arrived in Quito in September 1534, Diego de Almagro was already there, and Almagro and Benalcázar convinced Alvarado to accept 100,000 pesos to give up any territorial claims. Benalcázar was declared

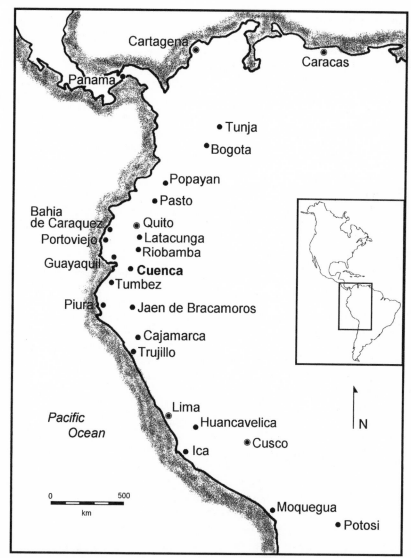

**Figure 4.** South America, with cities mentioned in the text.

lieutenant governor of Quito (Montes de Oca 1983:85). In 1536 Francisco Pizarro named the first 29 *encomenderos* (Spaniards with Crown authority to collect tribute from a group of Indians) in the region of Quito, dividing the region into *encomiendas* (a grant of Indian peoples to an encomendero). The large highland encomiendas, with diversified communities in different ecological zones, probably represented pre-Incaic social organizations (Salomon 1983:106). Gonzalo Pizarro, Diego de Sandoval, and Rodrigo Núñez de Bonilla all received large encomiendas in the region of Tumipampa (Newson 1995:226).

By the 1540s it is said that a population of Spaniards had taken up residence in the area of modern Cuenca, along the river edge in what is now Todos Santos. There is reputed to have been a plaza at the center of the settlement on the block to the north of what is now the Todos Santos church (Figure 3) (Municipio de Cuenca n.d.:10). The eminent nineteenth-century Ecuadorian historian Federico González Suárez related an old tradition that stated that the Todos Santos church dates to before the founding of the city of Cuenca (González Suárez 1983 [1891]:24). It is quite plausible that the church, which is in an unusual location not typical of Spanish ideals of town planning, may be built on a pre-Hispanic religious site. Archaeological excavation at the Todos Santos site in this neighborhood revealed the remains of Spanish mills and associated canals, all built reusing finished Inka masonry, particularly large stone lintels (Agustín Landívar 1974:8–9). These are proposed to be the remains of a wheat mill built by Rodrigo Núñez de Bonilla, a *conquistador* and encomendero who was given rights to the immediate area of Tumipampa before the Spanish town of Cuenca was officially founded and set up mills on the riverbank. Documents from 1563 relate the sale of the mill formerly owned by Núñez de Bonilla (Agustín Landívar 1974:9).

Several nearby towns had already been formally founded as small Spanish centers before Cuenca, including Gualaceo and Oña (González Aguirre 1989:214). The first Spaniards in the area were attracted by the alluvial gold in rivers, such as the Santa Barbara at Gualaceo, and by the fertile land in the region. In 1544 there were 20 work groups of 50 to 80 Indians each panning for gold in the Santa Barbara River (Landázuri Camacho 1983:188).

From 1537 to 1548 was the period of the civil wars during which Francisco Pizarro attempted to consolidate his control of Peru. As one aspect of this he named his brother Gonzalo Pizarro governor of the Quito region, thus creating a *gobernación*. In 1541 a royalist supporter replaced Gonzalo as governor of Quito, and Francisco Pizarro was killed in Lima by the allies of Diego de Almagro (Landázuri Camacho 1983:169). Gonzalo was able to gain control of most of the former Inka empire, but by 1545 royalist forces under the first viceroy of Peru, Blasco Nuñez Vela, were still in control of the Quito region. Sebastián de Benalcázar, a native of Córdoba in Spain, had assigned the encomiendas in the Quito area in the 1530s. The rebellious forces under Gonzalo Pizarro were organized largely through their regional ties to the Pizarro's hometown of Trujillo in Spain.

The encomenderos of Quito were not from this faction and, therefore, were much more sympathetic to the Crown (Lockhart 1994 [1968]:15). Gonzalo Pizarro and his forces moved north in 1545, and in the battle of Iñaquito, which took place just outside Quito in 1546, Gonzalo's forces killed the viceroy (Landázuri Camacho 1983:171). The new viceroy, Pedro de la Gasca, arrived in 1546 and restored Crown control through bargaining with the encomenderos.

La Gasca's forces captured Gonzalo Pizarro at the battle of Jaquijaguana near Cuzco in 1548, and he was executed (Landázuri Camacho 1983:171). With the end of the civil war the encomiendas throughout the viceroyalty were redistributed to people viewed as loyal to the Crown, and Francisco Campos was named the encomendero of Tumipampa in 1549 (Chacón Zhapán 1990:34; Salomon 1983:111). The *Corregimiento* (province) of Quito was formed in order to place a corregidor (Crown appointed judge/administrator) in control over the encomenderos. The corregidor of Quito ruled over a region that included Guayaquil and Cuenca until the 1570s (Chacón Zhapán 1990:264).

The formal Spanish founding of the city of Cuenca occurred in 1557, by order of the viceroy of Peru and Marques de Cañete, Don Andres Hurtado de Mendoza. The city was named Cuenca after his hometown in Spain (Villasante 1965 [1573]:142). The town was initially very small, but was laid out as a typical gridiron town with a plaza at its center and plenty of room for orderly, geometric expansion. This gridiron pattern had developed over the early years of Spanish New World colonization. Such a pattern was not formalized in written law until the 1573 city planning ordinances contained in the Laws of the Indies. These written laws postdate the foundation of Cuenca by almost two decades (Crouch et al. 1982). Many of the features of the central core were set out from the time of the initial founding, including the position of the main church, which was on the east side of the central plaza. The first church on this property was built from 1565 to 1570 (Paniagua Pérez 1989:44).

The ideals of the founding of towns were never followed to the letter, as for instance with the Act of Foundation for Cuenca, which set aside a city block for a hospital, although none was ever built there (Cordero Jaramillo 1989:86). The Franciscans founded the monastery of San Francisco in Cuenca at the time of the city's founding. It was the only religious house in Cuenca for the first 20 years of the city's history (González Aguirre 1991:15). Sebastián de Palacios died in 1558 and willed two *solares* (or city lots) for the laying out of a plaza in front of the monastery of San Francisco (Municipio de Cuenca n.d.:13). This initial presence of the Franciscans was due to their early control of the Quito region, where they had much more influence than in the other Andean areas where the Dominicans and Mercedarians dominated (Lockhart 1994 [1968]:57).

Cuenca's first Libro de Cabildo (municipal council book) outlined the initial layout of solares granted to particular individuals in the town (González Aguirre 1991:15). Many of the names in Cuenca's Act of Foundation were not later recorded in the municipal records. In Andean towns this was a common occurrence since the founding soldiers frequently moved on elsewhere. The cabildo ordered Natives from the villages of Macas and Tiquizambe to construct the first public buildings in Cuenca, the 1560 city council building, jail, and city stores (González Aguirre 1987:27). The Act of Foundation designated two separate *ejidos* (common grazing lands), one covering the plain between the Tomebamba and Yanuncay Rivers, and the other on the plain to the east of the city (Chacón Zhapán 1990:97). These areas were communal grazing lands, an area where private property ownership and fences were supposed to be illegal.

Most Andean towns in this early period were more like military camps, with soldiers and priests living in huts or shacks on their solar, raising a few chickens and producing garden vegetables on their property, and raiding the countryside for gold and food. After a few months of living in an insect-infested straw hut many gave up hope of finding a fortune in the region and sold their rights of encomienda in order to join a new expedition to another region (Aprile-Gniset 1991:166).

## THE TOWN AND THE COUNTRYSIDE

Relations with rural areas and with the existing native communities were very strictly controlled by the interests of the Crown, in competition with the interests of the encomenderos who had been granted rights in the viceroyalty of Peru. The Laws of Burgos of 1512 had outlined the rights of Native peoples in the Indies, specifically stating that they could not be enslaved unless captured in war, and that they could own property and receive salaries. The Crown wanted to prevent the encomenderos from becoming feudal lords in the New World, and thus some Indian freedoms were in the interest of the Crown. Encomenderos were given the right to collect tribute from the Indian groups under their power and were responsible for conversion of those Natives to Christianity (Jácome 1983:148–149).

Up until the Toledan reforms the majority of Natives in the vicinity of Cuenca lived in dispersed rural communities, with the house of the kuraka (local ethnic lord or chieftain) as the ceremonial center of their local region and trade systems with lowland groups still intact (Salomon 1983:114). Control over these native groups was placed in the hands of the Spanish encomendero who had been given the rights to their labor. The town of Cuenca was initially entirely dependent on the labor of the local Native population, as was common in Andean colonial cities. One of the initial rulings of the Cuenca cabildo was that the Native kurakas, who basically controlled the countryside, had to supply food for Cuenca for Friday and Saturday markets. The kurakas provided the workforce that built the city, and worked the gardens and *estancias* (livestock ranches). The first Libro de Cabildo is full of petitions by *vecinos* for *mitayos* (Indian tribute laborers) to be assigned to them. With the creation of the Audiencia of Quito in 1563, land distribution in rural areas came under the responsibility of the Audiencia president, removing this power from the *cabildo* (Jácome 1983:138; Salomon 1983:120). With the consolidation of Spanish power over the rural hinterland there was sufficient agricultural production by Spanish estancias so that the obligation of kurakas to supply food for the Cuenca market was reduced to one day per week (Moscoso C. 1989:346–348).

In Cuenca the economy of the late 1500s centered on several mines, such as those of Cerro de Espíritu Santo just north of the city, Malal, Cañaribamba, and the mercury mine at Azogues (Figure 1) (Newson 1995:230). The Azogues mercury deposits were discovered in 1558, very soon after patio amalgamation processing of silver ore had been introduced into New Spain. The gold deposits at Zaruma were discovered in 1560, and by 1600 there were 30 mills for processing ore at the site (Anda Aguirre 1960:33). In 1560 significant silver deposits were discovered at Zaruma, south of Cuenca. This was the most productive of the early mines in the region, with other important centers at Gualaceo and Zamora (Jácome 1983:158). In 1563 the discovery of mercury at the Huancavelica mine in Peru provided a cheaper source for the metal. With a lack of Native laborers, the Azogues mercury mines closed by 1565 (Chacón Zhapán 1990:147; Pablos 1965 [1582]:269).

Insufficient Native labor caused by epidemics and community dislocations closed many of the gold and silver mines, and by the 1580s agriculture, mainly in cereals, and cattle had taken over from mining as the economic mainstays of the region (Newson 1995:231). Foodstuffs were produced locally, but from the beginning of the colonial period New Spain provided pitch, dyes, cotton, and many other products that were shipped south along the Pacific coast to Guayaquil then hauled overland to cities such as Cuenca (MacLeod 1984:369).

## TOLEDAN CUENCA

Under Viceroy Francisco de Toledo the reforms of the 1570s constituted a major reorganization of Andean rural villages and the imperial system in

general. The goal was to increase royal revenues and to alleviate labor
shortages. From the initial period of Spanish colonization all Native villages had been assigned to supply *mita* (tribute) labor to the encomendero
of their village. By the 1580s the audiencia of Quito experienced difficulties since a large percentage of the tributarios had fled their home villages
to avoid the onerous labor tribute demanded by the Spaniards (Powers
1990:313). These labor shortages became more acute with the massive
epidemics caused by the introduction of Old World diseases. From 1561 to
1591 the population of tributarios fell by half in the Quito region (Salomon
1983:108). The combination of mine labor, epidemic disease, and the flight
of Natives to avoid tribute burdens greatly reduced the Native population
in the Cuenca region, with an estimated decline from 58,000 Cañari prior
to Spanish conquest to perhaps 12,000 in the 1590s. The mines at Zaruma
and Zamora were the main factor in this decline, largely because of population dislocations as Natives fled the region to avoid mining tribute requirements. In the 1590s Cuencanos requested that both northern Natives
be moved into the area and that African slaves be imported for mine labor
(Newson 1995:236; Powers 1995:17–18, 37–38).

Viceroy Toledo founded the Corregimiento of Cuenca in 1579, and
appointed a Crown representative for the district (Chacón Zhapán 1990:273).
Many of the Native towns surrounding Cuenca were formally founded by
Toledan ordinances, although many were actually pre-Hispanic Native ceremonial or habitation sites. These towns included Azogues, Cañar, Girón,
Cañaribamba, Paccha, Gualaceo, San Bartolomé, Paute, Déleg, and
Molleturo (Chacón Zhapán 1990:58). The Toledan "founding" of such towns
meant that in theory a new town site was laid out with a central plaza and
a chapel. Natives who lived in dispersed settlements in the region were
forced to move into the town and to receive religious instruction.

Two other towns founded in the Toledan era were Sevilla de Oro and
Logroño de los Caballeros, both in the lowlands east of Cuenca. Gold had
been discovered in the rivers, but both towns were destroyed by a Native
Jívaro rebellion in 1579 (Chacón Zhapán 1990:297). The Amazonian regions
east of Cuenca were never really controlled by the Spanish in the colonial
period, and even in 1730 the town of Macas required military assistance
from Cuenca because of Jívaro raids (Chacón Zhapán 1990:301).

As Spaniards gained greater control over the highland rural areas
around Cuenca, the town began to grow. Throughout the sixteenth century Cuenca was a merchant transit point for goods going to the big
mining centers of Zaruma and Zamora (Moscoso C. 1989:347) and a
major trade center for agricultural products. In 1573 the town had 60
Spanish *vecinos,* or full-fledged citizens, with their houses, one church
with a priest, the Franciscan monastery, and town council buildings. The
mines one league away at Llingate and Xililcay were prosperous, and the

thermal baths in the town of Baños, with their curative powers, were also well known (Villasante 1965 [1573]:141–142). In the 1570s two other neighborhood churches were founded, the San Blas church to the east of the town, and the San Sebastián church to the west. Both were initially classified as simple *ermitas* (small chapels) and may have been founded on sites of pre-Hispanic religious significance (Chacón Zhapán 1990:460–462). By 1582 the small Spanish population of Cuenca had almost doubled, to 150 resident vecinos. One observer described the town as "neither more nor less than a town in Spain," with proper plazas and streets, and Franciscan, Augustinian and Dominican monasteries (Pablos 1965 [1582]). In the following year the San Blas ermita became the parish church for the Native Andean residents living in the area east of the town center (Chacón Zhapán 1990:460).

Besides the religious institutions and the town hall, the other major institution in Cuenca in the sixteenth century was the hospital. In 1582 the baths at Baños had been identified as a likely site to build it, but this was not to be (Pablos 1965 [1582]:267). Two years later the Hospital de la Caridad was founded beside the Todos Santos church, in the riverside area near the mills (Cordero Jaramillo 1989:87; Pablos 1965 [1582]:270). The hospital was presumably built by the Cofradía y Hermandad de la Caridad y Misericordia (Fraternity and Brotherhood of Charity and Mercy). This was an organization founded by audiencia president Hernando de Santillán in Quito in 1565, and also associated with the construction of hospitals in Riobamba, Otavalo, and Loja in the 1580s (Alchon 1991:44). In 1589 a typhus epidemic overwhelmed the small facility, and a new hospital was built in a central location on the northeast corner of the block directly north of the main plaza. Ironically, this property was available to the cabildo because the 1557 Act of Foundation had designated the site as the municipal slaughterhouse (González Aguirre 1991:15). Part of the hospital cemetery was revealed by recent road construction at the intersection of Gran Colombia and Luis Cordero (Cordero Jaramillo 1989:88). In 1599 the Order of San Juan de Dios, also known as the Hermanos Hospitalarios or the Hermanos Jandenianos, took control of the facility. Well known for their efficient hospital administration throughout Spain and the Americas, the order accepted the task of refurbishing the dilapidated building (Alchon 1991:70; Cordero Jaramillo 1989:89).

# FROM THE ALCABALA REVOLT
# TO THE VICEROYALTY OF NEW GRANADA

Throughout the late sixteenth century and continuing into the seventeenth Cuenca's mining and livestock economy remained outside the *obraje* system of textile production that dominated the northern parts of the audiencia of Quito (Phelan 1967:69; Poloni 1992b:280). The obraje system relied on workshops located on rural estates and in Native villages to produce fine woolens in huge quantities, which were exported throughout the empire (Brading 1984:430). In 1592 the imposition of an *alcabala*, or sales tax, by Philip II caused a revolt by the cabildo of the city of Quito against audiencia authority and Crown abuses (Landázuri Camacho 1983:201). Cuenca and the southern highlands, with little interest in textile exports, remained loyal to the Crown throughout the two-year revolt and sent royalist troops north to quash the rebellion (Chacón Zhapán 1990:279).

The agricultural production in the southern highlands was diverse, with sugar cane and fruit production in the lower valleys of Cañaribamba and Paute, and grain and livestock production in the higher areas around Cuenca (Espinoza et al. 1982:39). Livestock was traded overland from Cuenca as far as Lima in the seventeenth century (Aldana Rivera 1989:113). The Guayaquil market received Cuenca wool, cotton cloth, leather, tar, rope, bread, hams, cheese, and sarsaparilla. The supply of flour, biscuits, and bread to the coastal population appears to have been a particularly important part of Cuenca's economy. These goods were transported to the coast at Bola or Naranjal and from there on rafts to Guayaquil (Anonymous 1992 [1605]:20, 27).

In return Guayaquil supplied Cuenca with imported goods from various parts of the empire. By the late sixteenth century Chinese silks and porcelains transshipped from Manila galleons arrived in Guayaquil for sale. Wine, olives, and olive oil from Peru were all imported into Guayaquil. The Guayaquil region itself produced cacao from the late 1500s onward, and shipments to New Spain were quite large, even after 1615 when the Crown banned cacao exports to New Spain (MacLeod 1984:369, 373). All of these products were available to Cuenca's elite, who were in constant contact with Guayaquil merchants.

Up until the early seventeenth century the economy of the audiencia and much of its agricultural production relied on the tribute extracted from encomienda privileges over Native communities. By the mid-seventeenth century Native groups had lost much of their control over rural land, and the emphasis shifted from tribute to large-scale Spanish land ownership in rural areas (Jácome 1983:137). Throughout the sixteenth and seventeenth centuries Indians in the audiencia of Quito moved away from their home villages in huge numbers, settling in the cities, on other haciendas, or in other Native villages, in order to avoid the heavy burden of their local mita tribute obligations. By the early 1600s the majority of tributarios abandoned their communities in search of new lives. The *caciques*, or leaders, of Native villages still paid tribute for all of these individuals, and in 1651–52 the situation led to a crisis in Cuenca in which the local caciques were imprisoned for failure to pay the tributes for absentee community members. They were released after a desperate petition stating that tribute money could not be paid unless the caciques were freed to find the missing community members (Powers 1995:149).

The migrants who left their home villages usually became Crown forasteros. These were Indians who did not live in their place of origin, and thus did not have mita obligations to a particular encomendero. Instead these forasteros paid cash tribute to the Crown itself and were free to pursue wage labor as agricultural workers, artisans, and so forth. Many forastero communities undertook legal battles pitting Crown interests against those of the local elite. In Cuenca in 1666 the forasteros, who had been forced by the local elite to provide tribute agricultural labor, threatened to leave town unless this practice stopped. Karen Powers points out the inaccuracy of the traditional view of Native people in the audiencia of Quito tied to a particular parcel of land. Instead, such Native migration patterns were a form of power brokerage "akin to an oversized game of musical chairs with the *parcialidades de la Real Corona* as the most coveted seats" (1990:319).

The seventeenth-century economy of the southern highlands remained largely based on agriculture. Mine output fluctuated, and by 1628 the dwindling deposits at the important Zaruma mines signaled a regional decline in the mining economy (Jácome 1983:158; Jiménez de la Espada 1965:3:81–83). In the 1640s the Crown recognized the curative powers of quinine, obtained from the bark of the native cinchona tree collected in the highlands around Cuenca (Chacón Zhapán 1990:213), but this was exploited on a small scale at first, and only became a major economic force in the eighteenth century. The main boost to Cuenca's economy was provided by the decline of the obraje system in the northern part of the audiencia. From the 1690s onward disease in the north led to the destruction of the workshop economy and large-scale movements of Native Andeans into the southern highlands. The formal economy of the Cuenca region benefited from the influx of labor and the opening in the textile economy, and local cottage-level production of rough cloth for export expanded (Andrien 1995:33).

The number of religious orders in Cuenca expanded along with the economy. The Concepcionistas (Immaculate Conception) convent was founded in 1599, and after almost 30 years of opposition from the other religious orders the Jesuits established a church and school on the west side of the main plaza in 1643 (Chacón Zhapán 1990:482–484). The Carmelite convent, called the Monasterio del Carmen de la Asunción, was founded in 1682 (Muñoz Vega 1989:135). In 1692 the *ermita* (chapel) in the San Sebastian neighborhood became an official parish church (Chacón Zhapán 1990:461–462), perhaps in response to the growing population of forasteros moving into the peripheral neighborhoods west of Cuenca.

## NEW GRANADA

In 1717 Cuenca with the rest of the audiencia of Quito became part of the viceroyalty of New Granada, with the capital at Bogotá. This reorganization did not last long, and in 1720 viceregal control returned to Lima (Chacón Zhapán 1990:316). In 1739 the Crown transferred the audiencia of Quito once again to the viceroyalty of New Granada, and this became a permanent move. Cuenca remained under the viceregal authority of Bogotá for the remainder of the colonial period (Chacón Zhapán 1990:325).

The urban population grew slowly, reaching between 14,000 and 25,000 in the mideighteenth century (Merisalde y Santiesteban 1992 [1765]:374; Montufar y Fraso 1992 [1754]:342). Many of the newer urban inhabitants took up smallholdings surrounding the city, and the former ejido between the rivers south of the city became known as "Jamaica" and was taken over with small *caserios*, or hamlets, of freehold agriculturalists and craftspeople (Municipio de Cuenca n.d.:18). This urban population increase was matched by rural increases, as Native Andean immigrants arrived steadily from the northern audiencia, particularly Riobamba, from the 1690s to the 1780s (Andrien 1995:41).

Large haciendas dominated the rural areas of the southern highlands throughout the eighteenth century, with grain and sugar being the two most important crops. Livestock were also a large part of the economy and were exported to Quito. Trade with the coast was still important in the eighteenth century, and it appears to have been sent mainly through Bola, or Naranjal. Cuenca supplied Guayaquil with flour, sugar, and cloth. The cotton textiles of Cuenca were of good quality and sold as far away as Lima. Coastal products shipped to Cuenca included salt, cacao, wax, tobacco, rice, fish, and cotton. From farther afield, via Guayaquil, Cuenca received clothes and metal goods from Central America, dye from Guatemala, and ceramics, spices, and perfumes from the Far East via Acapulco (Merisalde y Santiesteban 1992 [1765]:374; Montufar y Fraso 1992 [1754]:336, 342, 362–363).

In the mid-eighteenth century the first stirrings of the Enlightenment were seen in Cuenca. An infamous incident occurred in 1739, with the arrival of the French Geodesic Mission in the city, under the command of Jorge Juan and Charles de la Condamine. The French surgeon accompanying the mission, Jean Senierges, offended the local Cuenca elite after incidents involving the assault and attempted rape of a young woman and the beating of a man believed to be a thief. When the Frenchmen attended a bullfight in the San Sebastián plaza a scuffle broke out between the surgeon and a relative of the woman who had been assaulted. The alcalde intervened and was himself attacked by the surgeon. At this point there were shouts that the French were armed, and a riot broke out as the crowd attacked the French academics. The French ran for their lives, and Senierges died later from wounds he received in the riot (Chacón Zhapán 1990:321). The incident is now thought of as an example of the resistance of Andean colonial populations to the new ideas of European Enlightenment thought, yet the actions of the surgeon seem more than enough to have caused a reasonable populace to take some form of action.

Public health in Cuenca had not changed much by the mid-eighteenth century. A 1736 report to the audiencia charged that the hospital, still nominally run by the order of San Juan de Dios, was dilapidated, cold, and damp. The food was seen as inadequate, and patients, who were largely Native, had to bring their own beds (Alchon 1991:109). Juan and Ulloa described the hospital in Cuenca in 1739 as badly administered and half in ruins due to lack of care (Juan and Ulloa 1978 [1748]:433). In an attempt to improve conditions, the hospital was transferred in 1742 to the control of the Bethlemites, and the name was changed to the Hospital de Belén (Cordero Jaramillo 1989:89). The Bethlemite order was known to have dedicated hospital administrators, and it was felt the conditions would be greatly improved by their takeover (Alchon 1991:108).

## THE BOURBON PERIOD AND INDEPENDENCE

In 1762 the British captured Havana as part of the Seven Years' War, and the Spanish Crown under Charles III had to act. The regime instituted new taxes and attempted greater efficiency throughout the Spanish New World colonies in order to gain more revenue for military support. The Peace of Paris in 1763 ended the Seven Years' War, but the Bourbon reforms toward increased centralization and exercise of Spanish civil authority in the colonies were lasting (Andrien 1994:189-191).

Administratively these reforms were felt in Cuenca in 1771, with the creation of the gobernación of Cuenca. This was roughly the area now made up by Azuay and Cañar, replacing the former corregimiento (Espinoza et al. 1982:33). The state fiscal bureaucracy in the audiencia of Quito was also reformed, and from 1775 to 1802 higher taxes and a more centralized taxation system resulted in a tripling of government tax revenues from the new gobernacíon of Cuenca. This was a more modest increase than that seen in other parts of the audiencia, because tax revenue in Cuenca was largely from Native tribute, and the tax base remained virtually unchanged in the region. Much of the increased revenue was sent to Spain, but the expenses of local Cuenca government also doubled over the 1770 to 1795 period (Andrien 1994:172–183). The new gobernación undertook extensive reforms in taxation, economic concerns, and public works (Achig 1980).

In the audiencia of Quito the economy changed markedly in the Bourbon period. In Quito the cloth market had declined massively in the early eighteenth century, as other Andean cities like Cajamarca and Cuzco increased their cloth production. The opening of the Cape Horn sea route, the industrialization of European cloth production, and Bourbon changes in trade law allowed Andeans much larger access to European cloth imports. By the 1780s Quito switched from producing quality cloth for markets such as Lima, and focused instead on coarse woolens for the markets of New Granada to the north (Brading 1984:431). The cacao production of New Granada, which had been supplying the huge Mexican markets, was diverted to the newly opening European market in the 1760s. This left the Mexican markets in need of cacao, and in Guayaquil cacao exports to Mexico increased steadily and massively from the 1760s until the end of the colonial period (Andrien 1994:172; Brading 1984:432).

Late eighteenth-century Cuenca and its region were economically dominated by agricultural and textile exports for the internal colonial market, and cinchona bark exports worldwide for quinine production (Andrien 1995:49–50; Montufar y Fraso 1992 [1754]:344; Palomeque 1982:121). The collapse of the Quito obraje system led to the development of a large-volume cottage industry in woolens and cotton, woven largely by women and children to supplement agricultural income in the villages surrounding Cuenca (Andrien 1995:72–74). Livestock and wheat were exported to the coast in large quantities, and textiles, cinchona, and livestock were supplied to coastal cities in Peru via Piura (Aldana Rivera 1989; Palomeque 1990:17; Vega Ugalde 1986:18–19). Exterior trade via Guayaquil was limited, and there was concern expressed that the steep and dangerous path from Cuenca to the coast at Naranjal needed to be improved (Requena y Herrera 1992 [1774]:525–526). The major export from Cuenca to Europe was cinchona bark, harvested from wild trees with machetes. The process killed many of the trees, and by the 1790s merchants began to complain about dwindling stocks of cinchona in the region (Andrien 1995:50).

Unlike the large-scale weaving workshops in the northern part of the audiencia, textile production in the Cuenca area was a rural cottage indus-

try. Dealers imported raw cotton from Lima and distributed it to rural
subsistence agriculturalists. These peasants wove rough bolts of cotton
cloth and blankets from locally produced wool. Most of this production
was exported to northern Peru and to Lima, and most luxury imported
goods in turn came from Lima to Cuenca (Palomeque 1982:121–122,
1990:17). European imports into Cuenca became significant after the opening
of free trade in 1778. Throughout the 1780s and 1790s a small but steady
supply of European luxury goods entered the region, largely through Lima
merchants (Andrien 1995:156–159). For the purposes of archaeology it is
important to note that the regional economy was very insular, and the
vast majority of people could not afford such luxury goods that had been
imported over long distances (Palomeque 1990:24).

Cuenca's urban population grew steadily in the eighteenth century,
and what had been 12 to 15,000 residents in the 1740s grew to over 31,000
people in the city of Cuenca and the parishes of San Blas and San Sebastián
in the 1780s (Andrien 1995:49). Along with increased urbanization, the
town was also subject to greatly increased intervention from higher levels
of government. Throughout the Spanish empire new taxes, new public
health measures, and many other forms of intervention became common
in the late eighteenth century. Cuenca changed rapidly under the administration of audiencia president José García de León y Pizarro (Andrien
1994:190–210). The first house-to-house census of the city was conducted
in 1778, a measure designed in part to take control of the workforce away
from landowners and put it in the hands of the imperial government
(Espinoza et al. 1982:42). The physical layout of the city was also altered
and improved. Urban landowners were ordered to pave the streets with
cobbles and whitewash their houses. The municipal buildings were reconstructed, including the town hall, two new jails, and the new *rollo de la
justicia* (pillar of justice) in the northeast corner of the city core, at what
must have been an important entrance to the city coming from Quito
(Municipio de Cuenca n.d.:18). The rollo is still standing today, and it is
likely that the municipal buildings on the south side of the main plaza,
which were torn down in the 1960s to make way for modern government
offices, were the original Bourbon jail and town hall (Municipio de Cuenca
n.d.:18).

Urban public health was another area of wide-ranging concern for
Bourbon administrators. The butchering of animals within private households or in religious houses "in a furtive manner" was banned by the
cabildo in 1779. Instead instructions were given on the correct procedure
of showing the live animal in the main plaza, and then taking it to one of
the secondary plazas to kill it. An alternative was to use the municipal
slaughtering area one and a half blocks from the main plaza, near the

hospital (ANH/C C.94.055). The spread of smallpox within the empire was a serious concern to the Crown, and the royal ordinance of 1784, based on the latest scientific evidence from Europe, ordered that victims of smallpox in urban areas be removed from their homes and placed in hospitals. Church cemeteries in urban areas were to be closed (Gil 1983 [1784]). When received in Cuenca, the ordinance to remove the sick from their homes caused opposition (ANH/C L. 2 f.37r). The Cuenca cabildo responded quickly, however, to the demand for removal of the cemetery. The cabildo petitioned the church and hospital authorities and financed a new cemetery in Cullca, on the northeastern outskirts of Cuenca (ANH/C L. 11 f. 39r). All of these measures reflected the newly proactive measures of Bourbon administrations in the lives of urban people throughout the Spanish colonies.

In religious terms the Bourbon period was marked by the 1779 creation of the office of bishopric of Cuenca, separate from the bishopric of Quito, an idea that had first been suggested in 1752. The first bishop of Cuenca was José Carrión y Marfil. The Bishopric extended from Jaen de Bracamoros in the south to Alausí in the north, and included the coast from Guayaquil to Portoviejo (Martínez Borrero 1983:49). A more profound change was the expulsion of the Jesuits in 1767 by Charles III from all of his realms. Ostensibly because of the 1766 riots in Spain that were blamed on the Jesuits, the expulsion was really more a matter of the Jesuits' refusal to accept royal authority over that of the pope. Five hundred Jesuits were expelled from the viceroyalty of Peru alone, including those of the Jesuit college on Cuenca's main plaza. The Jesuit schools were a preeminent force in the education of the colonial elite in cities such as Cuenca. Until their expulsion this, combined with their extensive landholdings, made the order a very powerful force within the colonial system. In concert with Bourbon administrative reforms, the end of Jesuit scholasticism was a key step in the transformation of intellectual life in the Spanish colonies to Enlightenment ideals of experimentation, the observation of nature, and inductive reasoning (Barrera 1956:29–30; Batllori 1965; Ronan 1978). Ironically, the first example of an Enlightenment-style history of the region was the *Historia Natural del Reino de Quito* completed by the exiled Jesuit Juan de Velasco in 1789. His effort paralleled that of other Jesuit exiles who wrote passionate histories of the regions in which they were born. Such volumes later helped crystallize patriotic sentiment in various parts of Latin America in the period leading up to the Wars of Independence (Barrera 1956:29–30; Martínez Borrero 1983:38; Velasco 1981 [1789]).

The crisis in the Spanish monarchy in 1808 led to Spanish-American opportunities to rework their allegiances and relationship to Spain. In the city of Quito in 1808-1809 a group of wealthy creole landowners rebelled against the president of the audiencia. The dissatisfaction of the Quito elite was partly due to the decline of textile exports following the Bourbon commercial reforms. The initial rebellion was short-lived, and neither Guayaquil nor Cuenca joined in the rebellion. Forces loyal to the viceroy of Peru eventually regained control of Quito, and the creoles were brutally massacred. These events served to create more support for reform, and from September 1810 to February 1812, a "revolutionary congress" drafted a constitution of the "Free State of Quito." Guayaquil and Cuenca remained royalist strongholds, however, and in November 1812 forces from these cities took Quito once again. In the first decade of the nineteenth century, Cuenca was largely economically independent of Quito, with strong ties to northern Peru and to Guayaquil. The region also had a certain degree of political independence through its new Bourbon status as a gobernación, which decreased its ties to Quito (Bushnell 1985:95, 101-103, 117-118; Luna Tamayo 1987:110-111; Lynch 1986 [1973]:236-237).

The revolutionary period from 1809 to 1822 was one of considerable change. An economic shift occurred as Guayaquil began to replace Lima as the major coastal connection for goods to and from Cuenca. The town managed to maintain relatively stable imports of goods until 1812, but after this date the level of imports dropped (Palomeque 1980:139-140, 1982:123). The centralized bureaucracy of the audiencia of Quito lost much of its power, and Quito, Cuenca, and Guayaquil operated as largely independent entities (Andrien 1994:184). Rural people, who had previously gained considerable portions of their income from cottage textile production, suffered the most from the breakdown of trade ties. In the early nineteenth century many Native Andeans left the southern highlands to look for cash labor on the coast (Palomeque 1990:128-138, 168-184).

By 1820 Símon Bolívar had liberated the areas of modern Venezuela and Colombia, and the newly independent nation of Gran Colombia took shape. In October 1820 the city of Guayaquil established a revolutionary *junta*, and Bolívar was worried that the forces of José de San Martín would reach the audiencia of Quito first, to incorporate it into an independent Peru. Bolívar sent General Antonio José de Sucre to Guayaquil, where in May 1821 he established an alliance between Guayaquil and Gran Colombia (Lynch 1973:245-246). Bolívar advanced on Quito from the north, but could not break through; Sucre advanced from the coast, and José de San Martín sent a combined Argentine-Chilean-Peruvian force through the highlands. In May 1822 Quito was liberated from royalist hands in the Battle of Pichincha. Quito and Guayaquil had already become part of Gran Colombia by the time San Martín met Bolívar in Guayaquil in July 1822 (Bushnell 1985:143; Lynch 1986 [1973]:247).

# GRAN COLOMBIA AND
# THE INDUSTRIAL REVOLUTION

State control of Cuenca was never very solid throughout the period that it was a part of the new republic of Gran Colombia (Andrien 1994:184). The Wars of Independence had destroyed much of the local economic base and had made former trade connections tenuous. By 1826 English cloth imports coming through Guayaquil and Lima ended the market for South American cloth production (Palomeque 1982:124–125). Símon Bolívar's decree of 1829 prevented trade with Peru because of fears of annexation of the new nation. Combined with English textile imports, this edict destroyed the Cuenca cotton textile industry (Palomeque 1990:21). Much of the import-export commerce that did take place through Cuenca was contraband, including the importation of cotton and salt from Peru through Loja to Cuenca (Palomeque 1990:34).

The Wars of Independence had reduced Cuenca once again to a regional agricultural economy. The royal cinchona bark monopoly, which had preserved wild trees from overexploitation, was replaced by private harvesting that killed many of the trees, and by 1835 cinchona bark had lost its export importance (Palomeque 1990:19). In rural areas many of the haciendas were raided and destroyed in the Wars of Independence, and difficulties with the market system meant that from about 1820 to 1850 production of food was mainly on a smaller scale and for regional consumption (Palomeque 1990:147).

The religious orders lost a great deal of their power during the Independence period. Formerly some of the largest landowners, they saw a massive decline in their landholdings in the first half of the nineteenth century (Palomeque 1990:152). In 1832 the Augustinians abandoned their convent in Cuenca (Muñoz Vega 1989:135).

In 1826 Gran Colombia's credit collapsed, and in 1830 the country broke into three new republics: Venezuela, New Granada, and Ecuador. Ecuador was initially led by General Juan José Flores, who by 1843 had proclaimed a new Ecuadorian constitution, based on a Napoleonic model (Deas 1987:208; Safford 1987:67).

The Ecuadorian economy after 1830 was driven by exports of cacao and Panama hats, both of which initially came from the coast. Ecuador after 1830 remained a world leader in cacao production, and the coastal regions experienced demographic growth and industrial modernization much more quickly than the highland regions. The coastal elite gained considerable economic and political power in the new republic (Deas 1987:213). Regionalism and strong provincial rivalries were widespread from Independence up until the late nineteenth-century in Ecuador, and

Cuenca's nineteenth-century economy, based largely on cinchona bark, textiles, and livestock, was focused on trade with Guayaquil and northern Peru rather than with Quito (Luna Tamayo 1987). Violent local revolts were not uncommon as rapid economic and political changes destabilized local populations (Deas 1987:224–225).

The economy of Cuenca was stagnant from 1830 to 1860. The tax base dropped drastically during the Wars of Independence and did not recover to Bourbon levels again until the 1860s (Andrien 1994:185). Living conditions, particularly for rural Native people, were very poor, and Native resistance, through migration to other areas or localized violence, was a constant feature of the early nineteenth century. During this period Native people attempted to avoid the crushing burdens of church and state taxes, involuntary participation in public works projects, and constant threats to their remaining communal properties, which were frequently sold off to large landowners (Achig Subía and Mora Castro 1987; Vintimilla 1981).

One of the major developments worldwide in the midnineteenth century was the new scientific basis for medicine in European thought. A new emphasis on public health and hygiene led to an ability to safely increase the size of cities and house urban workers through sanitation and isolation of the ill. Cuenca remained a midsized town, never becoming a large industrial center, but the public health aspects of the Industrial Revolution were reflected in the 1831 movement of the hospital out of the city center to prevent the spread of infectious disease (Cordero Jaramillo 1989:90).

During the 1850s Guayaquil entered world markets, and Cuenca followed. Many different Ecuadorian products were exported to the world through Guayaquil, dominated by cacao, which continued to be Ecuador's most important export from the 1890s up until the 1920s. From this export economy the coast continued to gain prominence in national political and economic power. Quinine exports from the highlands were also important from 1850 to 1885, involving a harvest of wild trees that killed many of them. In the 1880s cinchona grown on Dutch and English plantations in Java, India, and Ceylon flooded the world market, and wild Andean cinchona bark was never marketable again (Deas 1986:669–670; Palomeque 1990; Rappaport 1990b:97).

From the 1850s to the 1880s the big regional haciendas surrounding Cuenca were subdivided, and many of the Natives who had been debt peons moved to tiny independent smallholdings. Imprisonment for debt was abolished in 1916, and from then until the 1950s the horrors of *concertaje*, or coerced labor, in the rural highlands slowly diminished (Ayala Mora 1991:688; Deas 1986:670; Palomeque 1990:126–130).

Cuenca never became a large factory town, but several industrial-level factories were set up in the town in the 1850s and 1860s. A quinine sulfite factory, textile mill, and iron foundry were important elements of the late-nineteenth-century economy (Palomeque 1990:52–53). Cottage industries have always been important to Cuenca, and in 1845 the Ecuadorian government, in an effort to diversify the stagnant economy of the region, founded trade schools to develop the Manabí craft of *paja toquilla*, hat making, in Cuenca (Palomeque 1990:128). The paja toquilla hat was a large regional export from the 1850s until fashion changes after World War II led to a decline in the market (Deas 1986:670). The hat is better known to North Americans as the Panama hat, because of its introduction during the 1849 California gold rush. Miners bought the hats when they traveled overland across Panama on their trip from the eastern seaboard of North America.

With a new focus on world exports there was an opening up of Cuenca for imported consumer goods in return. The urban elite of the 1850s acquired a taste for European and North American tablewares, glassware, cloth, furniture, and many other items (Palomeque 1990:56).

Unfortunately for the purposes of architectural preservation, this new wealth also created a desire for "French" style household architecture to replace outmoded colonial styles (Palomeque 1982:124). Many of the houses of the colonial elite in the urban core were entirely replaced or greatly modified in the mid-nineteenth century.

The 1895 Liberal Revolution brought General Eloy Alfara into control of the republic along with the coastal oligarchy that supported integration into the international economy, a railway from Quito to Guayaquil, and the separation of Church and state powers. In highland regions such as Cuenca, however, conservative landowners remained in power, and the Church remained a major political force into the twentieth century (Ayala Mora 1991:687–688). From the 1850s onward the churches began to be rebuilt in Cuenca. In 1860 the Padres Redentoristas reoccupied the abandoned Augustinian convent and rebuilt the entire complex (Muñoz Vega 1989:135). The new cathedral of Cuenca was begun in 1866 on the former Jesuit property on the main plaza, a huge building and an appropriate symbol of Cuenca's late-nineteenth-century optimism.

# The Domestic Architecture of Colonial Cuenca | 3

In the mid-1970s, Sidney Markman briefly studied the historical architecture of Cuenca, under contract for the municipality. His conclusions provide a rather depressing picture for the preservation of colonial architecture in the city. He points out that the majority of houses in the city center, far from being colonial, are "late nineteenth-century Parisian" in style. If this were not bad enough, since 1950 a "bad interpretation" of the International style has destroyed much of the feel of Cuenca's historic core, which has in any case been abandoned by the elite in favor of the suburbs. His recommendations for the preservation of Cuenca's colonial architecture are if anything even more depressing. Markman felt that the conservation of houses in poor neighborhoods, where sewage and water facilities are absent, would be a gross misuse of limited resources and would "mummify" the city into the form of a museum as bad as Colonial Williamsburg (Markman 1979:18–19).

After spending ten months from 1993 to 1994 searching for the remaining colonial-era houses of Cuenca, I cannot disagree with the substance of Markman's assessment, but his pessimism does seem a bit strongly put. The colonial architecture of southern highland Ecuador is in imminent danger. The large numbers of colonial houses visible in photographs of the city taken in the 1940s have for the most part disappeared. Of the eight houses outlined in this chapter, the owners of the Posadas, Cachaulo, and Challuabamba examples would like to have them demolished in order to replace them with modern buildings, while all the other houses show the results of heavy alteration for more modern uses. The people of Cuenca have concentrated on very admirable efforts to preserve the rich heritage of colonial religious architecture in the core of the city. Unfortunately the Yanuncay house is the single example of colonial domestic architecture in the southern highlands, urban or rural, that has been slated for any sort of preservation or restoration effort. With this book I would like to make a small contribution to that preservation effort, in presenting eight houses that at least partially maintain their colonial architectural layout.

I would not advocate turning Cuenca into a giant Colonial Williamsburg-style museum any more than Markman would, but I think there is very

47

little danger of that. The city is the third largest in Ecuador and is a vibrant place. It is true that many Cuencanos express a great admiration of modernization efforts. I also heard everyone from municipal officials to taxi drivers to the owners of many of these houses express a love of the older architecture of Cuenca and the memories of a bygone era which the old houses represent. I believe that several of the houses presented in this volume will be around for some time to come.

## THE GRIDIRON TOWN

In 1557 the city of Cuenca was founded on the ruins of the Incaic center of Tumipampa. Cuenca is a fairly late example of the state-controlled foundation of urban gridiron towns which dominated the entire sixteenth-century Spanish New World empire. From the 1513 Crown instructions for city planning until the 1573 ordinances issued by Philip II, the Spanish New World colonies developed a very regulated system for the laying out of urban areas, which reflected the ideals of Renaissance Europe.

Where did the ideas that are manifest in the plan of Cuenca's urban core come from? The gridiron plan was instituted in the New World from the earliest Spanish settlements (Deagan 1995a; Gutiérrez et al. 1986b:59) and has been characterized as one of the clearest representations in history of European colonial control and oppression (Crouch et al. 1982:xx; Foster 1960). Andean gridiron towns like Cuenca have been seen as descendants of Roman imperial designs, the ideas of Vitruvius, European Renaissance rationality, the *bastides* of France, and the garrison towns of the Spanish reconquest of Iberia.

It is clear that Spanish colonialism in the sixteenth century used models of Roman imperialism in organizing new towns. The Toledan reductions in the Andes, and Spanish colonialism in general, turned particularly to the ideals of the Roman architect Vitruvius as the basis for its own town plans (Gutiérrez et al. 1986b:61). Vitruvius was a Roman military architect, and his most famous book, *De Architectura*, or *Ten Books of Architecture*, is one of the cornerstones of Western architectural history. The work of Vitruvius was based on three centuries of Roman imperial experience and on Greek practices dating back seven centuries prior to Vitruvius's life (Crouch et al. 1982:33). The Italian architect Leon Battista Alberti rediscovered *De Architectura* in the fifteenth century. He first published it in 1485. Both *De Architectura* and Alberti's own architectural writings were known in Spain by the first quarter of the sixteenth century. It is seen as a key influence on both Spanish colonial town planning and architecture (Crouch 1991:25; Stanislawski 1946:105–120).

The marking out of *insulae*, or city blocks, the concentration of public buildings around an open central *forum*, and the porticoes that lined the streets were key features in Roman urban planning, particularly where new colonial towns could be laid out. The Spanish in the New World adopted all of these ideals (Crouch 1991; Thébert 1987:339). It was not just in the work of Vitruvius that sixteenth-century Spaniards could have picked up these ideals. In hundreds of towns in Western Europe, such as Barcelona and Leon in Spain, the Roman layout was still visible in the medieval town plan (Crouch 1991:26). In the eyes of one historian of European urbanism, "Everything west of the Rhine and south of the Danube has inherited something of Roman traditions and urban spatial order" (Claval 1984:33).

The medieval Spanish city was far different, however, from the Roman. Streets were often quite small, and although arranged in city blocks, they were not in a grid pattern unless laid on top of previous Roman streets (Begoña 1986:40). It is in the late medieval period that another major element of what was to become the Spanish colonial urban ideal developed. This was the concept of the *plaza mayor*, which began to be seen in Spain in the twelfth and thirteenth centuries. The *plaza mayor* grouped the municipal offices, the cathedral, and the governor's mansion all on the same central square, creating "a density of central functions and a symbolic hierarchicalization of the sacred and the secular, which were nowhere as marked in any other part of Europe" (Claval 1984:36).

The *plaza mayor* was at least in part a function of the reconquest of Iberia from the Muslims, and as such was a reaction to Muslim urban ideals. In Muslim cities the plaza or town square was deliberately eliminated. Muslim rulers of conquered lands saw open plazas as dangerous, because they could be used as a secular meeting place. The courtyard of the mosque was the only valid open meeting space in the Muslim urban form. Thus, the Spanish *plaza mayor* deliberately contradicted the ideals of Muslim religion in creating an open space where secular and sacred met (Claval 1984:33; Crouch et al. 1982:41–42). The adoption of regular urban plans, with city blocks and a central plaza, can also be seen as a Spanish reaction to the traditional Arab towns of Spain, where winding streets created what appeared to the Spanish to be a disorderly labyrinth. Cities rebuilt during the reconquest of Iberia, such as Granada and Santa Fe, had a fortified rectangular plan based on models adopted from the French bastide towns of the eleventh to thirteenth centuries (Kubler 1948:70; Reps 1965:31; Violich 1962:177). The Renaissance ideals of Spain should not, however, be seen as a complete rejection of Muslim architecture. The private gardens of Islamic palaces such as the Alhambra, with gridlike patterns and formal arrangements of plants and fountains had a strong influence on Spanish ideals of both private and public plazas and patios (Low 1993:82).

Michel Foucault (1984:239–240) situated the beginning of explicit writings on the relationship between architecture, city planning, and good government in Europe in the eighteenth century. What Foucault is referring to actually comes from tradition dating back at least to Vitruvius. For the New World Spanish colonies there were specific regulations on city planning set out initially by the Council of Castile, and later by the Council of the Indies. The first major Spanish urban center founded in the New World was Santo Domingo, in what is now the Dominican Republic. The city was founded in 1496 and then moved to a new position in 1502 by Nicolas de Ovando. The 1502 layout of the town exhibits many of the basic features that are seen in Cuenca's plan 50 years later, with a central plaza next to the cathedral, straight and wide streets, and rectangular blocks (Low 1993:86–88). The very general 1513 Instrucciones para poblar (Instructions for Colonization) issued by the Council of Castile postdated the founding of Santo Domingo, but they were a clear attempt to standardize the practice of founding New World towns. Over the next sixty years many other sets of Crown regulations were issued, addressing different aspects of urban planning and architecture. In 1573 Philip II set out the definitive instructions, an amalgamation of 149 ordinances from previous sets of regulations (Crouch et al. 1982:23–24).

The sixteenth-century cities of the Spanish New World were not purely European constructions. The brief mention of the influences of Native American urban planning on Spanish colonial cities by many architectural historians (Crouch et al. 1982:37, 58, 91–92; Foster 1960:34) is a serious underestimation of the Native American contribution to Spanish colonial urban form. From Taino villages in the Caribbean to Cortes's first views of Tenochtitlán in 1519 (a city that was probably the largest in the world at that time), the Spanish were profoundly impressed with the planned nature of the Native American urban areas they conquered in the sixteenth century. These influences were integral to the development of sixteenth-century Spanish colonial urban planning (Low 1995:754–756).

The contribution of the Native American urban form to Spanish colonial cities is denied because of the perception that the Spanish were ethnocentric and generally perceived the New World as totally "without culture" (Crouch et al. 1982:xvi). This could not be further from the truth, as the organization of pre-Columbian cities was greatly admired by the Spanish. Cities like Tenochtitlán and Cuzco had large central ceremonial plazas that were integrally tied into the street plans of the cities themselves. The Spaniards who first entered these cities were very impressed by them (Low 1995:749). In many cases the Spanish founded their cities directly on top of pre-Columbian urban centers, often simply co-opting the plan of these areas and the system of plazas and streets already in existence (Low 1995:756). Thus, rather than seeing the colonial city as an "instrument of colonial domination and control," Low urges us to look at colonial cities with an eye for "the cultural tensions of conquest and resistance" that are encoded in its architecture (1995:759).

Fifteen years after the conquest of the Aztecs the Spanish encountered the Inka empire. Most of the Spanish urban centers in the Andes were founded on preceding Inka centers, and in the fine masonry and ordered urban living of these cities the Spanish found something that they compared favorably to the achievements of European antiquity (Fraser 1990:27). The discourse between European and Native Andean versions of urbanism is clear in the Spanish "founding" of Cuzco in 1534. During the ceremony Pizarro had the all-important gibbet, a symbol of Spanish judicial authority, built on top of what was probably the Incaic ceremonial ushnu in the middle of the main plaza in the Inka capital (MacCormack 1991:72). The street plan of modern Cuzco still follows the radiating Inka streets, and yet Spanish artists of the sixteenth to eighteenth centuries portrayed the city as an ideal square, with symmetrical rectangular city blocks (Gutiérrez et al. 1981:3–8).

As with Cuzco, Cuenca was founded on the ruins of an Inkaic and pre-Inkaic Cañari center. It is not clear how large the Inka city of Tumipampa was, or what parts of Cuenca are pre-Hispanic in layout, but the main plaza and grid plan of Cuenca was laid out in 1557 around 1,200 meters northwest of the central plaza of Inka Tumipampa (Uhle 1983 [1923]). The spirit of the later 1573 royal ordinances was followed, and Cuenca was founded "where it would be possible to demolish neighboring towns and properties in order to take advantage of the materials that are essential for building" (Crouch et al. 1982:9). The houses built around the main plaza still contain Inka dressed stone blocks, often in the almost metaphoric function of providing strong pre-Columbian cornerstones for post-Columbian adobe houses. It was clearly not just the building materials that the Spanish were interested in when they laid out Cuenca's urban grid, but also the inherent authority already vested in this pre-Hispanic center of Inka and Cañari power. The core of the modern city is the colonial grid (Figure 3). The grid is bounded, however, on the south by the natural barrier of the river, and on the north and east by roads outside the grid system, roads that have very likely been in existence since before the arrival of the Spanish (Hyslop 1990:96–99).

The Spanish foundation of an Andean city could only occur with the consent of the Crown. The Act of Foundation was a ritual that was not always the same, but had several key steps. At the founding of the city all would gather in the area of the future *plaza mayor*. The designated official would take possession of the area for the Crown, and then the *rollo y*

*picota* (pillar and pillory/gibbet) would be set up in the middle of the
future plaza as the symbol of royal justice. A cross or several foundation
stones would be erected on the site of the future church. This done, the
municipal councillors, and other town officials would be named. Following
this the solares, or city lots, would be measured out and assigned, the first
to the church, the second to the founder of the town, and then others for
the principal citizens (Aprile-Gniset 1991:190; Fraser 1990:51-63). The
foundation of Cuenca in 1557 followed this pattern, with a rollo y picota
set up first, and then the plaza and other city blocks set out and assigned
to their owners (Chacón Zhapán 1990:95).

As with other built forms, the urban area that defined colonial Cuenca
structured the world for the people who moved through it, reproducing
the social relations of the colonial system daily (Bourdieu 1977 [1972];
Foucault 1975; Giddens 1979; Rabinow 1989). Spanish colonial cities were
"conceived and executed as propaganda vehicles, symbolizing and incar-
nating civilization" (Crouch et al. 1982:xx). The gridiron plan of Spanish
New World towns was in a certain sense unique, in that none of the royal
ordinances ever really specified that blocks had to be square and all the
same size, and many Renaissance architects advocated all sorts of other
street layouts for the ideal city. The Spanish colonial city was almost
always laid out in square blocks when possible, and it would appear that
the gridiron was a metaphor, whether conscious or not, for the orderliness
of the people that lived within the town (Fraser 1990:41). This can be
related to the Renaissance European fascination with "abstract space,"
the formal relationship of geometric spaces so evident in the perspectival
art of the period (Lefebvre 1991:48-49). The colonial gridiron town was
essentially "an instrument of production" that provided a superstructure
foreign to the original space. The city provided a base with which the new
colonial social and economic structure could gain a firm foothold (Lefebvre
1991: 151-152). Even the Spanish term for the urban core of the city, the
traza, literally meant the "plan" or "layout" (Fraser 1990:72).

At the center of the grid was the plaza, an area that was and still is
the urban center for public displays in the Latin American city, an area of
interaction among people, and interaction between people and material
culture, architecture, and space (Richardson 1982). The plaza in modern
Andean towns has been severely altered from its colonial roots. Even in
the late nineteenth century the majority of plazas were very open areas,
where market stalls and street vendors dominated at times, and at other
times bullfights, theater, and military and religious processions would be
staged. Generally all sectors of the city would take part in public events. In
the twentieth century many Andean plazas have been redesigned with
formal walkways and gardens, severely curtailing their function as mul-
tiple-use spaces (Gutiérrez et al. 1981:30-32).

The church overlooked the plaza, and the 1573 royal ordinances specified that the principal church should be visible from all sides and raised above ground level in order to "acquire more authority." The secular council chambers and customs house were also to be placed on the main plaza "in a manner that would not embarrass the temple but add to its prestige" (Crouch et al. 1982:15).

The spirit of this later edict is clear in the 1557 layout of buildings around Cuenca's main plaza (Figure 3). The centrality of the church in the colonial Andes was obvious. The church was usually the largest property owner in colonial Spanish cities. In Lima in 1644, for instance, a quarter of all urban houses were church-owned (Aprile-Gniset 1991:374). The main church in Toledan reduction towns was usually placed parallel to one side of the plaza, to create a more evident "presence" of the church on the plaza (Gutiérrez et al. 1986b:63). In Cuenca the original church on the main plaza has exactly this configuration, whereas the Republican period cathedral was placed with the main entrance on the plaza and the body of the church running down the side street. Churches and convents were usually the largest buildings in Spanish colonial cities and often took up whole city blocks. As is the case in Cuenca, urban space was basically structured around church architecture, just as the Church dominated the thoughts and daily lives of the citizens (Aprile-Gniset 1991:375). The plaza, with Church and state buildings gazing down upon all activities, is not, however, the only position to view the city from. In Cuenca, as in other colonial Spanish cities, it was the domestic architecture that took up the majority of the space.

## DOMESTIC ARCHITECTURE
## IN THE SPANISH COLONIAL CITY

The tension between private property and the goals of state and Church are reified in the gridiron plan. Ordinance 126 of the 1573 royal ordinances stated that no lots on the plaza should be assigned to private individuals. Ordinance 134 encouraged the municipal officers to ensure that private houses were "all of one type for the sake of the beauty of the town" (Crouch et al. 1982:15–17). There was more than beauty at stake. Conflicts between the authority of Church and state and the desires of colonial vecinos for more local power were manifested in the subordination of the architecture of urban private homes. The gridiron plan of the colonial city meant that private house facades that were not on plazas were always seen at an angle, because an observer on the street could not step back any great distance to admire a large facade (Aprile-Gniset 1991:211). After the founding of most towns in the Andes an official plan would be drawn up, and official inspections by a magistrate and architect would be taken frequently to ensure that buildings that disfigured the shape of the city street plan were rebuilt (Fraser 1990:73). This tension has deep historical roots in Western ideals of urban planning. Aristotle felt that private houses were more agreeable and convenient if the street plan of the city was "regular" (González Aguirre 1989:209). The idea of aligning house facades with the street comes from the Renaissance "ideal city" and privileges state authority, in that the position of the street was decided in the laying out of the town before the houses were constructed (Gutiérrez et al. 1986b:61).

The orientation of the peaks of house roofs in congested urban areas can be related to these ideals. In northern Spain Renaissance houses could have a roof peak that ran parallel to the street, a form that has been proposed to be more Mediterranean. Alternatively, the peak ran perpendicular to the street, creating a more imposing peaked front facade, something that is perceived to be northern European (Begoña 1986:3). In Cuenca older houses in the urban core clearly follow the Mediterranean example. Roof peaks generally run parallel to the street, and at the end of rows of houses the roof will be "hipped." This demonstrates that for the colonial Cuenca domestic architect open peaks were seen as "unfinished." Urban housing thus became one continuous roofline along the whole block (Begoña 1986:81–82).

With such enforced uniformity in facades and roofs, it is the position of the house within the city that is the most easily manipulated architectural symbol of status. If private homes were banned from the *plaza mayor*, then the most elite and expensive house lots in gridiron Andean colonial towns were on the four blocks whose corners formed the plaza. Each of these locations was visible to those entering the plaza, and each corner lot controlled two streets entering into the plaza (Aprile-Gniset 1991:223). Such rules only applied if houses were kept off the plaza itself. In the Spanish colonies this rule was quickly broken, as elite citizens bought up house lots with facades on the *plaza mayor* in the late sixteenth century, despite Crown regulations against this practice (Aprile-Gniset 1991:190). In Cuenca there has been no definitive archival search done to determine when the first private houses were placed on the *plaza mayor*. Gil Ramirez Davalos, the founder of the city and its first corregidor, received the two lots on the west side of the plaza for his property (González Aguirre 1991:15), but these later came into the hands of the church. The earliest document I have come across listing a private house on Cuenca's *plaza mayor* is the will of Pedro Ortiz Dávila, the *fiscal* (crown prosecutor) and *relator* (court reporter) of Cuenca, whose house in 1672 was on the *plaza mayor* (ANH/C L520, ff.603r–632r). The positions of houses within the city were very clearly related to status throughout the colonial period.

Throughout the cities of the Spanish colonies the regulation of house-holders was a concern of the municipal councils, particularly in the late eighteenth century, when increasing regulation of household affairs by municipal councils refelected Bourbon concerns for more efficient government. There are several activities that were particularly subject to regulation. The first was the enclosure of private properties. The councils were always attempting to have property owners build walls around their property, thus clearly delineating its boundaries. Walls and fences also stopped livestock, particularly pigs, from running loose in urban areas and contaminating the open water canals. In Cuenca during the Bourbon period this legislation included the replacement of *cabuya* (agave plant) hedges with adobe walls and the whitewashing of these walls to beautify the city (ANH/C L8, f.144 [1786]).

Water control was another major area of concern, as private house-holders would frequently divert water from public canals. Flooding was also a problem. Street maintenance was another important part of council legislation. In general each property owner was responsible for the street in front of their property, and the main council complaint often was that the street had not been properly paved with cobbles and was impassable.

Lighting at night was often a concern as well, and all shops and taverns were expected to light a lantern on the street each evening (ANH/C L8, f.144 [1786]). The maintenance of private property was a reflection on the inhabitants of a house. In eighteenth-century Cali, in what is now Colombia, one cleric was sure that individuals of properties with piles of material in the yards and no fences were "committing many sins against God" (Aprile-Gniset 1991:407).

This tension between private property owners and the municipal council was also manifest at times of community celebrations in Bourbon-period Cuenca, in the requirements to decorate house facades. For Christmas of 1786 urban property owners in Cuenca were required to place lit decorations in their porches, doors, and storefronts in the evenings (ANH/C L.8, f.136 [1786]). For the King of Spain's birthday the following year the same regulation was restated (ANH/C L.8, f.103 [1787]). For the Corpus Christi festival there were even more stringent regulations. Urban property owners were ordered to decorate their front balconies with hangings and to clean or employ Natives to clean the street and water canal in front of their houses. Elite citizens would sponsor altars that would be temporarily placed at significant intersections along the parade route (Chacón Zhapán 1990:235). From these regulations it is clear that the house facade was an important point of interaction, where the life of the urban community met with the lives of those within each household.

# VERNACULAR VERSUS
# FORMAL DOMESTIC ARCHITECTURE

Who designed and built the houses of colonial Cuenca? In the colonial Andes domestic architecture was part of an artisan's tradition, built by carpenters and masons. This is different from larger public works such as churches, when a foreman or master architect would direct the work, creating a more formal architectural style (Téllez and Moure 1982:13). Such masters had no formal architectural schooling. They would have reached their position simply by years of practical experience working with other builders (Fraser 1990:103-104). In the case of more formalized styles, the essential "filters" for the transfer of particular architectural features from Spain to the New World were these master artisans, who used what they considered to be the best from diverse regions of Spain in their designs. In church architecture and on elite houses, it is the decorative elements that they chose that most clearly reflect the "classical" European world (Téllez and Moure 1982:15).

These decorative elements, and the geometry of their arrangement, can be traced back to several professional guides to architectural design that were first published in the 1500s and were popular in the New World throughout the colonial period. These included Diego de Sagredo's *Las Medidas del Romano* (1526); Andrea Palladio's *Los Quatro Libros de la Arquitectura* (1570), and the works of Sebastiano Serlio (1475-1554) and Iacomo Barozzio da Vignola (1507-1573). Vignola's *Tratado Práctico Elemental de Arquitectura o Estudio de los 5 Ordenes* (1562) was particularly influential (Téllez and Moure 1982:49, 200). Echoes of the styles advocated in these volumes were seen in door frames, balustrades, and pillars on elite houses throughout the colonial Andes.

The choice of one style over another appears to have been based on the aesthetics of the architect or artisan in charge of the construction. In many Andean cities it is clear that a variety of styles was popular throughout the colonial period, with very little variation of any chronological significance (Corradine Angulo 1981:74; Téllez and Moure 1982:203). The construction of a "proper" facade required proportions and dimensions for pillars, an architrave, and a cornice. Thus, the work had to conform to the basic structure of classical European decoration, but the decorative elements used could vary greatly in their details (Fraser 1990:127). This has led to great difficulties in dating the construction of houses, as stylistic changes are rarely related to any chronological progression.

The work of Vignola was a particularly popular guide and went through many printings in Spanish until its final edition in 1736. Vignola defined the aesthetically simple *toscano* (Tuscan) style, which was also called *dórico toscano* (Tuscan Doric) by other authors, and was very popular in the Spanish colonies (Téllez and Moure 1982:49). This was a popular style in late eighteenth-century Cuenca and is seen in the pillars of several of the houses discussed below. Thus, at least some of the aspects of domestic architecture in Cuenca came from printed volumes on architecture, but much of it did not.

## COLLECTING RAFTERS IN THE WANING MOON

Most of the workers who built the colonial buildings in the Andes were Native Andean people. In Cuzco in the late 1500s and early 1600s building contracts abound in which a Native Andean was the *albañil* (builder) in charge of the construction of large and important urban houses (Mesa 1979:250–251). Between 1559 and 1560 in Cuenca the public buildings on the plaza, including the municipal buildings, royal smelting house, and the jail, were all built by Native Andean tribute laborers from the villages of Macas and Tiquizambe (Chacón Zhapán 1990:20–21). Spanish encomenderos with rights to Native labor tribute usually had Native laborers build their houses, while others would pay Native wage laborers (Fraser 1990:84).

It is therefore surprising that Native Andean influences on this architecture appear to have been extremely minimal. It would appear that formal training created builders, carpenters, and artisans who were well versed in European building skills and loath to create more Andean style buildings in colonial urban areas. Very soon after the Conquest the Spanish began to train Native Andeans in the skills of brick and tile making, mortar work, carpentry, and a host of other construction skills (Fraser 1990:90–98). In Cuenca Native Andeans are frequently listed in late sixteenth-century apprenticeship documents as apprentice carpenters, masons, bricklayers, and tile makers (Chacón Zhapán 1990:71). The colonial architecture of the Andes thus represents a form of domination by Spanish colonists over the labor of Native Andeans. The adobe and wattle and daub walls and thatched roofs of early colonial Andean architecture are technologically similar to pre-Hispanic Andean architecture, but in the layout of buildings and the decorative elements of door frames and pillars, we see unmistakable European influences (Fraser 1990:4–5, 19).

Andean architectural style was far from simple in its influences. The design books discussed above were influential, but there were also many other regional and vernacular architectural influences that were imported from Spain. One example of this was the survival of medieval European beliefs in the construction of houses. In Cuenca this is represented in a

1593 building contract for a house, in which it was specified that the wood for the construction should be cut during the waning moon (ANH/C L.490, f.480v [1593]). Surviving printed agricultural almanacs give evidence of rural beliefs in early modern Europe, which equated the phases of the moon to changes in the amount of moisture taken up by plants and animals. Wood and other crops were therefore cut during a waning moon to ensure proper drying, while it was advisable to plant crops during a waxing moon (Curry 1989:97–98; Thomas 1971:296–297). Such beliefs came to rural Europeans from the astrology of the ancient Greeks. Both Ptolemy and Pliny the Elder described how the waxing moon provided moisture to living creatures, while the waning phase dried them out (Barton 1994:102, 107).

I have not encountered this belief in modern Ecuador, and yet in both Puerto Rico (J. Ostapkowicz, personal communication) and in Venezuela (Margolies 1979:217) rural woodworkers still restrict the harvest of wood to periods of the waning moon, so that the wood is dry and resists insect infestations. Andean colonial builders thus brought to their work knowledge gained from pre-Hispanic Native American practices, academic architectural knowledge from Europe, and more vernacular European architectural traditions.

In order to look at regional European influences on the design of domestic architecture in the Andes we would need a clear idea of where in Europe immigrants to Cuenca came from. The regional origins of Spanish immigrants may have contributed to the introduction of distinctive architectural features in the southern highlands, but such regional origins have not yet been researched in detail. It is generally held that the "founders" of Cuenca in the mid-sixteenth century came from Estremadura (González Aguirre 1989:212). This view has not been demographically proven, but it is probably accurate given that Castile, Estremadura, and Andalusia provided most of the emigrants to the Andes in the early colonial period (Cook 1990:58). Migration to Cuenca from Spain was a continuous process throughout the colonial period, however, and there is little doubt that the places of origin of immigrants changed over time, particularly as economic conditions on the Iberian peninsula changed (Cook 1990:58).

Immigrants to Cuenca were from a wide variety of places. To take a specific example, we can look at the daughters of Gabriel Maldonado de San Juan and Estefania Ramirez de Heredia, a prominent seventeenth-century Cuenca couple whose daughters married peninsular men in the 1660s to 1680s. Of three of the daughters Maria married a man from Santiago, in Galicia, and her sisters Luisa and Tomasa married men from Carrion and Burgos respectively, both from the province of Castilla la Vieja. Their maternal grandfather was a southerner who had come from

Guadalcázar in Andalusia sometime before 1625 (ANH/C L.525 f.1042r [1686]; L.528, f.90r [1693]; L.533, f.649r [1691]; Borrero Crespo 1962:37–38, 133, 292–293). By the late seventeenth century immigrants to Cuenca came from a wide variety of regions in Spain. Each would have brought with them their own ideals of proper household architecture, but by the time they arrived in Cuenca perhaps a local style of household architecture, based on the earlier immigration of Spaniards from Andalusia and Estremadura, had already created a standard Cuenca style of house. As Germán Téllez and Ernesto Moure (1982:13) suggest of the colonial houses of Cartagena, Colombia, the houses of Cuenca represent a uniquely American mix of regional Spanish styles, with an emphasis on basic Mediterranean construction systems.

## COLONIAL HOUSES IN THE URBAN CORE

In the colonial Andean city the domestic architecture tended to follow a developmental trajectory from the period of the city's founding onward. A city block would be initially divided into four quarters, or solares, and on each of the four properties a small *bahareque* (wattle and daub) house with thatched roof would be built. These were usually built on the corner of the lot, with a kitchen of the same material in a separate building behind. This situation is illustrated on maps of Cartagena in the 1560s and maps of La Palma and Tenerife, Colombia, from the 1580s (Aprile-Gniset 1991:210; 245; Téllez and Moure 1982:14). As the urban area became more established each property was walled off and more substantial buildings were built along the street, usually starting at the corner of the block. The center of each block would generally remain treed or would become garden space. Over time the property would be divided into smaller more intensely used spaces, and two-story houses would begin to appear (Aprile-Gniset 1991:365).

In Cartagena by the 1580s substantial two-story houses were the norm in the city core (Téllez and Moure 1982:14), but even in 1578 in Caracas the vast majority of the houses were wattle and daub, with just a few examples of adobe houses with tile roofs (Margolies 1979:213). In Quito by 1573 there were large numbers of solid adobe houses with tile roofs, with the more substantial houses having two rooms, a patio, garden, and corral (Anonymous 1965 [1573]:221). It is clear that the density of property ownership was a large factor in the increasing density of buildings. In many Andean cities it was not until the late eighteenth century that urban blocks were so built-up as to present a continuous facade of houses on all four sides of the block. The division of urban properties into smaller lots was also a gradual process (Aprile-Gniset 1991:212; Gutiérrez et al. 1981:46; Téllez and Moure 1982:20).

The houses in Cuenca's core were typical in their development over time, although contemporary published descriptions of the domestic architecture of the city are rare. In 1582 the houses of Cuenca were described as:

> like those in Spain, built with stone, mud, and adobes made from earth; there are no tapias [pounded mud walls], because the earth is not good for that. Because there is no lime or bricks, there is no construction using these, because it would be very expensive. The houses are roofed with tiles. (Pablos 1965 [1582]:269, my translation)

Throughout the seventeenth and eighteenth centuries, a wide variety of domestic architecture existed in Cuenca's city core. The earliest two-story house noted so far was being rebuilt in 1603, and by the seventeenth century most of the houses in the urban core had tile roofs. A wide variety of house sizes existed in the seventeenth-century core, including one-room and two-room houses and several with multiple rooms, including store-fronts on the street. Some urban houses were, however, still roofed with thatch until at least 1710 (Jamieson 1996:84).

From the mid-eighteenth century onward we see a distinctive build-up of densely urban houses in the core of Cuenca. In 1748 the urban houses were described as built of "adobes, tiled, and most of them with an upper floor" while "those in the outer neighborhoods were disorganized and rustic because they are occupied by the Indians" (Juan and Ulloa 1978 [1748]:432, my translation). From the mideighteenth century onward the urban houses frequently consisted of four or more rooms, there was no mention of thatch roofs, and two-story houses were commonly listed (Jamieson 1996:84). By 1786 the houses throughout the city were described as being:

> generally of adobes, or unfired bricks with mud, with the exception of a very few which have mortar, stone, and fired bricks. All of these are large, comfortable, and fairly decent, and all without exception roofed with tiles of such an excellent quality that they do not lose their vibrant red colour, even after many years, a property which is attributed to the purity of the water and air. (Velasco 1981 [1789]:395, my translation)

A 1797 description by a Mr. Laporte confirmed that "the houses are adobe, roofed with tiles, and many of them with an upper floor: those of the *barrios* or *arabales* are unkempt and rustic, because these are where the Indians live" (León 1983:257, my translation). The development of larger, more substantial, houses in Cuenca's urban core may have been heavily tied to the textile boom of the late eighteenth century (Andrien 1995:72–74). This economic boom may have led to considerable house construction in Cuenca's core, something that would have ended with the chaos of the 1810 to 1830 period as the Wars of Independence destroyed such regional trade.

Several surviving examples of the late eighteenth-century houses in Cuenca will be the subject of the rest of this chapter. From archival documents a picture of the inhabitants of these houses can be created. It is from the architecture itself, however, that we can access some of the less explicit, but equally important, ideological concepts that shaped the lives of colonial Cuencanos. Moving through houses reinforced the way in which colonial people interacted with one another and with the world around them. Through the spatial arrangements of domestic architecture both inhabitants and visitors were inculcated with cultural principles and had those principles continuously reinforced (Bourdieu 1977 [1972]:89). These much-neglected buildings, many of them abandoned and on the brink of collapse, can tell us much about life in eighteenth-century Cuenca.

## A NOTE ON ARCHITECTURAL RECORDING

What follows is a presentation of five urban houses, all of which preserve, to a greater or lesser extent, colonial architectural features. For each house an isometric drawing is presented, showing the house in three dimensions as it stands today.

Accompanying these isometric drawings are permeability diagrams, a form of dendritic diagram taken from the methodology of Bill Hillier and Julienne Hanson (1984). These diagrams begin at the bottom with the "carrier space," or the space surrounding the buildings in question, represented by a cross within a circle. In Hillier and Hanson's methodology (1984:93–94) circles are used to represent "spaces" (in the case of buildings, the rooms within them), and lines represent "relations" between these spaces (in the case of buildings, a door or opening between the spaces).

I have slightly modified Hillier and Hanson's diagramming conventions. In this chapter the permeability diagrams include both circles, representing rooms that may have existed within a given house in the colonial period, and squares representing those rooms that are clearly postcolonial in date. In this way each permeability diagram represents the current access patterns within the house, while the contrast between circles and squares gives some idea of the colonial room arrangements.

Hillier and Hanson (1984:93, 104) feel that the permeability diagrams allow us to examine spaces in terms of "syntactic relations," allowing the basic properties of "symmetry-asymmetry," and "distributednessnondistributedness" to become visible. I would agree with this basic methodology, but I disagree with Hillier and Hanson's attempt to equate these spatial relationships to more anthropological concerns. Rather than using the diagrams to demonstrate totalizing concepts such as how "ritualized" or "conformist" the spatial arrangement is (Hillier and Hanson 1984:145), I prefer a more contextual approach to architectural meanings based on the history of colonialism in the context of Cuenca itself.

## THE HOUSE OF THE THREE PATIOS

For several reasons there are very few examples of intact colonial period houses left in the urban core of Cuenca. Since the 1940s the urban core has been abandoned by the wealthier segments of Cuenca's population, who have taken up residence in the suburbs. The large houses of the wealthy have been subdivided into smaller rental units, a process that has been one of the major threats to colonial period domestic architectural preservation in many Andean cities (Aprile-Gniset 1991:370; Gutiérrez et al. 1981:47). In the process of subdividing and rebuilding large buildings much of the architecture that survived from the colonial and Republican periods was heavily altered. At the same time areas of the urban core have become thriving and modern business districts, and the offices and retail shops that now take up much of the space in colonial residential areas have found the eighteenth- and nineteenth-century architecture insufficient for their needs. As a result historic houses have been heavily altered or entirely replaced. There is little doubt that many of the houses in the urban core retain some walls and doorways dating to the colonial period, but much of the architecture is so altered that reconstruction of the builders' original intentions is nearly impossible.

The Tres Patios, or House of the Three Patios, at Calle Bolívar 11-28 (Figure 3) is an example of a colonial residence that has been altered to house several businesses. For many years the main floor of the building has served as a restaurant (Figure 5). The upper floor has recently been renovated to serve as offices and retail shops. The back patios, consisting of modern concrete architecture, are the residence of the restaurant owners, and I was unfortunately unable to gain access to that section of the house. It is in these back patios that the less substantial colonial period outbuildings, including the kitchen, storage areas, garden, and so forth, would have been located.

Measured drawings and photographs of the front section of the house allowed the creation of isometric drawings (Figure 6) that delineate the remains of a late-eighteenth-century house encased within the later archi-

**Figure 5.** The facade of the Tres Patios house.

tecture. The doors of the central and eastern entrances on the lower floor facing the street are all hand-carved. The two pillars on the southern part of the interior patio on the lower floor are round in cross section and hand-carved in a "Tuscan" barrel-shaped style (Figure 7A). These pillars are probably late eighteenth century in date. This is in sharp contrast to the nineteenth- and twentieth-century machine-turned pillars and balustrades throughout the rest of the house. The adobe walls of the front section of the house are very thick, another indication of a premodern house. There have been many alterations of this property over time, but some vestiges of its colonial arrangement still remain.

The facade is the first clue that the Tres Patios house is quite old. It has a large central pair of doors (Figure 8A) flanked by two smaller sets of doors. The western set appears to be a modern reproduction, but the eastern set is hand-carved and is probably colonial in date. There are two upper floor windows with small balconies. The doors and windows of the facade are not in any strict geometric placement, which is of great interest when compared to North American work on domestic architecture. In North America geometric facades have come to be associated with the Georgian worldview of the late eighteenth century, as vernacular and medieval traditions were replaced with a concern for the geometric facade

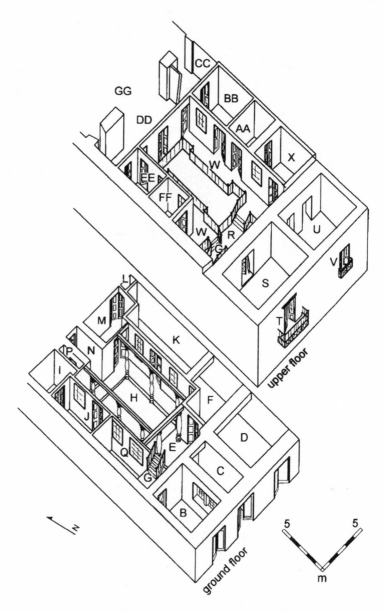

**Figure 6.** Isometric drawing of the Tres Patios house.

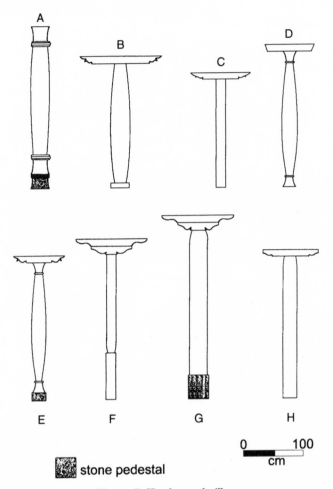

stone pedestal

**Figure 7.** Hand-carved pillars.

as a demonstration of an academic design overriding functional consider-
ations (Glassie 1975; Deetz 1977a). For Henry Glassie (1990:279) the geo-
metrically symmetrical facade is a "mask," something that is shaped from
social distrust, an attempt to repel social disorder.

Little research has been done on domestic architecture in Latin America
to compare to the North American idea. In the colonial houses of Cartagena,
Colombia, the doors, windows, and balconies of colonial house facades are
not placed in geometrical symmetry, nor do there seem to be any strict
stylistic rules for their placement. It seems that design occurred more

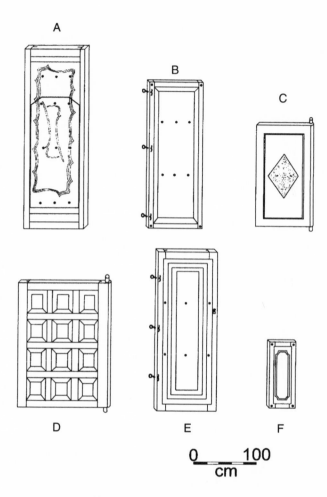

**Figure 8.** Hand-carved doors.

from the inside looking out, with basic room layouts and construction techniques determining where the most convenient places for windows and doors would be (Téllez and Moure 1982:21). In Cuzco preserved seventeenth- and eighteenth-century facades also ignore any concern with a strictly measured geometry in the placement of doors and windows (Gutiérrez et al. 1981:110–197). This is also the case for the Tres Patios house.

What is the significance of this lack of symmetrical geometry? For Henry Glassie (1990:279) this represents a "thick, face-to-face, neighbourly experience." Could the facade of the house in the colonial Andean town represent a relationship between public and private where face-to-face relationships were still more important than the strict categorizations of social roles?

There is another aspect to the facade that is important to its relationship with the public space of the street. The architecture of the Tres Patios house has been built up to the edge of the sidewalk, leaving no space for anyone to stop in front of the building. In order to gain access to the building interior one must pass through the heavy central doors. The control of movement at the front of the Tres Patios house is thus entirely in the hands of the property owner.

The front rooms of the Tres Patios appear to be typical of a prosperous late eighteenth-century Cuenca house. The main features are the entrance hall, or vestibule (Figure 6C), with two *tiendas* or shop fronts (B and D) on either side of it. The entrance hall is called a *zaguan*, a term derived from Muslim architecture (Gutiérrez et al. 1981:44). It creates a transitional space between the street and the interior patio (H), making the interior space more private. It is interesting to note that unlike examples discussed below, there are no preserved adobe benches built into the house facade, zaguan, or interior patio of the Tres Patios house. The construction encourages the flow of traffic through the zaguan into the first courtyard, but discourages any interaction between people in this transitional space from public to private.

The tiendas (6B and D) served as spaces that could be used by the property owner or rented to others, with easy access to the street. As early as 1584 the municipal council ruled that all tiendas and workshops in the city of Cuenca were to be within the *traza urbana* (urban core). This was so they would not be "in other depopulated places where justice could not visit or see them" (Chacón Zhapán 1990:206; my translation). Such legislation was common in many Spanish American cities and was also related to the visibility of sales so that items could be taxed (Aprile-Gniset 1991:420). This shows that at least in the sixteenth century the urban grid defined the limits of the "civilized" populace. This was the area where the safety of citizens could be guaranteed by government inspection of commercial activities. It has been suggested that the origins of the two-story house in the colonial Andes is exclusively related to merchants, with the lower floor front rooms always used for street-front shops (Aprile-Gniset 1991:228). This room arrangement was common in the Roman Empire, where separate shop entrances from the street occurred frequently in urban architecture (Thébert 1987:356).

Between the two tiendas the zaguan (6C) leads from the main entrance to the house at streetside to an interior corridor (E) adjacent to the patio (H). The corridor (E) beyond the zaguan is colonial in date, with thick barrel-shaped hand-carved pillars (Figure 7A). The corridors and rooms on the other three sides of the patio (I through Q) were clearly built after Independence. This is also the rule in Cuzco, where colonial period houses almost never have corridors on all four sides of the interior patios (Gutiérrez et al. 1981:46). The patio was the center for the circulation of movement within the colonial house. The justified permeability diagram (cf. Hillier and Hanson 1984) for the Tres Patios (Figure 9) shows that the patio (H) still serves this function in the modern restaurant.

Where did this system of patios come from? Architectural historians in the Andes are generally agreed that the model is from Andalusia in southern Spain (Aprile-Gniset 1991:370; Bayón 1979:159; Crespo Toral 1976:75; Téllez and Moure 1982:16). From there the origins are said to be generally Mediterranean, although there is disagreement whether these origins are Muslim (Aprile-Gniset 1991:370; Low 1993:82) or Roman (Crespo Toral 1976:75).

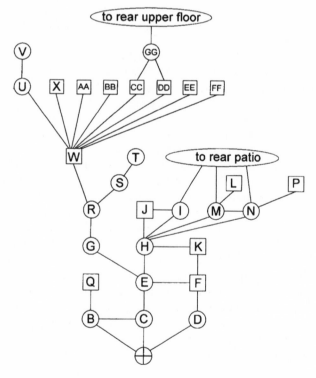

**Figure 9.** Justified permeability diagram of the Tres Patios house.

The Greeks were early users of the *peristyle,* or central courtyard, surrounded by columns around which the parts of the house were arranged (Thébert 1987:325), and this was passed on to the Roman world, where urban architecture was built around the peristyle. In the Roman Empire, as in the Spanish colonies a thousand years later, some peristyles were utilitarian, with packed earth floors and a well or cistern. In other cases the peristyle could be paved with mosaics, with central fountains, decorative plants, or even fishponds (Thébert 1987:361). The colonnaded courtyard was a solution for using homogenous space for heterogeneous activities depending on the time of day, with rooms arrayed around the courtyard, rarely with internal access from one to the other. Both "public" and "private" rooms could thus be flexibly located around the same courtyard (Thébert 1987:408).

Although rarely achieved in the Spanish colonies, the ideal of the courtyard house had corridors on all sides and a fountain in the center of the patio. It is evident that this ideal private patio is a miniature model of the ideal *plaza mayor,* which was also intended to have arcades on all sides and a fountain in the center. The house is thus an attempt to create a microcosm of the larger urban society, with its centralized meeting place for more "public" activities (Aprile-Gniset 1991:370).

From the west side of the corridor (6E) of the Tres Patios one can climb a staircase (G) to the upper floor. This is a typical eighteenth-century Andean staircase, placed within the interior corridor, in one corner of the patio, to one side of the zaguan. Here it joins the upper (R) and lower (E) corridors on the back of the main house (Gutiérrez et al. 1981:46; Téllez and Moure 1982:38, 228). Despite the nineteenth-century addition of galleries around the other sides of the patio (Figure 6), no new staircase was built for the Tres Patios. This is unusual, as many houses in Cuzco had symmetrical dual staircases introduced into the other side of the patio when nineteenth-century modifications were made to the house (Gutiérrez et al. 1981:46).

At the top of the stairs one arrives at a large number of upper floor rooms arranged around the central open space, but only the front two rooms (6S and U) are colonial in date. The corridor (R) is colonial, but the balcony (W) running all the way around the interior is quite modern. The building owner reported that before the recent renovation rooms S and U had clay tile floors, supported by a layer of earth on top of a wooden subfloor. This is typical of eighteenth-century Andean elite houses, as tile floors were considered more desirable than a simple wooden floor (Crespo Toral 1976:78; Téllez and Moure 1982:48).

Rooms S and U are interesting in that their position on the permeability diagram (Figure 9) gives them some of the greatest privacy of any of the rooms in the house. Each of the rooms has a balcony (V and T) that overlooks the street. In both Spain (Begoña 1986:3) and the Andes (Crespo Toral 1976:78) the use of small independent balconies on the front facade of houses is seen as a feature of elite architecture. Although not the case on the Tres Patios house, such balconies in the Andes were at times completely enclosed in wooden fretwork, a feature that is taken directly from Muslim architecture (Crespo Toral 1976:78). In the Muslim world these enclosed balconies are very much associated with the segregation of women, enabling women to see the street without being seen by males (Mahfouz and Serageldin 1990:86). Such balconies can be related to the act of surveillance (Giddens 1984:127), in which elite members of society have the opportunity to collate information on the activities of subordinates through the direct observation of their activities. With the use of the balcony the most private upper rooms in the Tres Patios house are open to the street, but much more in the sense of those looking out from the rooms rather than for those looking in from the street.

## THE OWNERS IN THE URBAN CORE

The ethnicity, gender, and social position of those who bought and sold houses in the urban core is clear from Table 1. Many of the males held professional titles, and all of the owners, whether male or female, were vecinos, implying that they were Spanish or mestizo in ethnicity rather than Native Andean. Although almost two-thirds of the property transactions were conducted by males, it is important to note the relatively large number of female property owners for these urban properties. Urban houses were viewed in the Spanish colonial Andes as valid types of property for females to own and were often built, financed, and inherited entirely by females (Lockhart 1994 [1968]:159; Wilson 1984:310). Public office holding and rural property ownership were areas of the political economy that women were largely excluded from, but women could and did own urban property in colonial Cuenca.

The total lack of property owners listed as "Indian" in Table 1 shows that Native Andeans were largely excluded from the city core, although this was not entirely the case. An extensive study of Native land purchases in the province (Poloni 1992) revealed that in the 1592–1620 period about 19% of recorded property transactions involved Native Andean purchasers or sellers, and about 26% of these purchases were for land in the urban core. From 1621 to 1661 19% of transactions were undertaken by Native Andeans, but only 6% of these involved land in the urban core, suggesting a distinct drop in Native land ownership in the core. In the 1662-99 period

Table 1. Some Property Transactions in the Traza of Cuenca

|  | 1592–1649 | 1650–99 | 1700–49 | 1750–96 |
|---|---|---|---|---|
| Don/vecino (male citizen) | 3 | 6 | 11 | 2 |
| Captain | – | – | 6 | – |
| Priest | – | – | 2 | – |
| Doctor | – | 1 | 1 | 1 |
| Monseigneur | – | – | 1 | – |
| Councillor | – | 1 | – | – |
| Licenciado (graduate) | – | 1 | – | – |
| Rector | – | 1 | – | – |
| Total males | 3 | 9 | 22 | 3 |
| Doña/vecina (female citizen) | 3 | 4 | 11 | 2 |
| Average size | 1323 m$^2$ | 1640 m$^2$ | 917 m$^2$ | N/A |
| Average price | 200 pesos | 1845 pesos | 1171 pesos | 796 pesos |

Source: Jamieson 1996:98.

about 43% of transactions involved Native Andeans, a jump caused by increased recording of land sales by notaries, but of these only 2.5% of transactions involved land in the urban core (Poloni 1992:306, 309). These data demonstrate that Native Andeans made up a very small part of the landowners in the urban core, but were not entirely absent. The first household census of Cuenca, done in 1778, shows that over 30% of the inhabitants of the urban core in the late eighteenth century were Native Andeans, but rather than being property owners a large percentage may have been renters, domestic servants, and so forth (Espinoza et al. 1982:44–45).

In conclusion, the Tres Patios house, although severely modified, still gives us some idea of the architecture of a late-eighteenth-century Cuenca urban house. Although archival data specifically related to this house could not be located, the house was probably owned by a wealthy Spanish or mestizo family, with the possibility that Native Andean servants were also living on the property.

# OUTSIDE THE GRID: OTHER URBAN NEIGHBORHOODS

Throughout the Andes colonial Spanish cities began to attract Native Andean migrants soon after their foundation, despite early colonial legislation prohibiting Natives from living in towns founded by the Spanish (Aprile-Gniset 1991:182, 215). In Quito by the late sixteenth century there were semirural neighborhoods surrounding the city, with solares for gardens and textile production. The informal urban economy gained much of its vitality from the contributions of rural workers, and most of the food supplied to Quito came from Native Andean markets (Minchom 1989:197-201).

From the foundation of the city of Cuenca the municipal council attempted to encourage the separation of Native Andeans into their own neighborhoods (Moscoso C. 1989: 354). The parishes of San Blas and San Sebastián were set up to the east and west, respectively, of the urban core (Figure 3). It has been suggested that both of the parish churches in these neighborhoods are situated in the locations of pre-Hispanic waqas (González Aguirre 1989:215), although no clear evidence has been given for this assertion. It is clear that the names of the two parishes correspond to, and probably take their names from, the parishes of San Blas and San Sebastián in Quito, which were set up by the bishop of Quito in 1565 specifically as "Indian" parishes (Salomon 1983:119).

Native Andean urban land transactions give a picture of the increase in Native isolation in the neighborhoods of San Blas and San Sebastián in the mid-seventeenth century. This was followed by a drop-off in the late seventeenth century as the Native population expanded in the more peripheral areas outside the city (Poloni 1992:309).

In the mid-eighteenth century there was a polarization in the domestic architecture of Cuenca, with the houses of the peripheral neighborhoods described as "disorganized and rustic because they are occupied by the Indians" (Juan and Ulloa 1978 [1748]:432), a contrast to the adobe structures of the urban core. Between the 1744 visit of Juan and Ulloa and the 1778 municipal census, the city continued to grow, and the urban population doubled in size, from 15,000 to 30,000. Much of this population increase was in the parishes of San Sebastián and San Blas (Andrien 1995:49). In the 1778 census Native Andeans dominated the population of San Blas parish, but San Sebastián had become a mostly white and mestizo parish (Espinoza et al. 1982:44–45). Total ethnic segregation, however, was never the case in either parish.

## LA CASA DE LAS POSADAS: A COLONIAL "INN" ON THE EDGE OF THE CITY

A single house two blocks west and one block north of the San Sebastián parish church, on the edge of the colonial urban core (Figure 3), was included in this study. The house is called the Posadas or The Inn, perhaps because it served such a function for a part of its existence. Its location on one of the main roads leading out of town would make this a not unreasonable function. Today the house is a private residence in a very poor state of repair, but it appears to represent the best preserved example of late colonial domestic architecture still in existence in Cuenca.

When the Posadas house is approached from the street its most obvious initial feature is its portico, which dominates the entire facade (Figure 10). This style of facade is common in the colonial architecture of southern Ecuador, with a balcony supported by pillars running the full length of the house front (Figure 11). The plaza of the town of Gualaceo, 25 kilometers east of Cuenca, has several well-preserved examples of very similar facades. Much has been made of this style, which has been described as "of a freedom of design that escapes all classification and generally situates the very beautiful balconies at the center of the definition of the facade" (Crespo Toral 1976:84).

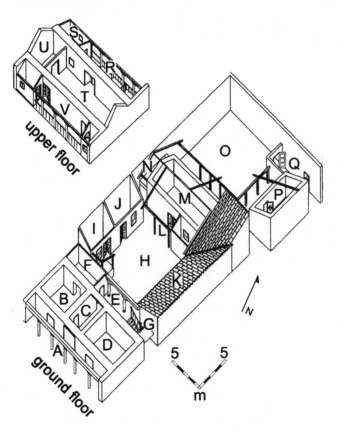

**Figure 10.** Isometric drawing of the Posadas house.

**Figure 11.** The facade of the Posadas house.

The construction of such porticoes is common in Spain and is seen as a "universal" trait of Mediterranean architecture (Begoña 1986:73, 568 fig. 243). Its origins are from Roman domestic architecture. The Roman urban house was usually lined with pillars along the facade, which created an ambiguous space between the public street and the private house. This was a contested space in the Roman city. On main thoroughfares the city would at times replace the front portico pillars of all the houses on the street in order to create one long facade. In other parts of the town private citizens would be more in control of the portico space, and in some cases it would be enclosed to increase the domestic interior space (Thébert 1987:331–332).

The advantages of the portico system were emphasized in colonial urban planning in the Andes. Ordinance 115 of the Laws of the Indies, issued in 1573, specified that porticoes should be built on the facades of all buildings facing the central plaza and along the four principal streets emerging from it. This was explicitly for the convenience and shelter of street merchants (Crouch et al. 1982:14). In many Andean cities the *portales* or porticoes surrounding the colonial plaza are still preserved (Fraser 1990:144-145).

In 1712 the Jesuits in Cuenca petitioned the municipal council for permission to erect two-story porticoes on the front of their college, which faced the main plaza. The fact that they had to petition the council suggests that the portico was to be placed on the public plaza rather than on the Jesuit property. The Jesuits gave several interesting justifications for the construction. They suggested that the portico would create a more beautiful plaza, shelter from sun and rain for the public and the vendors using the plaza, and make the area cleaner, as it was currently filled with garbage and manure (Chacón Zhapán 1990:442–443). These concerns show the intimate relationship between aesthetics, sanitation, and crowd control in the municipal regulation of city streetscapes.

Similar porticoes to those on the Posadas house were also present on the colonial municipal council building and jail on Cuenca's main square. Both of these buildings were torn down in the 1960s and new municipal buildings were erected. The jail had round stone pillars supporting the upper balcony, and the municipal council building next to it had large square brick pillars on the lower floor (Centro de Investigación y Cultura 1991: 25, 27, 56, 141).

Two tiendas flank the main entrance to the Posadas house, with one tienda (Figure 10B) currently open to the house interior through the zaguan (C). The other tienda (D) has no entrance to the house, and, therefore, could have easily been rented out for use as a separate shop or small residence. The arrangement of the tiendas is almost identical for the Posadas and Tres Patios houses.

In both urban houses one passes through the zaguan (10C) to enter the central courtyard. In the Posadas house an adobe bench has been built to the left of the zaguan in the interior corridor (E). Both the portico and the zaguan are transitional spaces from the public street to the private central courtyard. In the case of the Posadas house the builders decided that the interior corridor was a good place for a bench, suggesting that those entering the residence would often wait there to be received by the occupants. The portico itself suggests that the Posadas house was a more "permeable" structure than the Tres Patios house, with more interaction with the life of the public street beyond. The positioning of a bench in the corridor (E), and the lack of benches in the portico (A), suggests that the designer felt it more appropriate for the residents to interact with visitors in the patio rather than in the street-side portico.

From the corridor (10E) a set of stairs (G) leads to the second story of the house. The stairs built into the corridor are a clue to the house's eighteenth-century construction date, as with similar stairs in the Tres Patios house discussed above. The staircase in the Posadas house, however, also preserves the original construction materials. It is built with two ramps doubling back on each other, with a landing halfway up. The stairs are tiled in plain clay tiles, and the edge of each step is edged in wood to hold the tiles in place. This system of stairwell position and construction is the same as that described for eighteenth-century houses in Cartagena, Colombia (Téllez and Moure 1982:228).

At the top of the stairs one reaches the upper corridor (10R), which overlooks the interior patio. One can monitor the movement within most of the household from this position. From this corridor one can move into a small side room (S), perhaps used for storage, and the main upper floor room (T). The double doors leading into room T and the single door leading into room S are all identical. They are hand-carved, with a single central panel surrounded by beading. The planks from which they are constructed are attached to the door frame with decorative wrought nails with large heads (Figure 8b). These two rooms are two of the least permeable in the house when placed on a justified permeability diagram. The upper floor main room (T) was probably the room occupied by the family who owned the premises.

Off of this main living area there is a small room (10U), perhaps best referred to as an alcove. This is a small space and may have been used for storage of items not immediately in use in the main living room (T). This is the least permeable space in the entire house and thus the personal belongings, such as clothing and jewelry, of the family that owned the house were very likely stored here.

The construction techniques used in the main upper floor room preserve several aspects of colonial architectural technology. The floors of the entire upper story are tiled with 30 × 30 centimeter terracotta clay tiles. These have a layer of earth underneath them, presumably over a board subfloor. This is an intact example of the colonial flooring technique that was recently destroyed in the Tres Patios house. The use of such tiles as upper-story flooring material in colonial Cartagena is considered a sign of a higher status house, as simple wooden floors would have been much cheaper (Téllez and Moure 1982:48). The dating of the floor is difficult, although it should be noted that the refectory of the Carmelite convent in Cuenca, which was remodeled in the 1790–1800 period, has similar 30 × 30 centimeter tiles (Martínez Borrero 1983:143). This size of tiles is no longer used in Cuenca, but there is no current way to determine the timespan in which they were produced.

There is no ceiling in the main room (10T), so the frame for the roof is clearly visible. The framing of the roof is a typical Spanish colonial system known as *par e hilera* (pair and stringer), and thought to be Islamic in origin. If the more complex Spanish colonial roofing system of *par y nudillo* (pair and tie) was used then a tie beam would have been placed between each pair of rafters, giving the roof added strength and thus allowing for a wider, less steeply pitched roof (Téllez and Moure 1982:47). The weight of the roof frame in the Posadas house is balanced on the top of soleras (beams) that run along the tops of the adobe bearing walls. This system is common in Ecuadorian highland colonial architecture, with the rafters called *tijeras* ("scissors") and the beams along the tops of the walls referred to as *costaneras* (Crespo Toral 1976:77). The design is also common in colonial buildings in Cartagena, Colombia, and in Spain, so presumably it was fairly standard throughout the empire. It is described in a popular colonial book, the *Breve Compendio de la Carpintería de lo Blanco y Tratado de Alarifes* (Brief compendium of carpentry, joinery, and treatise of builders) by Diego López de Arenas, published in Seville in 1633 (Téllez and Moure 1982:47).

Returning to the main floor, the rear corridor of the house (10E) is held up by three pillars that are of great interest. These are barrel-shaped, very wide in diameter, and have wide, hand-carved capitals with simple scrollwork decoration at the ends (Figure 7B). These pillars are probably late eighteenth century in date. Directly above these, supporting the roof of the upper corridor (R) are five pillars that are also hand-carved, in a slightly different shape. They are square with slightly rounded corners in cross section, and smaller, but identically shaped capitals to those on the lower floor (Figure 7c).

The central patio (E) is paved entirely with river cobbles, a construction technique that was common in Cuenca up until the early years of this century for both patios and the city streets themselves (Centro de Investigación y Cultura 1991). This is a patio that even today serves multiple purposes. It is the center of movement between many of the rooms of the house, and is also a workspace that includes the water taps and sinks on the south side, a bread oven in the southwest corner, and various pieces of household material scattered in various parts of the patio. The central patio was also the most versatile space in the colonial Andean house, serving as work area, corral, and an area used to receive visitors. Some have suggested that the eighteenth century saw a generalized change from the central patio as work area to a formal garden for receiving visitors (Corradine Angulo 1981:29). It is more likely that the formal garden was present throughout the colonial period, but only in the most elite colonial houses. In most houses in Cuenca such formal gardens probably did not appear until the nineteenth century if at all. In the Posadas house the main patio is still a multiple-purpose space and has not been adorned with any of the decorations of a formal garden.

The central patio is flanked by a series of rooms on the west and east sides (10I, J, and K), which are all modern in construction. These rooms are where the current residents of the house spend the majority of their time, and the eastern wing (K) was not measured in order to avoid disturbing the privacy of the occupants. It is quite likely, however, that these rooms are simply replacing colonial versions of the same room arrangement, perhaps originally built of wattle and daub.

There is also a room (10F) with its door facing onto the front corridor (E). It is clear that room F is also a modern addition, enclosing what used to be a section of the corridor. A door used to lead directly from the tienda (B) into the corridor (E), but this door was walled off when room F was built.

At the back of the patio a small corridor (10L) has been roofed over, and directly behind this is a large, rectangular room (M). This room was very likely the dining and reception room of the house in the colonial period. It is solidly built and large, with considerable privacy. Both the family and guests coming from the main patio (H) can access the room. It can also be accessed from the rear patio (O) where the servants presumably prepared meals.

Meals were an extremely important part of the life of an urban household in the colonial Andes. The furnishings and tableware of the dining room were very important indicators of the status of the family. The positioning of the dining/reception room at the rear of the first patio in the Posadas house is an arrangement dating back to the Roman house, where the *triclinium* (dining and reception room) was usually directly to the rear of the peristyle (central courtyard) (Thébert 1987:365).

From the corridor (10L) a narrow roofed passageway (N) leads to the rear patio of the residence. This patio is not cobbled or tiled, but has a pounded earth floor. In the northwestern corner of the patio is a small kitchen garden (O). This is the area in which a few animals may have been kept, some vegetables grown, and the meals prepared in the colonial period.

On the east side of this garden is another room (10P), with a single small door entering into it. This door is hand-carved from a single slab of wood, with a bevel around the edge, and an ornate carved floral motif within a diamond lozenge in the center of the door. It has no metal hinges, but is set into the frame using a "pintle" system (Figure 8C), thus minimizing the need for metal. All of this suggests the door is colonial in date, although it is impossible to determine whether this was its intended original location.

In the roof of room P is a simple chimney, consisting of a small raised section of the roof that allowed smoke to escape. The entire interior of the room is blackened with smoke. Such a kitchen was common in the lower-class houses of eighteenth-century Spain, where a central fire was surrounded by benches under the *campana volada* (literally bell tower, suggesting the shape of the chimney). In the upper-class houses of eighteenth-century Spain there were usually several fireplaces, in the kitchen, main room, and largest bedroom. These would be "French style," or built of brick and embedded in the walls (Begoña 1986:102). Such high-cost fireplaces were probably a symbol of high status in colonial Cuenca and were never installed in the Posadas house.

Finally, to the north of the kitchen was a second entryway (10Q), with an exit from the house leading into a rear alley. This arrangement was common in the colonial Andes, but is rarely preserved today as so many urban alleyways have been removed because of pressure on space in urban areas. In Cuzco it is suggested that most houses had a rear "false door" from an alley, which allowed servants, supplies, and commercial transactions to enter and leave the house without using the main entrance. Most of these rear entrances are now gone (Gutiérrez et al. 1981:103). This rear entrance is very important to the permeability of the Posadas house. The rear entrance means that the kitchen garden (O) and the kitchen (P) have much greater access to the exterior than would otherwise be the case.

## The Use of Space in the Posadas House

The Posadas house appears to be a fairly intact example of a late-eighteenth-century Cuenca house of modest proportions. Two descriptions from late-eighteenth-century household inventories describe houses that were very similar to the Posadas house. The house of Doña Maria Leon, a vecina who lived in the San Francisco parish, is described in the inventory accompanying her 1797 will:

> [It is] composed of one upper room, whitewashed, and tiled, with a door and its lock and key, a balcony appertaining to the principal street which is not completed, its pair of doors with latch, an alcove with *bahareque* wall, a lower room with a small *tienda* on the street, and the corresponding piece of land, with some old walls, where some *umbrales* [thresholds? foundations?], and other new walls which divide the patio with a small portion of adobes, which are noted in the overhangs, and another of stone. (ANH/C C.97.733 f.5v [1797]), my translation)

The single large tiled upper room of the Posadas house (Figure 6T), with its balcony over the street (V), alcove separated by a thin partition (U), and the lower floor tiendas (B and D), seem to match this description well.

The inventory of the house of Joseph de Alvarado at the time of his death in 1770 gives a picture of a house that was very similar to the Posadas house. The rare room-by-room descriptions of the house contents give such a vivid picture of what the material culture of the Posadas house may have looked like that it is worthwhile quoting the inventory in detail:

> f.2v—First a house of two storys built of adobes, plaster, and bricks, roofed in wood and tile, with doors and windows toward the street and corridors within, with its locks and keys, and within it two *tiendas* to the said street, and in the lower room a leather-covered table . . . seven chairs, six gilded and the other ordinary, all used; five paintings . . . two with gilded frames, one silvered . . . and two without frames . . . and two small prints with small gilded frames; an *estrado* (couch) with its rug . . . used f.3r—and in the upper room . . . with its corridor and veranda over the patio . . . thirteen paintings of several subjects without frames, four of them new and the other nine old, and an altar with its arch and two pidamires [?] of gilded balsa and in it effigies of Christ crucified . . . Saint John, the Magdalene, and a Saint Anthony all carved and of several sizes, a small broken silver-plated box and within it a Sorrowing Mary . . . and an *excesomo* [?] of the same with its arms, two Saint Anthonies, a Saint John, and a Saint Michael all carved and of different sizes; eight prints of balsa and leather, large and small, used; a round table with its drawer, lock and key; an *estrado* . . . used a desk with its lock and key, painted and empty; two leather-covered trunks empty and old with locks and keys; a new pine box without lock or key, empty; two wooden boxes one large, with a lid, lock and key, new, and the other medium sized; a sword and a pair of pistols, all new f.3v—firstly in the patio of the house which has already been inventoried one building which is half built of adobes without roof, another building where there is an old oven with wood and tile roof; twenty-nine boards . . . another building with its corridor, room, and two additions, roofed in tile, and a small garden in front of the corridor. Worked Silver: . . . one *fuente* [fountain], four small plates, two jars, . . . two bowls . . . , one gourd trimmed in silver with its straw of the same . . . a "Polish" saddle adorned with silver with bronze stirrups and bit, and silver spurs f.4r—a saber with hand-guard and sheath of silver; a sword-belt . . . ; a bronze brazier . . . ; two old copper jars; four copper pails. (ANH/C C. 97.102 [1770]).

Don José was clearly a man of military demeanor if not an actual militia member, and his house was under construction at the time of his death, so in a certain sense the material inventoried was unique to his situation. There are several important general points to be made, however, when comparing this inventory to the standing architecture of the Posadas house. The lower front room was some sort of reception room for visitors, dominated by table and chairs. The main upper room, with desk, altar, table, and a wide variety of boxes and chests, was the focus of Don José and his family's daily life, where business could be conducted, religion attended to, and intimate visitors received. The majority of the artworks in the house were in this room. This is similar to an eighteenth-century Cuzco house inventory, which shows that the upper floor rooms in a two-story house were used as bedrooms and a living room, while the entire lower floor was devoted to "service areas" (Mesa 1979:256). The patios of the ground floor were in some disarray, but contained the horse tacking, and consisted of several loosely described outbuildings. The garden receives a mention, as do items like the brazier and copper cooking implements. The inventory provides a picture of how a house like the Posadas house may have been furnished, but it is an incomplete picture, as items considered of little economic value are not listed.

The Posadas house provides us with what may be the best preserved example of a late eighteenth-century house in Cuenca and is thus very important in looking at spatial relationships within the household. The Posadas is a courtyard house based on Mediterranean traditions that date to ancient Greece and were also present throughout the Islamic world. The key design feature of the traditional courtyard house is the separation of the house interior from the outside world. The high walls and the entrance vestibule separate the house interior from the street, in a physical manifestation of the premium that Mediterranean societies put on the separation of the private space of the family from the public domain. This delineation of private space is explicitly articulated within Islamic law, in which a large number of rules relate to the privacy of the courtyard house interior. Under Islamic urban codes visual access of neighbors to house interiors is stopped by several construction techniques. Parapets block views, doors cannot be placed immediately facing the door of a neighbor, and restrictions on window placement prohibit the construction of windows overlooking the property of others (Nevett 1994:107). The fact that modern municipal regulations in Cuenca prohibit the placement of windows overlooking the interior courtyards of other urban dwellers suggests that such Mediterranean ideals have had their influence on Andean urban planning.

The colonial Andean urban house was clearly separated from the life of the city around it, but within a given household the rooms were not as compartmentalized according to activities as they are in modern Western houses. As with the Islamic courtyard house, the spatial segregation of women within the Andean colonial house was minimal. Rather than having separate areas of the house for men's and women's activities, women's activities took place throughout the house. Strangers were excluded from the house because of its walled nature, but when strangers entered, women could always move to another part of the house to avoid contact with them. In this way, despite widely differing gender roles within the functioning of the Spanish colonial household, women still had the ability to partake in activities throughout the household interior (Nevett 1994:105, 110).

There was little physical separation of the activities of different genders in the Spanish colonial urban house, but there was a clear separation of the homeowner's family from the activities of servants. The front sec-

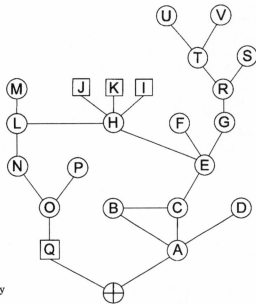

**Figure 12.** Justified permeability
diagram of the Posadas house.

tion of the Posadas house was taken up with the activities of the homeowner (or renter) and their family. The servants of the household, however, probably inhabited the back patio to a greater extent. Thus, the
spatial relations within the Posadas house suggest that in the colonial
period the family that lived there was of an economic level to afford
servants, who were probably either wage labor Native Andeans, or tributary Native Andeans assigned to the family by the state. The two entrances allowed the front entrance to be used by the owner and family,
while the rear entrance could be used for the interaction of servants with
the outside world, delivery of foodstuffs, and so forth (Figure 12). This
system is common in Mediterranean courtyard houses. The separation of
the daily activities of the servants probably did not extend to providing
the servants with their own private quarters. As in the houses of the
Roman Empire, it is likely that servants slept on cots in the house corridors (Veyne 1987:73).

In conclusion, the Posadas house is an example of a substantial
house on the periphery of the eighteenth-century city. It was a part of the
San Sebastián parish, a parish which by the late eighteenth century had
large populations of both mestizo and Native Andean inhabitants. The
Posadas house is a very strong statement of Mediterranean architectural
ideals. Although modest by modern standards, and not of the scale of the

large houses in the city core, the Posadas house was probably owned by a person with some economic means in the eighteenth century.

## THE RIVERSIDE NEIGHBORHOOD OF TODOS SANTOS

There were many much smaller houses in eighteenth-century Cuenca than those described above, and in the Todos Santos parish, immediately south of Cuenca's central core (Figure 3), there are several well-preserved examples of such lower-class urban colonial housing. The Todos Santos area was probably the first part of the city inhabited by Spaniards. In the 1540s, a decade before the city was formally founded, it is said that a population of Spaniards had taken up residence along the river's edge. They founded the Todos Santos church and laid out a plaza on the block immediately north of the church (González Suárez 1983 [1891]:24; Municipio de Cuenca n.d.:10). The church is in an unusual location in terms of Spanish ideals of town planning, and this may indicate that it was built on a pre-Hispanic religious site.

Excavation at the Todos Santos archaeological site, three hundred meters east of the church, revealed the remains of Spanish mills and canals for supplying water to the mills, all built of reused finished Inka masonry (Agustín Landívar 1974:8–9). These mill remains are supposed to have been built by the conquistador and encomendero Rodrigo Núñez de Bonilla, who was given rights to Native Andean labor in the immediate area of Tumipampa prior to 1557 and set up mills on the riverbank. Documents from 1563 relate the sale of a riverside mill formerly owned by Núñez de Bonilla (Agustín Landívar 1974:9). The water for these mills may have come from pre-Hispanic canals that were reputed to have been in existence when the Spanish arrived and to have continued in use up until the seventeenth century (González Aguirre 1989:220). A system of working canals would have been an attractive feature for initial Spanish settlement of Cuenca. In medieval Europe mills and canals were an important investment, often built by feudal lords, who in turn would charge peasants for grinding their grain. The mill excavated in Todos Santos and presumed to date to the mid-1500s is thought to have been a large horizontal waterwheel (Agustín Landívar 1974:24). This suggests that the excavated mill is indeed sixteenth century in date, as such mills were replaced by the more familiar and efficient vertical or "Vitruvian" paddle wheel in medieval and early modern times in most of Europe (Pounds 1989:174).

The water from the river was not only used for mills. Andean cities were generally built near rivers, and water for household use and sewage disposal were key factors in colonial urban planning. The municipality controlled access to canal systems, and municipalities, monasteries, and convents sponsored public fountains in the plazas. These formed points of interaction among the population who gathered in the plazas at fountains to get water.

When Cuenca was formally founded in 1557, the *plaza mayor* and quadrangular grid of city blocks were laid out to the north of Todos Santos. As in other Andean colonial cities, this quadrangular layout attempted to deny the geography of the adjacent river. The grid system was the center of imperial power. Along the river's edge the Todos Santos parish, as with other riverside areas in the colonial Andes, became a neighborhood for the urban poor, people who undertook the essential tasks of taking in laundry, tending animals, collecting firewood, and so forth (Aprile-Gniset 1991:196).

There was a distinctive ideology that went with these riverside colonial neighborhoods. The Spanish colonial mind saw the river's edge as a place of danger and wilderness. In Cali the municipal council constantly complained about the edge of the river, where criminal and sinful activities were undertaken under the cover of the plant growth. The river's edge was seen as a place of immorality, where the devil could easily gain a foothold among the urban population (Aprile-Gniset 1991:196, 424).

Cuenca was never a wealthy municipality. From as early as 1586 the council had occasionally encouraged the construction of a fountain in the central plaza of the city, but the lack of funds was still defeating the idea in 1754. Why was such a fountain important? The *procurador* (solicitor) of the Cuenca municipal council suggested in 1754 that if a fountain was built in the plaza it would give the poor access to water. He suggested that "many offences against God would be avoided, because among the hiding-places of the banks of the river and its gullies such offences are performed" (Chacón Zhapán 1990:441–442, my translation). It is clear that both church and state officials were concerned that colonial authority was not well established in this neighborhood. Its location outside the city core meant that "surveillance" (Giddens 1984:127) was not possible in the winding streets, gullies, and overgrown banks of the river, but this was probably of little concern to the urban poor who inhabited the neighborhood.

An examination of the property transactions in the Todos Santos neighborhood (Table 2) gives a picture very different from that of the central core of Cuenca, only three city blocks to the north. The Todos Santos properties were on average much smaller and much lower in price. The owners were evenly split between males and females, which means

**Table 2.** Some Property Transactions by Owner in the Todos Santos Neighborhood of Cuenca

|  | 1628–49 | 1650–99 | 1700–49 |
|---|---|---|---|
| Male citizen | 2 | 4 | 19 |
| Male resident | 1 | – | – |
| Male Indian | – | – | 1 |
| Ensign | – | – | 1 |
| Sergeant | – | – | 1 |
| Total males | 3 | 4 | 22 |
| Female unmarried Indian | – | – | 1 |
| Female citizen | – | 1 | 15 |
| Female Indian | 1 | 2 | 8 |
| Female citizen, widowed | 1 | 1 | 2 |
| Mestiza (female mestizo) | 1 | 1 | – |
| Total females | 3 | 5 | 22 |
| Average size | 1552 m$^2$ | 441 m$^2$ | 741 m$^2$ |
| Average price | 60 pesos | 107 pesos | 133 pesos |

*Source:* Jamieson 1996:119.

there were more female property owners in Todos Santos than in the core of the city. The most striking difference is in the ethnicity and titles of the property owners when these are listed. The upper crust of Cuenca colonial society lived in the urban core, and in Todos Santos the property owners were often vecinos, but could also be mestizo or Native Andean. Widows were fairly common, and this was a neighborhood of the urban poor. Throughout the seventeenth century only between 1% and 5% of Native Andean urban property transactions involved property in Todos Santos (Poloni 1992:309), suggesting that this was by no means an "Indian" parish, but rather a parish of the urban poor of all ethnic groups.

The inhabitants of neighborhoods like Todos Santos were key figures in the colonial economy, and yet their status as people on the margins makes them difficult to pin down. The only resident of Todos Santos in the colonial period whose occupation happened to be mentioned in a property transaction was Martin Pugo (a Native Andean name), who was a hatmaker (ANH/C L.618, f. 102r. [1745]). A significant proportion of the residents of Todos Santos would have been renters, as property ownership would have been well beyond their means. Many of the vecinos listed as property owners in the neighborhood may have been absentee landlords.

The presence of several widows and Native Andean women who were never married suggests that Todos Santos was one of the areas where many of the female market women lived. Ethnically they were frequently classified as *mestizas en habito de india* (mestizas in the clothing of Indians) or *cholas*. Native Andean women were more likely than men to live within the city of Cuenca in the seventeenth century. This suggests to the historian Jacques Poloni that there may have been a division of labor wherein women were more associated with urban marketing and men more associated with rural farming. Even these women's ethnicity was part of their marginal status, as declaring yourself a mestiza meant you could avoid paying tribute as an Indian, yet declaring yourself Indian meant you could avoid having to pay the sales tax on goods that you sold (Poloni 1992:291, 302). If such women led similar lives to their counterparts in seventeenth-century Quito, they generally rented their small houses or shops and took part in all sorts of marketing activities, both legal and illegal (Minchom 1989). The picture of the Todos Santos neighborhood emerges as an area of people who worked in the market, were artisans or craftspeople, and had very limited economic resources.

## THE TODOS SANTOS HOUSES

The colonial domestic architecture of the Todos Santos neighborhood was much smaller in scale then that of the core of Cuenca. The only pre-1650 house found in the notarial documents was a single room, with a thatch roof (ANH/C L. 511 f. 622v. [1646]). Such one-room houses, with thatch roof and often a bread oven on the exterior, were common in the latter half of the seventeenth century in Todos Santos (Jamieson 1996:120). In 1695 there is the first mention of a tile roof on the tienda of a house, which itself had a thatch roof (ANH/C L.527 f. 657v [1692]). In 1725 we see the first tile roofed house with multiple rooms, "a house . . . with two rooms for living, roofed in tile, and a bread oven with tile roof" (ANH/C L. 612 f. 465r–v [1725]). Up until the 1740s the single-room thatch roof house was still common in Todos Santos, but from the 1730s onward these began to be replaced with tile roofs. The vast majority of houses had only one room, although some two-room houses were present by the early eighteenth century (Jamieson 1996:121). Almost all the house descriptions fail to mention the construction material for the walls. A tile-roofed house specifies that the walls were wattle and daub (L.540 ff.485r–486r [1744]), so we cannot assume that most tile-roofed houses had adobe walls. The earliest specific mention of adobe walls (L.540 ff.401r–402r [1743]) suggests that the Todos Santos neighborhood was an area of one-room wattle and daub houses until the mid-eighteenth century. The only mention of a second story on a house is from 1741 (L. 617 ff. 255r–255v [1741]). Unfortunately no house descriptions dated after 1750 were found for Todos Santos.

The standing domestic architecture in the neighborhood today all appears to postdate 1750, but there are several examples of houses that probably predate the Wars of Independence. The main thoroughfare of Todos Santos is the Calle Larga (Long Street), which runs parallel to the river. Three houses along a two-block section of the north side of Calle Larga were chosen for this study (Figure 3), based on presumably colonial features in the facade and the permission of owners for access to the houses to undertake detailed measurements.

## House 2: Calle Larga 5-24

The house designated "House 2" for this study is located at 5-24 Calle Larga, just northwest of the Todos Santos church (Figure 3). The main building is entirely adobe brick, with a clay tile roof. The entrance portico of the house (Figure 13A) has modern pillars, presumably replacing colonial examples, and an earth floor with no visible tiles or stone cobbling.

The most prominent features of the portico (A) are the two adobe benches built into the west and north sides. This is the first example of a house with benches built into the portico, and their presence suggests that guests may have been received in this area, looking directly out onto the street. This is interesting in that rural houses surrounding Cuenca commonly have benches on the portico (Calderón 1985). Using the portico as the area to receive guests reduces the privacy of the household, making their relationship with others visible to those passing on the street. The unlit, single large interior room was probably not an ideal place to work, so the portico may also have been a place to undertake the daily work activities of the household. The portico seems to be abandoned now, and the family and friends were smoking, working, and socializing in the rear patio for the few hours that I spent with them while measuring the house.

From the portico a door leads to a small tienda (13B), inaccessible from the house interior. This small room would have been appropriate for a small family business or for rental to another individual. Two other doors lead to the zaguan (C) and the main room of the house (D). The zaguan is long and narrow and is cobbled, with floor tiles along the edges. The main room, tiled with 30 × 30 centemeter tiles, is still the combined living and bedroom of the family occupying the house, and there is very little privacy for this room, with its door leading directly onto the street. This door has been recently nailed shut, suggesting that modern urban life is not amenable to this older architectural arrangement.

From the zaguan (13C) one reaches a corridor (E), which is tiled on the eastern half and cobbled on the western half. Laundry and toilet facilities are currently located here, and it is the locus of much of the

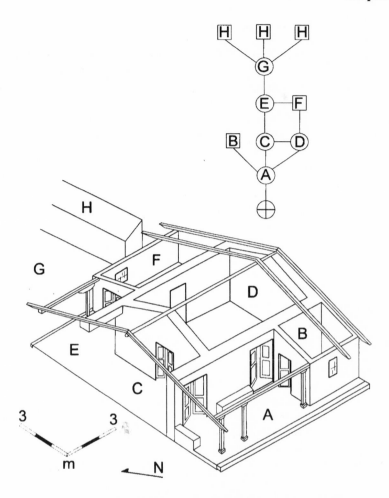

**Figure 13.** Isometric drawing and justified permeability diagram
of Todos Santos House 2.

daytime activity in the house. Accessible from this corridor and from the
main room (D) is a rear room (F). This is currently being used as a second
bedroom, but was not a part of the original house. There is an embedded
pillar in the rear wall, hand-carved and barrel-shaped, probably late eighteenth century in date. The pillar was embedded in the wall when walling
off a section of what had been the rear corridor of the house that created
room F. The walling-off of corridors to create more rooms is common in

Cuenca houses and suggests the increasing need for segregated and enclosed spaces in the modern era. The pillar in the wall of room F is one of the few clear suggestions that House 2 may indeed be colonial in date.

Beyond the corridor (E) there is a large rear open space, unpaved in any way, and surrounded by modern "lean-to" outbuildings (H). This space is walled on all sides with modern concrete walls, so that the colonial arrangement of this space is entirely unknown. There may have been a rear exit to an alleyway, but this is no longer visible. The modern outbuildings (H) were not measured or drawn, but one was serving as a kitchen and others as bedrooms and storage rooms. It is presumed that in the colonial period small constructions of wattle and daub and thatch may have existed in this rear yard.

## House 3: Calle Larga 4-78

The house designated "House 3" for this study was located one block east of House 2, at Calle Larga 4-78 (Figure 3). The main building is entirely adobe, with a clay tile roof. The portico of the house (Figure 14A and Figure 15) is striking because the slope of the street means that the portico floor has been raised above street level. The roof is supported by two hand-carved pillars, barrel-shaped, with very wide capitals (Figure 7D). These appear to be colonial in date. The portico is now poured concrete, showing no immediate evidence of its original floor. There are no preserved adobe benches on this portico, as there were in House 2.

From the portico one door leads to the zaguan (14C) and another to the main room (B). All the floors in this house have been rebuilt in poured concrete, so there is no evidence of the colonial flooring. Above the main room (B) is a large loft (D), with an open area so that the loft overlooks the main room. The loft is wooden and industrial-era in construction, with machine-turned balustrades and wire nail fasteners. Currently the building is a residence, and the loft is used for storage and for drying agricultural products. It is unknown whether the current loft is simply replacing an earlier example. It is possible that a loft existed there in the colonial period or that the roof was raised and the loft built at a later date to enlarge the house.

To the rear of the zaguan (14C) is a small corridor (E) facing onto a rear patio. A long narrow room (F) leads off of this corridor and was constructed by walling in a section of the corridor. Originally there was a door from the main room (B) through to the rear room (F), but this door has been walled off. The room (F) may be quite modern, and the door may have been walled off when the room was built. Beyond the corridor (E) is the rear patio (G), with several modern additions (H) on its western and

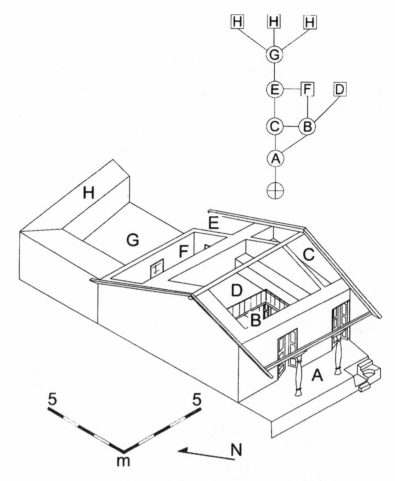

Figure 14. Isometric drawing and justified permeability diagram
of Todos Santos House 3.

northern sides. There is no evidence of any colonial architecture in the
rear patio area, and no visible rear exit from the residence.

## House 4: Calle Larga 4-130

Several doors west of House 3 but on the same block is the residence that
I designated House 4, at number 4-130 Calle Larga (Figure 3). The front of
the building is a small portico (Figure 16A), with three pillars. The pillars

**Figure 15.** The facade of Todos Santos House 3.

are barrel-shaped and hand-carved (Figure 7E), but only the western pillar has a preserved capital, which is embedded into the front wall of the neighbor's house and is only half-visible. This is an interesting feature that suggests the portico on the street was uniform along the facade of several dwellings. This may indicate that several buildings in a row may have had the same owner (and been rented out to the occupants) or the municipality may have had some control over this portico space, creating a uniform facade for this section of the street.

From the portico one door leads to the main room (16B) and another to the zaguan or entrance hall (C). The main room (B) has a rear door through to the main patio, but this was blocked off when the modern outbuildings (F) were constructed. As in House 3 the main room has a loft (E), which overlooks the room below it, and it could have been used as storage and sleeping space, particularly if the room below was used as a shop or business of some sort. The zaguan (C) provides a passage to the rear patio (D). A series of modern outbuildings (F) have been built along the western and northern sides of the patio, and because these were clearly not colonial in date they were not measured and drawn. These probably replace earlier wattle and daub outbuildings used for various purposes by the family.

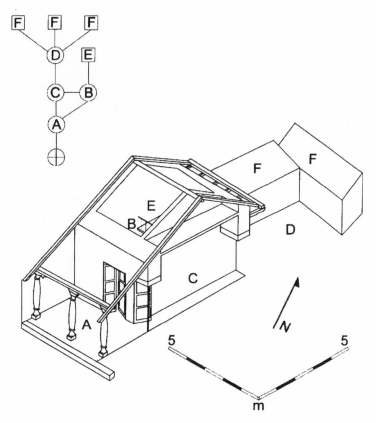

**Figure 16.** Isometric drawing and justified permeability diagram
of Todos Santos House 4.

## The Todos Santos Houses: A Summary

Combining the architectural and archival evidence, the three recorded
Todos Santos houses represent the architecture of the urban poor of late-
eighteenth-century Cuenca. The notarial archives suggest that houses with
adobe walls were not common in Todos Santos before 1750, so these
houses are probably all late-eighteenth-century in date. A comparison of
the permeability diagrams for the three houses (Figures 13, 14, and 16)
shows a very similar basic premise. Each was built as a single large adobe
room with a gable roof that extends to cover front and rear corridors. To
one side of the main room was a zaguan leading from the front to the
rear. Each of the three houses is a variation on this theme. The variation

consists of building lofts above the main room and/or enclosing the front portico or rear corridor to create other small rooms. To the rear of the main building is the yard of the family, now surrounded in all cases by modern outbuildings.

The subdivision of the main house into smaller rooms may have been an original colonial feature, but I would suspect most of the alterations are Republican or modern in date. The large single room of the eighteenth-century builders became insufficient in a modern world where specialized spaces were divided among a multiplicity of rooms and concerns for privacy became universal.

The houses of Todos Santos are small and very open to the street. Most of these buildings were probably not owned by their residents. Whether one owner constructed the row of houses or the porticoes was a matter of municipal ordinance, but their similar pillars running along the block would have given the street a very corporate aspect. The open front porticoes would have created a sphere for interaction between the residents of Calle Larga, who could have more easily interacted with one another as they worked and socialized in an area open to the street. The porticoes would have also fulfilled an objective of the colonial administration, allowing residents of the neighborhood and other passersby an opportunity to monitor the activities of each household. In this we see the preindustrial precursors of the housing of the Industrial Revolution in Europe. Such housing often included continuous galleries, so that all workers could see and visit one another easily, and each person's life was exposed, allowing others to monitor the "moral and intellectual standards" of the population (Markus 1993:298).

In a sense these three houses are similar to rural Native housing (Calderón 1985), with one- or two-room architecture, and benches on the porch where much of the day's activities would have taken place. But to live in the city house was to live under corporate regulation, rather than under vernacular traditions. It is to those vernacular traditions of the countryside that we will now turn.

# The Rural Architecture Surrounding Cuenca | 4

## ANDEAN VERNACULAR: HUASIYUC AND THATCH ROOFS

Vernacular architecture in the Andes is a vibrant tradition, and we can learn much about colonial rural relations in looking at the rural Andean house in the twentieth century. In many rural villages the act of building a house is a time for the expression of particularly Andean ideals.

The founding of a new house in a rural *ayllu* (a social unit of lineage or kinship) is an important symbol of the independence of a newly married couple in the Andes. Houses are built by co-operative work groups, led by a local expert without any institutionalized training but with extensive expertise in designing and building houses (Calderón 1985:29–30; Margolies 1979:218). In Saraguro, south of Cuenca, couples generally live with one of their parents for a few years after marriage, until they are able to afford to build a house of their own. At this stage the man becomes known as a *huasiyuc*, "a person building a house"; this is an important stage of married life in Saraguro. Delicate negotiations dealing with the obligations of the families of each marriage partner are undertaken before the materials for the house are purchased or harvested, and a communal work group assembled for construction. The huasiyuc must provide food and drink for all the participants in the communal building activities (Calderón 1985:19–20, 26).

There are ethnohistorical sources that give some idea of the symbolic and ideological importance of the house itself in Andean thought. An early seventeenth-century ceremony for the founding of a house in Cajatambo (200 kilometers northeast of Lima) demonstrates the embedded ideology of ancestors, gender relations, and the house at the local level of the Andean ayllu. In the belief system of the local *Cotos ayllu* the goddess Coya Guarmi was the sister and consort of the god Condortocas. Together they had come from the sea and were the founding couple of the ayllu. For the final roofing ceremony of a new house Coya Guarmi, represented by a small ceramic pitcher dressed in miniature female clothing, was brought from the chapel she resided in to the new house. She resided for three days in the area of the house where the *chicha* (beer, brewed by female household members) was to be stored. At the end of this time she was taken to the place where Condortocas, the male founder of the ayllu, was buried. When Coya Guarmi joined Condortocas the founding of the new house was complete (Duviols 1986:349–387).

The founding of a new household is also reenacted in the rural Andes each time a house roof needs to be rethatched. Both house construction and house rethatching work parties in a village in Apurímac, in southern Peru, for instance, involve the participation of a work party during a particular part of the annual agricultural cycle. Houses are rethatched just before the ripening and harvesting of crops, when the community is in transition from co-operative planting and weeding tasks, to the harvest season when each nuclear household focuses on its own harvest (Gose 1991:45). The work party that rethatches a house roof also participates in a complex part of the annual ritual cycle, in which reciprocity is important, and a mock wedding occurs to symbolize the ties of the house-owning couple to the rest of the community (Gose 1991:44, 56).

The single- or two-roomed rural house with thatch roof can still be seen in southern highland Ecuador. In the rural Andes the wattle and daub or stone one-room house with thatch roof remained the standard rural dwelling up until the 1930s. They are becoming more and more rare, however, as the industrial world is brought into the rural Andes. It was after World War II that thatch in the rural Andes began to be widely replaced by that symbol of modernity, the corrugated metal roof. Multiroom structures reflecting previously urban ideals of living room, kitchen, and bedrooms, with the associated industrially produced household furnishings, began to be more and more common in rural areas (Gutiérrez et al. 1986b:61; Margolies 1979:219–220). In southern highland Ecuador clay tiles, rather than corrugated metal, became the rural standard after thatch began to lose popularity in the 1920s and 1930s. In most rural villages there are farmers who are also part-time specialists in clay tile manufacture (Calderón 1985:23). Throughout the colonial period such rural thatch houses would have dotted the Andean landscape everywhere outside the larger towns; the vast majority of the inhabitants of the colonial Andes would have lived in such houses. Colonial examples of this architecture all disappeared from the landscape long ago, although with extensive areal excavations the footprints of these ephemeral buildings could be revealed archaeologically.

From initial Spanish contact in the 1530s up until the 1560s the majority of Native Andeans in the southern Ecuadorian highlands had lived in dispersed rural communities. The house of the *kuraka* (ethnic lord or chieftain) was the ceremonial center of their local region, and trade systems with lowland groups were still intact (Salomon 1983:114). With the Toledan reforms of the 1570s all of this changed, as dispersed rural inhabitants of the southern highlands were congregated in villages designed and founded by the Spanish (Chacón Zhapán 1990:58).

The logic of the Toledan program involved several important aspects, relating to Spanish religion, medical beliefs, and state ideology. In the writings of Pedro de Cieza de León it is clear that sixteenth-century Spaniards had little understanding of the Native Andean worldview and how it related to architecture. Cieza believed that people such as the Pastos, who lived to the north of the Inka Empire, had no religion at all. His proof of this was that they had no separate houses of worship (Cieza de León 1965 [1553]:88). A sixteenth-century Jesuit priest believed that the Indians in scattered hamlets had "not been able to learn the social and political skills that are a prerequisite to becoming capable of the law of God . . . they live in wild terrain like savages; even when they do join together in villages, their custom is to dwell in narrow poor quarters, dark and dirty, where they associate together and sleep like pigs" (MacCormack 1991:276).

Epidemics introduced by the Spaniards devastated Native Andean populations in the Cuenca region in the 1520s to 1580s. The Spanish were sure that one of the causes of this widespread disease was the extended family household in the Native villages, which tended to contain 20 to 30 individuals. The Spanish in the 1580s claimed that the formation of nuclear family residences in Native villages reduced personal contact and that this greatly reduced deaths from disease. It seems more likely that constant exposure meant the surviving Native populations had built up immunity by the 1580s (Newson 1995:234). The Spaniards were clear in their belief that Andean people could never become true Christians until they lived in centralized villages with nuclear households and a village church.

The Toledan reduction program was the physical manifestation of this Spanish ideology throughout the Andes. Juan de Matienzo outlined the ideal small Andean town, as it would be founded in the Toledan reductions:

> In one-quarter of the other block there must be a council house where meetings will be held to deal with all that concerns the community. In another quarter there will be a hospital, and in another the garden for the use of the hospital. In another quarter, the corral of the Council. . . . In another quarter there will be built the *Corregidor*'s house, all of these with tile roof. The house of the priest who preaches to them must be of two-quarters, next to the church with tile roof. The other quarter-blocks of the plaza must be the houses of married Spaniards who wish to live among the Indians. . . . To each *cacique* there must be given a block, or two quarter-blocks given to those who must have them, and in the two quarter-blocks behind the *Corregidor*'s house there must be the house of the *Tucuiruco* [Native leader] and the jail. (Matienzo 1967 [1567]:49–50, my translation)

The tile roofs were of key importance to the status and ideals of Spanish colonization in the Andes. All the major buildings of Church and state were supposed to have tile roofs in order to be valid. The hierarchical nature of seeing thatch as associated with a poorer type of building, and tile as more advanced, came from a European model. This model stressed a hierarchy of building materials, with stone and tile as the ideal, wood and adobe as acceptable secondary materials, and the thatch roof as a despised symbol of the lack of "proper" materials (Fraser 1990:26–27, 108). The tile roofs represented the coming of Spanish civilization, while thatch roofs symbolized the primitive. From this we can see how the transition from thatch to tile roofs in the colonial period was intimately tied to identification of a building with either local Andean village life, or to the larger Spanish colonial world.

From the 1582 Crown inquiry, which resulted in the Relaciones Geográficas, we can gain a glimpse of the Native rural architecture in the villages around Cuenca immediately following the Toledan reductions. The physical layout of Toledan villages, built on a quadrangular plan with the church on the main plaza, was a key element in Spanish colonial control of Native Andean peoples. The houses in these villages, however, were still designed and built by the Native Andeans themselves. Luckily for us, the priests who filled out the questionnaires for the 1582 inquiry took many different meanings from question 31, which asked what sort of houses Native peoples lived in, and what materials the houses were built of.

Basic house construction was described by the priest assigned to Cañaribamba, 50 kilometers southwest of Cuenca:

> [T]he order and manner of building their houses is to dig some posts into the ground, leaving a space the size that they would like the house to have; after placing the posts, they place mud to the thickness of a hand; and this is their construction technique. They cover the said houses with thatch, which they collect in the countryside, and which the locals call ichu. (Gómez 1965 [1582]:285, my translation).

These houses were built by ayllu work parties, as described by the priest of Pacaibamba (now the town of Girón, 30 kilometers southwest of Cuenca). He stated that "Their houses are of wattle and daub, which lasts six to eight years or longer, which they build with a minga, their word for a work party; and as all the village comes, in two days they build a house twenty feet wide and thirty long" (Arias Dávila 1965 [1582]:280, my translation),

In Azogues, 25 kilometers northeast of Cuenca, we have the first hint of a power relationship reified in village architecture, with a particular name for the houses of the caciques. The village was made up of

> some round houses with thin walls; they are one story with two terraces, one on each side. The caciques have large rectangular houses, and have placed

on the houses wooden constructions with thatch roofs, which the Indians call *rinriyuchuasi*, which is to say "house with ears"; and this is for their large size, which only the *caciques* build; they are of mud and wood, in the manner of thin walls, as I have said; and they do not make them any other way, because this is their ancient building method; and this is general in the entire Cañari province. (Gallegos 1965 [1582]:278, my translation).

In Paccha, ten kilometers east of Cuenca, the priest described the village houses in terms that succinctly summarize the relationship between architecture, the new colonial power, and the traditional reciprocity embodied in ayllu social relations. The village houses were described as being

> some round and others "large." The houses of the *caciques* have a patio at the entrance, where the *cacique* asks his Indians to gather and preaches and reminds them of their orders to do that which the *corregidor* and other justices of Cuenca demand, and how they must pay tribute to their *encomendero*; and having finished his speech, he must give them food and drink on the patio. (Angeles 1965 [1582]:270–271, my translation)

The Toledan reductions were above all an attempt to monitor the everyday existence of Native Andeans. Juan de Matienzo's ideals for Native resettlements emphasized this in the design of Native houses. In areas of the Andes where Native people had traditionally built round houses they were forced to build square ones, to "imitate the houses of Castile" (Fraser 1990:78). It was stated that houses should have two or three rooms, so parents could sleep separately from children. Everyone was expected to sleep on a bed rather than on the floor. Finally, the front door of the house was to face the street, so that those passing by could monitor the activities within (Matienzo 1967 [1567]:48–49, 53–54). Subtle forms of resistance by Native Andean peoples to such colonial efforts are still visible today in the rural Andes, in households such as those of the town of Saraguro, south of Cuenca. At formal meals in Saraguro the men sit at a table, while the women sit on a mat in the corner (Calderón 1985:26). The use of individual chairs for each person at the meal, as the colonial authorities began encouraging four hundred years ago, is still not the norm in Saraguro.

Rural Native Andeans in the colonial period had a worldview very different from the perceptions of the Spanish residents of urban areas. Their lived experience created a view of the landscape that was divided into three parts—valley bottoms, midslopes, and high mountain areas. During the colonial period the valley bottoms became associated with the Spanish landed estates, with the labor of the rural men who walked down to the valleys to work on these estates, and with a violent and exploitative colonialism. It is the midslopes that were the benevolent heart of the world, where the dispersed rural villages were positioned to maximize access to agricultural resources. Finally, the high mountain areas were associated with the upland herding done by women, with the wilderness and the uncontrollable, and with the mountain gods, who look down on them all (Isbell 1978:57–66; Skar 1981:37–40). In the valley bottoms the landed estates of the Spaniards in the Cuenca region were an architectural manifestation of the social boundary between forced tribute laborers and a landed upper class, whose worldviews clashed at a profound level. It is to these landed estates that we will turn now.

## YANUNCAY

The cluster of buildings now known by the two names of the hacienda Yanuncay Grande or *la Primavera* (Springtime), is located southwest of Cuenca on the Yanuncay River (Figure 2). One of the buildings is still a family home, although part of the complex is abandoned. The property has been purchased by an educational institution in Cuenca to be used as a rural retreat, and the buildings are being restored by the Ecuadorian Instituto Nacional del Patrimonio Cultural (National Institute for Cultural Heritage).

The large, adobe-walled, tile-roofed Yanuncay Grande house (Figure 17) was in no way typical of the houses in this area during the colonial period and was probably part of one of the few large rural holdings in the area. Prior to 1700 the notarial documents for the Yanuncay region described mostly one-room thatch houses in the area. The earliest house with a tile roof is mentioned in 1706, but all other eighteenth-century Yanuncay houses found in the archival sources had thatch roofs (Jamieson 1996:139). There is no mention in the documents of any house with multiple rooms built of adobe. It is very likely that this house was an elite rural residence, a relative rarity in the region. For this reason the small sample of documents has simply failed to reveal descriptions of any similar houses in the area in the colonial period. It is thus through the architecture and archaeological remains alone that we gain some understanding of this elite Yanuncay colonial residence.

The Yanuncay Grande hacienda is a series of buildings entirely surrounded by high adobe walls. On approaching the house from any direction the first impression is that it is a very enclosed space (Figure 17). The walls that surround the buildings are blank on most sides. Fieldstone walls, some of them recently knocked down in several places, border the lanes approaching the house, making access to the building even more difficult. The house complex can be entered by two doors. The first entrance is approached from a short, narrow lane (Figure 18A), and it would

**Figure 17.** The Yanuncay house.

be the logical approach for people coming from the roadway to the south. At the end of the lane are the main double doors of the house, assembled from milled lumber, and therefore probably twentieth century in date. These doors lead through to the main patio (B).

The second entrance is to approach the house from the riverside to the north. This involves walking up a wider, long lane with stone fences on either side (18U). The lane is quite well constructed, and it seems likely that it has been used since the time of the construction of the house as the lane to get water from the river and to lead animals out of the patio (B) and into the fields. A pair of milled lumber gates enclose the entrance to the patio. Just to the west of this entrance is the bread oven for the house, located outside the main patio enclosure (B).

Once standing within the main patio (18B) much of the house layout is revealed. The patio is now grassed, but test excavation has shown that the space is still cobbled with river-rolled rocks directly beneath the sod. There is direct access to several areas from this patio, including a storage room (G) against the south wall and lean-to enclosures currently being used to stable animals (E) against the south and west walls. Room F, against the west wall and adjacent to the rear house entrance, has a dirt

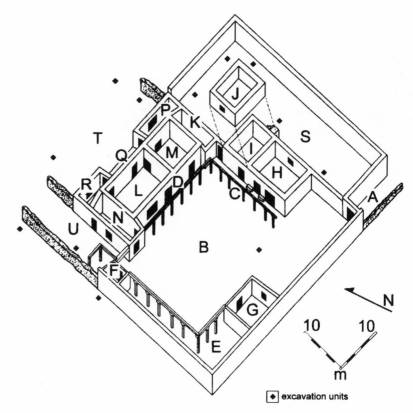

**Figure 18.** Isometric drawing of the Yanuncay house.

floor and still contains the adobe construction elements for a stove in its
northwestern corner. Clearly this room was a kitchen at one time.

On the eastern side of the main patio is the largest building of the
complex, a two-story residence. The interior corridor of the building (18C)
is supported by plain square pillars of milled lumber and has a dirt floor.
Two adobe benches are built into the wall of this corridor, suggesting this
area was a place where visitors could be met. From this corridor a pair of
double doors and a separate single door lead into room H. The double
doors appear to be colonial in date. They are hand-carved, and each consists of a frame containing twelve recessed beveled rectangles, without
any further carved decoration (Figure 8D). These doors are one of the few
clues that this building is colonial in date. The interior room (H) has a dirt
floor and is currently being used as a kitchen and living area, with a large
adobe brick stove. Also accessible from the corridor (C) is a second room

(I), currently used for storage. The door to this room is identical to the double doors on room H. There is no interior door connecting rooms H and I. This is a typical feature of the Mediterranean courtyard house (Thébert 1987:408), in that all rooms would have access to the courtyard, but without internal passages from one room to the next. Room H has one tiny window, with shutters but no glass, facing east, while room I is windowless. This suggests a construction date predating access to glass for windows. Oral testimony from a previous owner of the house suggests that this building was built in the 1820s, but the architect for the Instituto Nacional de Patrimonio Cultural has suggested that the hand-built doors with pintles instead of hinges suggest a colonial construction date (Miño S. n.d.:6).

To the north of the main building there is an exterior passage leading from the corridor (18C) to a walled garden (S), which the tiny window in room H overlooks. This is a convenient space for kitchen vegetable gardening, as the walled space is thoroughly separated from marauding livestock. Exterior stone stairs lead from this garden to the second story of the colonial house, which consists of a single room (J) proposed to have been a granary. There is no interior access to this room from the lower floor.

The northern portion of the building complex is taken up with a building accessed from a second corridor (18D) overlooking the central patio. From the corridor (D) there is access to two central rooms (L) and (M). Room L, used as a living room up until the current restoration, has an interesting configuration of tiles, with large (32 × 32 centimeter) square tiles on the western part of the room and smaller (18 × 18 centimeter) square tiles on the eastern half. Room M, currently a bedroom, has yet another style of tiles, 19 centimeter diameter hexagonal tiles, which also cover the floor of the corridor (D). The hexagonal tiles have been suggested to date to the 1860s (Miño S. n.d.:8). The floor tiles suggest certain alterations to the central rooms of this building. If we propose that a wall once ran north to south through room L, the small square tiles may demarcate an area of a central passage or zaguan leading from corridor D to the rear corridor Q. This suggests that the core of this building originally had an arrangement of two rooms flanking a central corridor, as in the lower floor of the urban Posadas and Tres Patios houses described above.

Surrounding these central rooms are a chapel (18N) and three rooms currently used as bedrooms (P, R, and K). All of the doors and hardware in this building are of milled lumber and industrial metal, suggesting extensive renovations to this building in the Republican period. The presence of windows in most of the rooms also indicates a Republican date for the modifications. A former owner stated that the building was remodeled in the 1890s (Miño S. n.d.:9), and it appears that in the colonial period this was a two-room structure with corridors on all sides, with a hip roof. The long and narrow rooms added around the perimeter (N, P, R, and K) were probably built by simply walling off sections of the former exterior corridors. This remodeling has severely altered the permeability diagram of this property (Figure 19) from what it may have looked like in the colonial period. The most significant alteration is the door that leads directly from the rear entry lane (U) into the chapel (N). The chapel is Republican era in date, and contains a beautifully painted wooden altar. The door to the chapel from the lane is the only way to access the interior of the building complex without passing through the main patio (B). The arrangement of rooms around a main patio would appear to be a "rule" of eighteenth-century Cuenca construction, and this Republican-era chapel breaks those rules, creating greater permeability. This was probably a function of convenience for those visiting the chapel from outside the household, including the priest administering the services in the chapel.

The architectural form of the Yanuncay Grande house complex focuses attention inward, with high walls obscuring almost all views of the countryside from within the buildings, and preventing outsiders from seeing the activities in the gardens and central patio. It has been suggested that the courtyard house is simply an arrangement that is environmentally sensible in hot climates, providing covered outdoor workspace

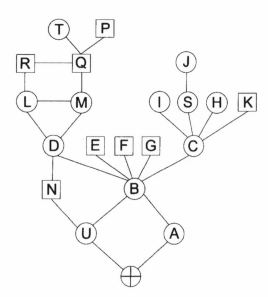

**Figure 19.** Justified permeability diagram of the Yanuncay house.

within the house. Lisa Nevett suggests that veranda houses, with the porticoes facing out over the exterior landscape, rather than inward, would work just as well in terms of the environment (Nevett 1994:108). Thus, the desire for privacy, rather than environmental concerns, was the key factor in the development of courtyard houses like Yanuncay Grande. This was a popular architectural arrangement in the late-eighteenth-century southern highlands. The figure of a rural hacienda in the Carmelite convent refectory in Cuenca, which was painted between 1792 and 1801, has a very similar array of buildings and walls (Martínez Borrero 1983:216). A 1796 description of a rural elite estancia in the Cuenca area is preserved in the Conceptas convent archives in Cuenca. The document describes several buildings forming a square enclosure, with an interior corridor running around a central garden with benches for sitting on. The main rooms were the living room, two or three minor rooms, the bedrooms, the kitchen with oven, and the chapel. Attached to this main area were outbuildings such as a granary, tool shed, and horse barn (Chacón Zhapán 1990:122).

Enclosed agricultural complexes like Yanuncay Grande were a physical manifestation of the Cuenca colonial elites' relationship to their rural surroundings. The walls and fences, which enclosed the fields and corrals of the valley bottom, redeployed power over the land. These fences and walls not only delineated the new colonial property relationships, but also decorporealized the experience of the landscape for its inhabitants. The inward gaze of the house itself, surrounding a central patio and avoiding views of the surrounding countryside, set the housing complex clearly apart from the rural "hinterland" that surrounded it. This reinforced the view of the elite inhabitants that this house was not a part of that hinterland (Johnson 1996:73–74; Lefebvre 1991).

## The Historical Context of Yanuncay Grande

The location of the Yanuncay Grande house is significant in providing some historical context to its use. The land it sits on, between the Tumipampa and Yanuncay Rivers, was the ejido or communal grazing land for the city in the colonial period. In the eighteenth century, however, the area was taken over by recent immigrants to the city, who set up small rural agricultural holdings throughout the river floodplains (Chacón Zhapán 1990:97; Municipio de Cuenca n.d.:18). It is reasonable to suppose that the Yanuncay area and the adjacent ejido lands had a similar mix of inhabitants in the late eighteenth century. In the 1778 census the population of the ejido was reportedly very mixed, with 52% Native, 46% white/mestizo, and 2% slaves and free blacks (Espinoza et al. 1982:44–45). These "suburban" areas were places where all ethnic groups lived side-by-side.

The Yanuncay Grande house was not within the original ejido lands, but was immediately west of this area. Notarial documents from Yanuncay show that in the early eighteenth century what had been an area of large rural landholdings was subdivided, and as property sizes went down, property prices went up (Table 3).

The creation of many smallholdings in areas such as Yanuncay was at least partially due to the decline of the obraje system in the northern part of the audiencia of Quito, which led to large-scale movements of Native Andeans into the southern highlands (Andrien 1995:33). The suburban parishes of Cuenca were particularly attractive regions throughout the eighteenth century, as migrants from depressed regions such as Riobamba moved south. These migrants purchased small freehold farms to supply the markets of Cuenca with foodstuffs (Andrien 1995:115). Many of these migrants became forasteros de la Real Corona. These were Native Andeans who did not live in their place of origin, and thus did not owe labor tribute obligations to a particular encomendero. Instead these forasteros paid cash tribute to the Crown itself and were free to pursue wage labor as agricultural workers or artisans (Powers 1990:313, 317). Felipe Torres, who bought a small property with a thatch house on it for 75 pesos in Yanuncay in 1710, was one example of this migration, as he is specifically identified as a forastero de la Real Corona (ANH/C L. 534 f.884r [1710]).

The Yanuncay Grande house does not fit well into this picture. It was clearly a much larger and more elaborate housing complex than that of

Table 3. Some Property Transactions in the Yanuncay Region

|  | 1592–1649 | 1650–99 | 1700–49 | 1750–96 |
|---|---|---|---|---|
| Male citizen | 1 | 5 | 9 | 1 |
| Priest | – | – | 2 | – |
| Doctor | – | – | 1 | – |
| Male Indian | – | 1 | 3 | – |
| Indian tailor | 1 | – | – | – |
| Total males | 2 | 6 | 15 | 1 |
| Female citizens | – | 1 | 3 | 2 |
| Widowed citizen | – | – | 1 | – |
| Unmarried female citizen | – | 1 | 1 | – |
| Female Indian | – | 1 | 3 | – |
| Total females | 0 | 3 | 8 | 2 |
| Average size | 1 hectare | 25 hectares | 5.5 hectares | 8.5 hectares |
| Average price | 18 pesos | 40 pesos | 265 pecos | 375 pesos |

Source: Jamieson 1996:147.

the smallholdings that surrounded it. It was likely to have been part of a large rural estate, similar to the Cachaulo property described below. Unfortunately, no colonial period documents for any large estates in the Yanuncay area have been found.

## Challuabamba

> Vieja casona ancestral; con ALMA.
> acoje en tu seno al niño de antaño.
> Aqui mis abuelos, cantaron en coros
> cante y cariño a la madre de Dios.
> hoy es un recuerdo de tiempos remotos,
> es una nostalgia de ensueños mas puros,
> y aun que sus aleros estan todos rotos.
> huelen a plegarias sus vetustos muros.
>
> [Old ancestral house; with a SOUL.
> Receive in your bosom the child of long ago.
> Here my ancestors sang in choirs
> sang to and loved the Mother of God.
> today it is a memory from times long gone,
> a nostalgia for purer dreams,
> and although your eaves are battered,
> your ancient walls are steeped in prayers.]

The second rural house that was a part of this study is located near the village of Challuabamba, northeast of Cuenca on the north side of the Tomebamba River (Figure 2). The poem above was written quite recently on a wall on the second floor of the house. I copied it into my field notes when recording the architecture. It is without attribution, and presumably was written by a visiting member of the family that used to live there.

The house is abandoned, and the property is involved in an inheritance dispute among several members of the owner's family. I was eventually able to trace down the owners by asking several people in Cuenca. Permission to visit and map the house was gained from the owner, but unfortunately permission to conduct archaeological excavations was denied because of the ongoing property dispute.

From the exterior the house presents a rather gloomy appearance (Figure 20). The standing remains consist of the house itself, a separate chapel to the southeast and a large adobe gate to the north. It is clear from soil disturbances all around the standing house and chapel that there used to be several outbuildings around the standing architecture,

but all have been destroyed. There is no perimeter wall surrounding the
house complex, but the large adobe gate to the north of the house shows
that the house was at one time surrounded by a wall or fence. Without any
of this evidence it is impossible to gain a clear idea of how the exterior
space surrounding the house may have been ordered in the colonial period.

From the north side of the building the most striking feature is the
two-story porticoed facade (Figure 21). The large adobe gate to the north
is aligned with the center of this facade, and a raised pathway is still
visible under the grass of the front patio, running north to south from the
gate to the front of the house. The ground floor portico (Figure 21A) has
eight pillars, six of which are original.

These pillars (Figure 7G) are one of the clearest indications that this
house is colonial in date. The base of each pillar is a stone octagonal
block, 32 centimeters in diameter. Entirely hand-carved, the pillars are
undecorated except for a slight tapering toward the top. They are round to
slightly squared in cross section, with a 30 to 40 centimeter diameter.
These imposing pillars are not entirely straight, many of them retaining
some of the shape of the tree trunks from which they were fashioned. At
the top of each pillar is a double capital with some simple scrollwork.

**Figure 20.** The Challuabamba house.

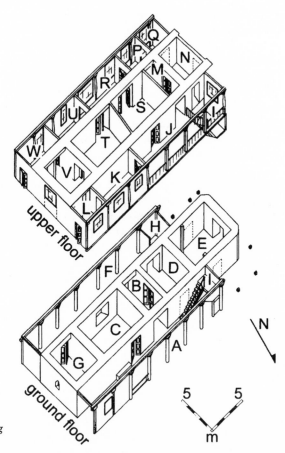

**Figure 21.** Isometric drawing of the Challuabamba house.

These double capitals are unique to this house among the examples in this study, and their significance is unknown. They may be status-oriented and aesthetic, a device used to show the opulence of the architecture of the house.

The two eastern pillars of the portico are Republican-era and machine-cut and are resting on 25 centimeter diameter square stone bases. The eastern-most pillar has slots for beams on its eastern side, showing that at one time the building extended farther eastward. On examination of the entire house, it appears that the eastern-most rooms (21G and V) are Republican additions, perhaps added at the time the separate chapel was built to the southeast of the house. At the western end of the portico two additional square stone pillar bases are hidden in the grass, showing that the house at one point extended farther west.

The floor of the portico is made up of small river-cobble paving, although in the area in front of room C there is a tile floor made up of 25 × 25 centimeter square clay tiles. There is a single adobe bench on the east side of the entrance to room C, suggesting that visitors were received on this portico, and that room C may have been a public reception room for the estancia. There is also a balustrade preserved between the third and fourth pillars from the east, and holes for a continuation of the balustrade are present on the fifth pillar. The lack of such holes in the western pillars means that the balustrade only ran in front of room C, indicating that this "reception area" was the only part of the portico needing the barrier of a balustrade to separate it from the front patio of the house complex. The combination of balustrades, tile floor, and bench clearly separates this section of the portico. The stairs (21I) to the upper floor of the house are entered just west of the entrance to the zaguan (B). Each of the three original lower floor rooms (Figure 21 C, D, and E) has an entrance from the portico (A), although the doors to rooms D and E from portico A have been walled off.

On the south side of the building another portico (F) mirrors the portico on the north side. The pillars are the same style, and in this case all except the eastern-most pillar are original. The entire portico is floored with small river-rolled cobbles, and the eastern-most section of the portico had been walled off in the twentieth century. There is also a small room (H) that was built recently by simply walling in two of the pillars with wattle and daub.

The zaguan of the house (21B) can be accessed from either portico A or F, and is aligned with the front gate of the house complex. From the zaguan a door leads to room D, and one formerly led through to room C. This arrangement of the zaguan leading through the center of the house with a single room flanking it on either side is similar to both the Tres Patios and the Posadas houses, and is probably a standard feature of multiple-room late colonial houses in Cuenca.

Rooms C and D were originally both accessible from either the south (21F) and north (A) porticoes, although the south door of C and the north door of D have later been walled off. The two remaining functional doors have a pintle system identical to that in the kitchen door of the Posadas house. Both rooms have rough dirt floors, with the appearance that tiles may have been salvaged from the rooms after the house was abandoned. It is very tempting to propose that room C, the larger of the two, was the public reception room in the colonial period, while the smaller room D may have served as an office for the landowner. This is, however, purely speculation.

On the western end of the house is room E. The only current entrance to the room is through a door on the west side, but the outline of doors on both the north and south sides of the room are still visible despite having been walled in. These doors would have given access to the north (21A) and south (F) porticoes. Preserved square stone pillar bases to the west of this room suggest that another portico ran along the western side of the house, built in the Republican period but now destroyed. At the eastern end of the house room G is clearly a Republican period addition, with modern hardware, including glass windows.

Access to the upper floor is via the stairwell (21I) in the western end of portico A. The stairway is wooden and is clearly a later addition because it blocks a doorway into room D on the lower floor and makes use of a doorway to room N on the upper floor impossible. The location of the original stairway is not possible to determine, but it seems likely that it may have been located at the extreme western end of portico A before that western end collapsed. At the top of the stairs the balcony (J) runs the length of the north side of the house, although two rooms (L and K) have been added in the modern period by enclosing the formerly open balcony. The balcony flooring is 25 centimeter wide sawn boards, fixed in place with hand-forged nails, indicating that the upper floor is almost certainly pre-Independence in date. Six original pillars for the upper-story balcony of the house are still visible here, although three of them have been encased in modern wooden square frames. The original pillars (Figure 7F) are hand-carved, barrel-shaped, and undecorated, with double capitals mirroring the style of the larger lower floor pillars. They are 17 centimeters in diameter.

Rooms T and V, and an upper floor hall (21M) can all be accessed from the balcony (J). The hall (M) is floored with the same wide boards as the balcony (J). From the hall (M) there is a door to the eastern room N. Room N is quite small, and the west wall of the room is a thin wooden partition. It appears that the room originally extended farther west. This western portion of the upper story collapsed at some point, and a lean-to roof has been added to the exterior here in order to cover the exposed room E below. The entire arrangement is poorly constructed and is a modern attempt to maintain some of the colonial rooms as the building deteriorated. Room N also has former north and south doorways providing access to the balconies, both of which have been rendered useless by later modifications.

Rooms T and S form the core of the colonial upper floor. There is a thin wood and plaster partition separating the two rooms, and it is clear that they were once one large room, with two sets of double doors leading to both the north balcony (J) and the south balcony (R). The combined rooms T and S would have formed a large room that was probably used as the main living quarters of the family who owned the Challuabamba property. This probably contained both sleeping and living areas and would be equivalent to the large upper-story rooms in the Posadas house (Figure 10T) and the Tres Patios house (Figure 6S).

On the southern side of the upper floor is a balcony (21W, U, R, P, and Q) mirroring the balcony on the north side (L, K, and J). This south balcony has been divided into five rooms by simply filling the spaces between the pillars with wooden partitions. The modern window and door hardware show that this was done in the Republican period in order to provide a whole series of new small rooms. The eastern-most room (Q) has an adobe and clay tile stove built into its north side and was used as a kitchen up until quite recently. The colonial period pillars, identical to those on the north balcony (Figure 7G), are still visible at several locations in the south balcony embedded in the walls.

The western end of the upper floor has a single room (V), which has modern doors leading to room T and to room L on the north balcony, and is entirely open on the south side leading to room W on the south balcony. The most interesting aspect of this end of the house is that rooms W, V, and L all have doors that face west and lead nowhere. The house had a larger wing on its west side, probably built during the Republican period, but this is now gone.

To the southeast of the main house is a large chapel. This is Republican period in date, both because it contains large glass windows and because the altar and other hardware in the building are industrial. The most interesting feature from the perspective of spatial analysis is that the front facade of the chapel has a second-story window that is a modified door. It would appear that if the house extended farther east, a walkway probably existed from the upper floor of the house to the small interior balcony on the upper floor of the chapel. The eastern end of the house and the separate chapel building all appear to be Republican in date, but the architectural arrangement is still of great interest. Members of the landowner's family could have used this arrangement in order to move from the private rooms on the upper floor of the house to the chapel balcony. They could then have watched the service in the chapel without the necessity of mingling with the people on the main floor of the chapel, who would have been principally the estancia workers.

## The Use of Space in the Challuabamba House

The Challuabamba house has been heavily altered since the colonial period, and all the perimeter walls and outbuildings except the chapel have been destroyed. This makes any reconstruction of the use of space in the colonial period difficult. There are several points that can, however, be made. The first is that when the Republican-era rooms built onto the balconies are removed, we are left with a house that is very long, but only one-room deep. This conforms to the other colonial houses mapped for this study and appears to be a universal rule in Cuenca colonial architecture. The Challuabamba house, as a rural residence, is different, however, from the urban houses described above in that there is no "street" facade. The north side of the house faces toward the road several hundred meters to the north, and it has been constructed as an imposing facade. It faced directly onto an enclosed patio, and guests were greeted on the north portico. The south facade faced the river, and it would seem that this side of the house was associated with the day-to-day agricultural operations. There were no balustrades on the lower south portico (F), suggesting it was a more "open" area. The colonial lower floor rooms (21C, D, and E) were permeable from both sides of the house, thus making this lower floor the central hub between relations with the outside world (toward the road) and with the agricultural production (toward the river). These lower floor rooms were probably used as reception rooms and offices.

The staircase from the north portico leading to the upper floor delineated this as the space for the family. Rooms S, T, and N would have provided the living space for the family, which is quite private space on the permeability diagram of the Challuabamba house (Figure 22). The least permeable part of the colonial house, however, was the south upper balcony (W, U, R, P, and Q). This balcony overlooked the rear patio of the house and the land all the way to the river. It is very likely that most of the outbuildings of the estancia were located within the view provided from this balcony. In this way the property owners were provided with a very private space from which all activities in the core of the agricultural complex could be taken in at a glance. Such a balcony would have been a very useful tool in the administration of a colonial estancia, and it is a wonderful example of the interaction of ideology, architecture, and political economy in colonial Cuenca.

# CACHAULO

The final rural house recorded for this study is located six and a half kilometers north of Cuenca, on the east bank of the Machangara River (Figure 2). The house is about a kilometer south of the tiny village of Ochoa León and is marked as "Cachahuco Grande" on the topographic map for the area, although the name of the house was actually "Cachaulo." The house is now abandoned and is owned by a family who lives in

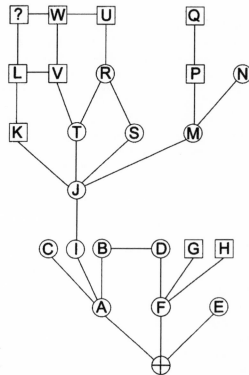

**Figure 22.** Justified permeability diagram of the Challuabamba house.

Cuenca. They gave permission for me to record the architecture of the house and to undertake archaeological excavation on the property.

A fortuitous accident led to the discovery of a documentary record for the property. I was reading the 1664 will of Doña Luisa Maldonado de San Juan (ANH/C C.116.404a) when I came across a reference to a large rural property called "Cachaulo." The similarity to the name of the hill above the large rural house was striking, and further archival research with the help of Deborah Truhan allowed the history of the property to be set out. The location of the house on the Machangara River and the description of the architecture in a 1740 document (ANH/C C. 617 ff. 49v–50r) confirm that Cachaulo is indeed the name of the property. The fact that the buildings can be tied into the documentary record in the Notarial Archive means that a history of the property can be pieced together.

The earliest known owner of the property was Augustina Ortiz Dávila, a citizen of Cuenca with a house in the city itself, as well as several other rural properties. When Augustina sold Cachaulo in 1658, at a price of

4,400 pesos, the property was a two hundred-hectare mixed grain and sheep farm, with six hundred sheep and several pairs of oxen to work the land. There were no buildings listed on the property (ANH/C L515 ff.209r–211v; L514 f.593r [1658]). Although not a large property by Andean standards, both the size and its cost are quite large for seventeenth-century Cuenca.

The property included the services of four mitayos, or tributary Native Andeans, who came from the villages of Macas, Sigsig, and Sibambe (ANH/C L514 f.593v [1658]). The colonial system of mita labor had been set up by the Viceroy Francisco de Toledo in the 1570s and was a colonial reworking of the *mit'a* labor system of the Incan empire. The mitayos were used as a form of state patrimony, assigning a village to supply a certain number of workers on a rotating basis to a mine, city, or Spanish citizen such as Augustina (Stern 1982:82). The mitayos who worked the land and herded the animals at Cachaulo were from villages up to one hundred kilometers from Cachaulo, emphasizing the labor shortages caused by the sixteenth- and seventeenth-century decimation of southern highland villages (Newson 1995). Each of the four by definition was an adult male, and he probably brought a family to live at Cachaulo for their limited labor turn. No buildings were listed in the contemporary documents describing the property, but the mitayos must have been housed somewhere and presumably had built their own wattle and daub houses.

In 1658 Luisa Maldonado de San Juan bought the property from Augustina. Luisa, a widow twice over, had been married the second time to Juan Rodriguez Fernandez. Both were citizens of the mining town of Zaruma (Figure 1) in the mid-seventeenth century, where they appear to have been cloth merchants. It is likely that Luisa participated actively in the cloth trade, as the wives of merchants often participated in the administration of the family businesses, particularly when their husbands were away on trading trips (Borchart de Moreno 1992:364–365, 373). Juan died sometime before 1656, and Luisa was left with considerable investments. As a widow Luisa sent someone to Panama to buy 8,000 pesos worth of clothing in 1660. She owned hundreds of yards of cloth in her shop in Zaruma at the time of her death in 1664 (ANH/C C116.404a, ff.26v–29v, 50r, and 59r [1664]).

After 1656 Luisa's position as a widow gave her an opportunity to own and manage property. The fact that Spanish colonial women often married much older men meant that widowhood such as Luisa's was not a rare occurrence (Equip Broida 1983:28). Widowhood in early modern Spain or in its colonies left women solely responsible for the ongoing tasks of family businesses and properties (Couturier 1985:298; Vincente, 1996). Many women, when their husbands had abandoned them or died, used their inheritances to take part quite openly in the management of their own economic resources (Borchart de Moreno 1992; Wilson 1984).

From 1656 to 1659 Luisa purchased at least 7,700 pesos worth of rural and urban properties in the southern highlands of Ecuador, including the Cachaulo land. The architecture on the property at the time of Luisa's death in 1664 was simple, consisting of an "old house with a thatched roof with wooden doors and windows and a small padlock . . . another thatched building for a kitchen . . . two small old thatched houses where the Indians live . . . and a large building for storing the crops" (Jamieson 1996:159).

Upon Luisa's death the Cachaulo property was divided among her heirs, following Spanish laws of partible inheritance, which guaranteed each legitimate child, male or female, an equal share in the property of his or her mother or father (Lavrin and Couturier 1979:286). It was essential to the family, however, that such a property be maintained intact as a functioning enterprise. In theory daughters had inheritance rights equal to sons. In Spanish colonial practice this meant that a male heir usually inherited or bought up rural agricultural properties, while urban houses were frequently owned and inherited by women (Couturier 1985:296–300; Lockhart 1994 [1968]:159). This may to a great extent have kept rural properties out of the hands of colonial elite women (Goody 1983:257; Wilson 1984:308). In the case of Cachaulo, Luisa's nephew Alexandro Maldonado de San Juan slowly bought out or inherited the bulk of the property from the 1660s to 1701 (Jamieson 1996:159).

In 1740 Alexandro Sr. was dead, and his widow sold the property to their son, Alexandro Jr. When Alexandro Sr. acquired the property in 1701 there were no buildings worth mentioning on the property, but by the time Alexandro Jr. acquired it the property was described as

> an *estancia* of wheat . . . in the location of Cachaulo . . . with 130 *cuadras* of land . . . two large houses roofed with tile, the one wrecked which is of wattle and daub with its two corridors, and a house of double walls with its chapel with another two houses roofed in thatch of wattle and daub, one with its corridor, the other roofed in thatch with its bread oven . . . and the said chapel is divided in the same corridor of plaster and tile. ( ANH/C L617 f.49v–50r [1740], my translation)

The "double walled" (presumably adobe) house and chapel described here appear to be the same two buildings that form the core of the building complex at Cachaulo today. After 1740 I lost track of the Cachaulo property in the documentary record.

Approaching the abandoned building complex today it is obvious that it has changed considerably from its colonial appearance, with most of the architecture dating to after Ecuadorian independence (Figure 23 and 24).

Several of the walls or fences that once surrounded the building complex, particularly on the north and west sides, have been destroyed. A large adobe gate in the northeast corner, however, is still standing, and was clearly the main entrance to the building complex. Through this gate the visitor enters the main patio (Figures 23A and 24A). The patio is grass, and excavation revealed no evidence of pavement.

On the north side of the patio there is a new concrete and steel building with an open corridor on its south side (23B) and two rooms off of this corridor (C and D). It was built but never used and may replace an earlier building with the same configuration. On the east side of the patio (A) a stone wall is still partially standing.

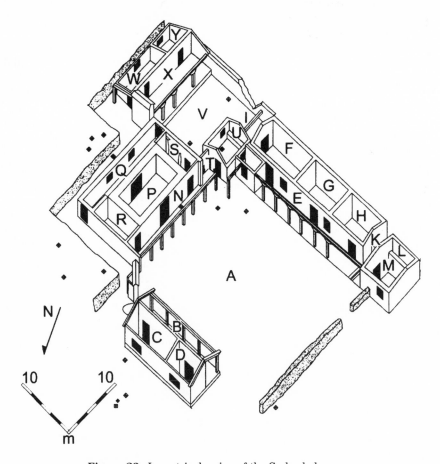

**Figure 23.** Isometric drawing of the Cachaulo house.

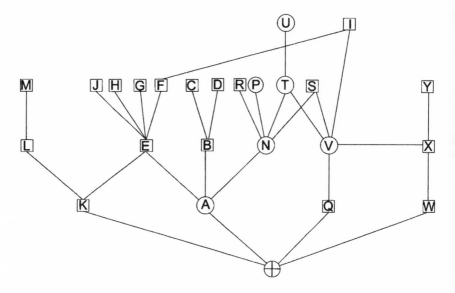

**Figure 24.** Justified permeability diagram of the Cachaulo house.

The entire south side of the patio is made up of a single Republican-period wing. The north side of this wing has a long open corridor (23E), with three rooms extending off it to the south (F, G, and H). All windows from these rooms face onto the central patio, with the southern exterior wall of the building being entirely windowless. The entire wing adds a large segment to the permeability diagram for the Cachaulo house (Figure 24E through J) that would not have been there in the colonial period.

To the south of this wing there is a small chapel built in the Republican period, with the same style of woodwork and hardware as the wing itself. It is made up of a main room (23M) with a large ornate wooden altar and a window on the north side. A narrow side room (L) was perhaps where the priest prepared himself for services or where religious objects were stored. The chapel roof overhangs a small entryway (K), which allows access to the south entrance of the building complex. The single wooden door at this entrance is built of hand-milled lumber, with two rows of decorative wrought nails on its exterior (Figure 8E). The permeability diagram (Figure 24K, L, and M) shows that the chapel is easily accessible from the exterior through this entrance, and also from the main patio (E). This was very likely a feature allowing both family members and others from the community to participate in services in the chapel.

On the eastern side of the patio the colonial house sits on top of a slightly raised platform built of large river-rolled cobbles. The west side of the house is a long corridor (23N) with square pillars and a dirt floor. The colonial portion of the house itself is a single windowless large room (P), with doors on its west and east sides. The walls of this room are built of large rectangular adobes and are a full one hundred centimeters thick.

To the north is a long, narrow room (23R); it is a former corridor, enclosed by filling in the spaces between the pillars on the north side of the colonial house. On the east side of the colonial house is another room (Q). This room has its own entrance from the exterior of the building complex, and a similar small door entering the second patio (V) from the south end of the room, as well as two windows on the eastern exterior of the building. The room has a raised floor, which Ecuadorian informants told me was an indication that the room was for grain storage, as the raised floor prevents the crops from rotting. The permeability diagram shows that this room has easy access from the building exterior, presumably for delivery of crops from the field. Access to the other entrance to the room is from the interior patio (V), suggesting an arrangement that made monitoring of the stored crops easy for members of the property owner's family.

On the south side of the colonial house there is another long narrow room (23S). This room was walled with small rectangular adobes and had doors both to the west corridor (N) and to the interior patio (V). The south wall of this room has two pillars embedded in the wall, both of which are hand-carved barrel-shaped plain pillars with wide capitals (Figure 7H). I would propose that rooms Q, R, and S are all Republican modifications of the building, and that the house originally consisted of the single interior room P. Open corridors surrounded this room on the west, south, and east sides, and possibly on the north side as well. This probably indicates that the house had a hip roof when it was originally built. The lack of a door on the north side of the room would have provided privacy from the exterior, while all the other sides gave easy access to the adjacent patios. The house has a modern second story, which was not completed before the house was abandoned. There is no stairway to this level, and the floors were never installed, so this upper story was not mapped.

The roof of corridor N continues south to cover a passage (23T), which has an east door leading to the interior patio (V) and a south door leading into the colonial chapel (U).the north facade of the chapel building has two cherubs painted on the plaster on either side of the entrance doors and a sprig of leaves painted lower down the exterior wall to the west of the doors. The entrance doors themselves are unfortunately gone, but the door frame preserves the holes from a set of double doors hinged using a pintle system so that no metal was needed. This appears to be a typical colonial door construction technique in Cuenca, also present on the Challuabamba and Posadas houses.

I was considerably surprised upon entering the small chapel interior (23U). The building has an intact roof, but cattle have been able to enter the room, and considerable portions of the wall plaster have been destroyed by the cattle and by seeping dampness from the floor. What is preserved of the wall plaster revealed a series of mural paintings covering the north, east, and west walls (Figure 25). The lower third of all three walls was painted in a tromp l'oiel technique to resemble wainscoting, with a small painted "shelf" running around the room at waist height. On both the west and east walls representations of vases resting on this shelf have been painted. There are two paintings of vases per wall, each done in blue to resemble stone. Each vase contains grapes on the north side and yellow lilies and stalks of wheat on the south side, with three pink roses in the center. Various small red, blue, and yellow flowers are interspersed among these. At ceiling height a tromp l'oiel curtain in orange, yellow, black, and white runs around the three sides of the room. The south wall of the chapel, where the adobe altar was located, was wallpapered during the Republican period. It has unfortunately been used for cooking fires and has also suffered damage from looters. There are no visible paintings on this wall, although removal of the soot and wallpaper might reveal an altar painting of considerable interest.

The chapel has single windows on its west and east sides, both of which may be colonial in date. These are *corrediza* or "sliding" windows. They contain no glass, but have an interior frame for the placement of a wooden board that could be slid open and shut. The corrediza system is thought by the local architectural historian employed by the Instituto Nacional de Patrimonio Cultural to be a typical feature of colonial window construction in the southern Ecuadorian highlands (Edmundo Itturalde, personal communication 1993). The shutters are preserved on the exterior of the east window and are hand-carved wood with forged decorative nails on their surfaces (Figure 8F).

There has only been one other set of mural paintings from an eighteenth-century private chapel reported in southern highland Ecuador. The chapel of the Susudel hacienda, located just west of the town of Oña, 65 kilometers south of Cuenca, was completed in 1752, at which point the hacienda was owned by Joseph Serrano de Mora. The artist who completed the chapel paintings was Juan de Orellana (Martínez Borrero 1983:100). Alexandro Maldonado de San Juan Jr. and his wife Victoria Serrano de Mora bought Cachaulo from Alexandro's widowed mother in

**Figure 25.** Eighteenth-century chapel wall painting at Cachaulo.

1740. It is interesting to note that Victoria and Joseph may have been related. If this is the case it is quite possible that the same artist could have painted both chapels. The paintings appear similar to the extent that both involve tromp l'oiel work in yellow and ochre colors (Martínez Borrero 1983:65, 81), but the Susudel Chapel is more complex, with several images of saints and other figures. I have been unable to locate any documents relating to the painting of the Cachaulo chapel murals, although the 1740 sale record describes a chapel on the property with several religious statues with silk and silver decorations (ANH/C L.617 ff. 49v–50r [1740]).

Mural painting was popular in elite domestic contexts throughout the Andes, and house restorations from Cuzco, Peru, to Tunja, Colombia, have revealed mural paintings dating throughout the colonial period

(Gutiérrez et al. 1981:85–92; Kubler and Soria 1959:317; Mesa 1979:258–260; Sebastián 1979; Téllez and Moure 1982:41). In many parts of Latin America such murals lost favor in the eighteenth century as oil painting on canvas became more common (Martínez Borrero 1983:63). In less affluent areas, such as southern highland Ecuador, mural painting appears to have remained popular. Late-eighteenth-century travelers in Ecuador commented on the paintings of "fruit, flowers and animals" that were done *alfresco* on the walls of colonial houses. Surviving examples of such murals are still little studied in Ecuador, and colonial paintings are threatened with destruction in many locations. In Azuay and Cañar colonial period mural paintings are very rare, with the two main examples being the Carmelite convent in Cuenca and the Susudel chapel. The paintings in the refectory of the Carmelite convent, which date to 1790, include a mixture of tromp l'oeil panels, vases, and so forth, and wall paintings with tromp l'oeil frames, complete with painted strings and nails for "hanging" (Martínez Borrero 1983:63–99).

The paintings in the Cachaulo chapel are simpler, but in some ways similar to both the Carmelite refectory paintings in Cuenca and the mural paintings in the copula of the Sagrario church in Quito, which were also done in the 1790s (Martínez Borrero 1983:72). An examination of the paintings by Juan Martínez Borrero confirmed that they are mideighteenth-century in date (Martínez Borrero, personal communication 1993). The chapel appears to be a rare example of a mideighteenth-century private hacienda chapel, and it is hoped that some action can be taken in the future to help preserve this small building before it is entirely lost.

The 1740 inventory of Cachaulo reveals that of all the inventoried rooms, it is the wealth of material in the chapel that stands out. The chapel contained a large table with woven cotton tablecloth, a wooden dais, an altar, and a bench. The art in the chapel consisted of a painting of a saint, two *bultos* or religious statues, one of which was a virgin with "descent" clothing and flowers in her hand, and the other of St. Joseph dressed in silk with silver woven into it. There was also a crucifix with silver rays coming out of it (ANH/C L617 ff. 49v–50r [1740]). These are rather expensive investments for what is otherwise a very rustic-sounding farmstead.

Cachaulo was not just a place where agricultural products were produced for urban consumption. It was also a place where an elite urban Spanish family came into contact with rural Native tribute laborers. Just as anyone else who had tribute laborers working for them, the Maldonado de San Juan family were responsible for the maintenance of "proper" religious practices by the mitayos who worked the land and herded the animals of Cachaulo. The ceremonies that took place in the Cachaulo chapel were a microcosm of the Native Andean relationship to the Spanish empire and the Catholic church. The investment in silks, silver, and painted decorations that were all placed in the chapel tells us that this room above all others at Cachaulo was an important expression of this relationship.

Cachaulo is similar to the haciendas of eighteenth-century Cali, Colombia, described as "productive haciendas which existed around an owner's residence constructed in a rustic and cheap manner, although always with a chapel" (Aprile-Gniset 1991:419, my translation). These rural Cali households led Jacques Aprile-Gniset (1991:419) to conclude that elite landowners poured their economic resources into their urban houses, where symbols of power were of great importance. For Aprile-Gniset the rural houses, far from any major roadway, had no money spent on them because no one "important" was there to see them. And yet there were people of utmost importance who were around to see these buildings—the mitayos who worked the land. Luisa and her family understood this. Their Cachaulo house was indeed "rustic," but it was also an enclosed space that created an inward-looking gaze, separating Spanish control from the rural wilds. Most important, the complex contained the chapel, where significant resources were expended on religious art. Such art was an essential material part of the ongoing relationship between Luisa's family and the mitayos and their families who worked the land.

From the corridor outside the chapel (23T), a small door leads through to the interior patio (V) of the building complex. Access to this patio is prevented from the exterior by a tall adobe wall on its south side. On the east side of the patio there is another small wing (W, X, and Y), which looks Republican in date. The room at the north end (W) has a door to the exterior and an intriguing arrangement of benches down both the west and east walls. It is unclear what the function of this room was, but its position on the permeability diagram (Figure 24), and the presence of the benches, suggests that the room may have been used for interactions between the landowner and the individuals who worked the agricultural lands of Cachaulo. Harvested crops may have been received here, and payment for services distributed. From this room there is access to the corridor (X) of the building, which overlooks the interior patio. From the corridor (X) another room (Y) is accessible, and was probably a room used for storage.

## The Use of Space at Cachaulo

The documentary record shows that up until the mid-eighteenth century the architecture of Cachaulo was entirely wattle and daub. None of this architecture has been preserved, although large areal excavations could possibly reveal the footprint of these buildings on the landscape. The only colonial buildings that do survive are the house (23P) and chapel (U) described in the 1740 sale record. These are now entirely enclosed with later phases of construction.

From what is known of colonial estancias in the rural areas surrounding Cuenca, it seems likely that the spatial layout of Cachaulo is similar to what it would have been in the colonial period. As at Yanuncay Grande, the buildings are arranged around central courtyards, each building only one room in depth, with all rooms accessed from the courtyards. High walls and this inward orientation of the buildings contribute to a spatial arrangement that clearly separates the interior spaces of the house complex from the surrounding countryside.

## CONCLUSIONS

What do the few remaining examples of colonial domestic architecture tell us about domestic space in colonial Cuenca? To our modern eyes, and in the eyes of modern Cuencanos, these houses are very segregated from the street or the countryside, but internally the original spatial arrangements provided little privacy and lacked small, compartmentalized spaces. As has been shown in various other parts of the world (Glassie 1990:279), the modern era has brought with it a change toward the compartmentalization of domestic spaces, creating more and more spatial divisions that facilitated the "routinized specification and allocation of tasks" (Giddens 1984:135) within the household. The houses of late-eighteenth-century Cuenca were only partially suited to such an ideology, and their simple one-, two-, or four-room spaces, with large exterior porticoes, balconies, and patios for workspace and social interaction, have been subdivided extensively in the Republican period to create more segregated interior spaces. Much of the hierarchy and complexity shown in the permeability diagrams of the houses in this study results from these Republican alterations.

When we look beyond these modern alterations, we see that the colonial houses of Cuenca followed several "rules" in their construction. The most important was the single-room depth of the buildings. Creating houses only one room deep does not provide for any hierarchy of the space within the architecture. The single-room house, with exterior porticoes and patios, was the reality for the urban poor of the Todos Santos district in the colonial period. The small houses of Todos Santos, with a single room bounded by exterior corridors, meant that much of the daily life in such households occurred in public view, in what Erving Goffman (1963) would have referred to as the "front region" of the architecture. Surveillance of the occupants of these houses was simple from the street. In the architecture of the Posadas house we see an intermediate step away from this design. The portico on the street is an area of public interaction, where the occupants could work or meet guests in full view of the surrounding population. Behind the central doors, however, the inner patios of the house were entirely private. In the case of the Tres Patios house in the city core, a closed facade strictly separated the activities of the household from outside view, and there was no exterior space in which to stand or sit in view of the street.

The constant interaction between people on the street and people on the front porticoes of the Todos Santos houses would have served as a form of reflexive monitoring of action (Giddens 1984), a factor not only in the "surveillance" of the people of Todos Santos by the elite, but also in the community solidarity among the people of the neighborhood itself. Thus, the architecture of Todos Santos could have contributed to enabling the community to function more closely outside the exploitative colonial system, but simultaneously to constraining the gaze of passers-by.

For the residents of the Tres Patios house such surveillance would have been an insult, and perhaps their own complete immersion within the colonial economic and ideological system made any such surveillance unnecessary. The large houses of the elite, with buildings arrayed around a courtyard and enclosed within a wall, created an inward-looking and inherently private household, with strong barriers against entrance from the outside world. Such enclosure or confinement of particular activities within strictly segregated spaces was an important part of the disciplinary power of Spanish colonialism. The enclosed walls separate the house from the surrounding town, and thus cut off intrusive encounters, routinizing the tasks of the householders (Foucault 1975; Giddens 1984). These tasks are further defined within the architecture by the addition of multiple patios, such as the two patios of the Posadas house. In the rear patio the mundane tasks of servants and cooks and the tending of animals in the urban household were completely separated from the family life of the front patio.

The addition of a second story in the Tres Patios and Posadas houses greatly increased the ability to create hierarchical space within such elite urban houses, when the single-room depth of the architecture makes such hierarchy difficult on the ground floor. Such two-story buildings were most common from the early colonial period in buildings in the urban cores of Andean cities, in the residences of the colonial elite. The stairs provide a natural barrier separating the upper-floor rooms from those on the ground floor. The upper-floor space is thus inherently more private. In this way Goffman's "back region," or the private space, of an elite family was much larger in size than that of nonelite families such as those living in the Todos Santos neighborhood. The positioning of these rooms in the upper story allows those who gain access to them the ability to undertake surveillance. Such surveillance allowed elite householders to collate information on subordinates and to supervise subordinates directly. This would have been greatly facilitated in the Tres Patios and Posadas houses by the presence of balconies overlooking the street from the upper floor and a corridor overlooking the interior courtyard. Surveillance was an essential part of the creation of the modern capitalist world (Foucault 1975), and in these balconies we can see the Spanish colonial antecedents for such eighteenth- and nineteenth-century obsessions.

In the rural areas elite domestic architecture was built on very similar principles, but the exigencies of the landscape created different problems to be solved. The position of these rural houses, on river floodplains overlooking the best agricultural land of the region, helped in their control over what the colonial Cuencano elite doubtless saw as a wild rural hinterland. The walls, fences, and architecture of the valley-bottom estancias redeployed power over the land. For rural Andeans the fencing in of private properties rearranged the historical boundaries of community lands based on kinship and geography. Instead, as with the transition to merchant capitalism in the rural European world, the Andean colonial estancias around Cuenca created newly geometric and "abstract" spaces based on standardized measurements and the legal language of private property (Johnson 1996:73–74; Lefebvre 1991:48–49). As with urban houses, the complex of buildings at the center of these estancias was the physical manifestation of an inward gaze, toward central patios and avoiding views of the surrounding countryside. Neither the Yanuncay house nor the Cachaulo house has any windows overlooking the exterior of the building complexes. Rather than a series of buildings set in the landscape around it, these rural estancias with high walls and central patios show in their permeability diagrams the regulation of the flow of traffic within their walls, always passing through the central patios. This spatial segregation and control was one aspect of the disciplinary power of landowners over the system of forced labor on rural agricultural complexes. The Challuabamba house went beyond this, and in a rural setting re-created the two-story house of the urban elite. In this case the house is positioned so that the private upper-story corridors of the family overlooked the courtyards and fields of the whole property, creating an efficient system of surveillance over the agricultural production process. To the Spanish mind there was not only economic wealth in the rural Andes, but they

believed the devil was waiting in the "remote solitudes" of the rural highlands to lead people away from civilized areas to deceive them more easily
(MacCormack 1991:147). The blank exterior walls of Cachaulo and Yanuncay
were a barrier, separating the controlled Spanish household from the
uncontrollable rural territory around it.

# Excavations | 5

## INTRODUCTION

The archaeology of domestic sites dating to the Spanish colonial period in the Andes is a very new and, so far, a very limited field. My excavations in the Cuenca area were one of the first attempts to expand this area of research into the Andean region. Spanish colonial archaeologists, however, have been researching domestic life at least since Charles Fairbanks and Kathleen Deagan began the program in "backyard archaeology" at St. Augustine, Florida, in the early 1970s. Fairbanks, Deagan, and many others made the study of domestic archaeological assemblages from the Spanish colony at St. Augustine the focus of their research (Deagan 1974, 1985; Fairbanks 1975). This interest by the University of Florida's Department of Anthropology has now expanded to many other regions of the Spanish colonial world (Deagan 1995d; Ewen 1991; McEwan 1988).

In Andean South America there have only been a few excavations of domestic Spanish colonial contexts (Flores Espinoza et al. 1981; Smith 1991; Van Buren 1996). There is a great need for more excavation of such contexts in the Andes before we can conclude much about the overall picture in the region.

In order to gain an idea of the colonial material culture of the rural area around Cuenca, Ecuador, test pitting was carried out at two rural sites, the locations of which are shown in Figure 2. The two main factors in choosing sites for excavation were the presence of standing colonial architecture and the ability to gain permission from property owners for excavation. The focus on excavating areas with well-preserved colonial architecture has created a distinct bias toward elite houses. The vast majority of the rural colonial population in the region lived in wattle and daub buildings that have not survived the ravages of time. It is clear from the historical record that the adobe houses that survive from the colonial period on the landscape around Cuenca are the remains of the houses of the elite. Doing archaeology around these houses has thus become a study of the material culture of the Cuenca colonial elite.

The bias toward elite material culture because of its greater visibility is recognized in historical archaeology (Paynter and McGuire 1991:10), but this does not mean that a study of elite ideology through material culture is not a valid exercise (Leone 1984, 1987). I hope that future research in the Cuenca area can extend the study of colonial material culture to the material culture of other classes. The rural locations of the ephemeral wattle and daub houses of colonial estancia workers and Native peoples could be located through surface surveys of plowed fields and would form an essential counterpoint to the data presented here.

## CACHAULO

The first site to be test pitted was the rural estancia of Cachaulo, 6.5 kilometers north of Cuenca on the Machangara River (Figure 2). The history of the property and its standing architecture has been described in Chapter 4. The property was called Cachaulo in the historical documentation and has been abandoned for over a decade. A total of 15 test pits were placed around the historic building cluster in an effort to detect colonial middens or other features for a sample of domestic refuse. The test pit locations are given in Figure 23.

One test pit was placed in the interior of the colonial chapel (Figure 23U), but revealed no evidence of any rebuilding episodes. The complete lack of industrially produced artifacts in this test pit confirms a colonial date for the construction of the building.

The test pits in the south corner of the central patio (23A) revealed no sealed stratigraphy or features, apart from a concentration of broken adobe bricks used to raise the west corridor (N) of the colonial house above the level of the river floodplain.

Six test pits were placed to the north and west of the building complex, outside the walled patios, in the hope of encountering midden deposits. This proved fruitless, as only a scattering of artifacts were found in a mixed surface loam. Four test pits to the east of the colonial house contained a similar mix of colonial and Republican period artifacts in mixed contexts, with no midden build-up. Two test pits in the small patio (V) hit sterile sand at 20 centimeters below surface (BS), and contained almost no artifacts, suggesting that the patio was kept clean throughout the history of the house.

### Cachaulo Archaeology

The estancia of Cachaulo is located on a flat river terrace and may be subject to occasional flooding. Many of the test pits had large river-rolled cobbles in their lowest level. It is clear that river-rolled cobbles are deposited throughout the property. They have been collected from plowed fields and piled up for generations to create the dividing walls between fields. The ones near to or inside the buildings were deliberately piled up before the construction of the buildings to create solid, flat platforms and retaining walls for house foundations.

By far the largest amounts of material were recovered to the north and east of the main house, outside the complex of walled courtyards. It would seem that an attempt was made to keep the enclosed areas of the building complex clean.

Site assemblages from domestic sites in the Spanish colonies tend to be over 90% ceramic artifacts (Deagan 1995c:440), and the Cachaulo house lived up to this expectation (Table 4). The ceramics were almost evenly divided between coarse earthenwares, which were usually plain or slip-decorated, and fine earthenwares, the majority of which were decorated in rough majolicas. Three fragments of plain pearlware date to the 1775 to 1830 period (Miller 1980:16). These provide archaeological evidence of a colonial occupation at this house. The presence of pearlware at a Spanish site in the rural Andes can be taken as an indicator of elite access to foreign trade goods, and also as evidence of the English domination of the world ceramic trade by the turn of the nineteenth century (Miller 1980:1). They were, however, a very minor part of the assemblage at Cachaulo.

**Table 4.** Cachaulo: Ceramic Artifacts

| Type | N | MNV | % of MNV |
|------|---|-----|----------|
| Coarse earthenware | | | |
| Plain | 97 | 5 | 6.8 |
| Red slipped | 34 | 3 | 4.1 |
| Thick red slipped | 12 | 4 | 5.4 |
| Tan slipped | 3 | 1 | 1.4 |
| Brown slipped | 17 | 3 | 4.1 |
| Orange slipped | 3 | 2 | 2.7 |
| Majolica | 1 | 1 | 1.4 |
| Fine earthenware | | | |
| Plain | 55 | 2 | 2.7 |
| Slipped | 17 | 9 | 12.2 |
| Green lead glazed | 7 | 2 | 2.7 |
| Majolica | 95 | 37 | 50.0 |
| Pearlware | | | |
| Plain | 3 | 2 | 3.6 |
| Refined white earthenware | | | |
| Plain | 3 | 2 | 2.7 |
| Hand-painted polychrome | 2 | 1 | 1.4 |
| Stamped ware | 1 | 1 | 1.4 |
| Total | 349 | 74 | 100.0 |

*Source:* Jamieson 1996:181–191.

Three sherds of hand-painted or stamped refined white earthenware date
to the 1830s to 1870s (Majewski and O'Brien 1987; Miller 1980). Their
rarity suggests that even in the late nineteenth century the residents of
Cachaulo were not using imported ceramics to any great extent. Locally
made earthenwares thus dominated the ceramic assemblage at this rural
site, the majority of them plain or slip-decorated, but with a significant
number of locally produced majolicas.

There were also a certain number of glass sherds, mostly from bottles
(Table 5). A small quantity of molded glass was also recovered, all late
nineteenth or twentieth century in date (Miller and Sullivan 1984). No
glassware diagnostic of the colonial period was found.

The faunal remains were minimal, with only one domestic species,
cow (*Bos taurus*) identified from the Cachaulo excavations (Table 6). This
is interesting when compared to the documents, which list the animals
being grazed on the property. Between 1657 and 1740 these are always
listed as being between two and ten oxen, and between two hundred and
six hundred sheep (Jamieson 1996:192). The main focus of the estancia
was sheep production, yet the only species identified archaeologically was
cow. Sheep were used for wool production, but they were also a very
popular source of meat when available in the Spanish colonies, and many
of the young sheep would have been sold to urban markets (Reitz and
Cumbaa 1983:183; Reitz and Scarry 1985:71).

**Table 5.** Cachaulo: Nonceramic Artifacts

| Artifact | N |
| --- | --- |
| Earthenware construction tile | 239 |
| Toy | |
|     Glass marble | 1 |
| Container glass | |
|     Colorless bottle glass | 12 |
|     Brown bottle glass | 6 |
|     Green bottle glass | 2 |
| Glass tableware | |
|     Colorless pressed glass | 2 |
| Flat glass | |
|     Colorless window glass | 3 |
|     Mirror glass | 2 |
| Fastener | |
|     Wire nail | 2 |
|     Hand-forged square spike | 2 |
|     Hand-forged nail | 1 |
| Lithic | |
|     Black chert flake | 1 |
|     Beige chert flake | 1 |

Table 6. Cachaulo: Faunal Remains

| Taxon | NISP |
|---|---|
| UID mammal | 20 |
| Artiodactyl | 1 |
| Cervid (probably Odocoileus virginianus) | 1 |
| Bovid | 2 |
| Bos taurus (cow) | 1 |

Source: Jamieson 1996:178–189.

The cervid bone, probably from a white-tailed deer (*Odocoileus virginianus*), came from northeast of the main house. The presence of deer is of interest, as Pedro de Cieza de León (1965 [1553]) and Hernando Pablos (1965 [1582]:268) listed deer as one of the major hunted species in Cuenca in the sixteenth century. In both the Ecuadorian coast and highlands wild deer, usually *Odocoileus virginianus*, were quite common and frequently hunted in the sixteenth and seventeenth centuries (Estrella 1988:326–327). One of the eighteenth-century paintings on the wall of the Carmelite convent in Cuenca shows an elite Cuencano out hunting deer and birds in the countryside (Martínez B. 1983:33). In Spain deer were protected by royal decree and could only be hunted by noblemen (Reitz and Cumbaa 1983:155), so deer hunting by elite Cuencanos must have been seen as a very pleasurable activity and a significant status indicator. In eighteenth-century faunal samples from St. Augustine, Florida, deer were more common in elite household assemblages than in those of the poorer members of society (Reitz and Cumbaa 1983:183).

## Comparison to Cachaulo Documentary History

The overall history of Cachaulo and its architectural history have been given in Chapter 4, but the notarial documents also provide extensive data for the material culture of Cachaulo in the colonial period. From the first known document to refer to the property in 1657, up until a 1701 sale document, the material culture at this property is listed as being very basic (Jamieson 1996:193). The houses were of wattle and daub with thatch roofs, and when any mention is made of materials on the property it is to refer to agricultural tools, and particularly the plows, as the most valuable items.

There were between two and three mitayos (Indians serving terms of forced tribute labor) living on the property in the seventeenth century, presumably with their families. It is not known whether their houses were in the same location as the adobe buildings now on the property. The belongings of the mitayos were not listed in these sale documents, so we do not know what material goods they brought to the property.

The only extensive inventory of the property that I was able to locate dates to 1740 (ANH/C L617, f49v–50r). At that point the adobe buildings had been erected, and the property owner had set up a household on the property. The only items listed in the document that would survive archaeologically are the ceramics, which included an *ollita* (small pot), two tinajitas for water, and two large tinajas. Tinajas are usually defined as very large coarse earthenware jars, wide mouthed, with everted rims and flat bases. This is a form that came from Andalusia with the Spanish colonists in the sixteenth century and was used for storage of drinking water and agricultural products like liquids and beans (Lister and Lister 1987:100–101; Marken 1994:182–183). The tinajas of eighteenth-century rural Cuenca may have been imported from Spain, but it is equally likely that they were made in the Andes. Most agricultural production, particularly of liquids like olive oil and wine, had associated pottery production areas to make botija and tinaja containers on site for transport, such as in the Moquegua Valley in Peru (Smith 1991:89). No sherds of Spanish "olive jar" paste were recovered from Cachaulo, suggesting that by the eighteenth century Cuenca botijas and tinajas for agricultural products and water storage were probably made somewhere in the Andes, if not locally in the Cuenca region.

Significantly the 1740 inventory makes no mention of any glass tableware or imported ceramics. From both the inventory and from the archaeological evidence, it would seem that up until the late eighteenth century there were few if any imported "luxury" tablewares at Cachaulo. Unfortunately, no notarial records were recovered dating after the 1740 inventory, but the archaeologically recovered pearlwares suggest that perhaps as early as the 1780s, and definitely by the 1820s, imported English ceramics played a role in the tableware at Cachaulo. Thus, throughout the colonial period locally made earthenwares appear to be the only material culture likely to survive at a site like Cachaulo. It is only in the late-eighteenth-century Bourbon period that imported ceramics began to appear on rural tables.

## HACIENDA YANUNCAY GRANDE

The Hacienda Yanuncay Grande is located southwest of Cuenca on the Yanuncay River (Figure 2). Because of the restoration activities being undertaken there by the Ecuadorian Instituto Nacional de Cultura (the federal agency responsible for Ecuador's heritage resources), it was possible to gain access to the property for test excavations to determine what colonial archaeological remains were present. A total of 14 test pits were judgmentally placed in hopes of encountering stratified colonial midden remains.

A 1 × 1 meter excavation was placed in the central patio of the buildings (Figure 18B). The excavation in the main patio (B) revealed a river-rolled cobble pavement, which is visible at various other places in the patio, and is still intact under the current loam surface. At some point in Yanuncay's history the cobbles formed a pavement over the entire main patio area, but no diagnostic artifacts were recovered to help in dating this feature.

Fourteen test pits were excavated in various locations surrounding the buildings at Yanuncay. Five were placed in the walled garden (18S), three in the walled corral (T), three in the walled lane (U), two outside the perimeter wall on the west side of the complex, and one in the southeast corner of the main patio (B). None of these test pits revealed any significant build-up of midden deposits.

The artifact collection recovered from all the test pits is similar to the Cachaulo collection in many respects (Tables 7 and 8). The vast majority of the artifacts were roofing tiles, very densely scattered in areas close to

**Table 7.** Hacienda Yanuncay Grande:
Nonceramic Artifacts

| Artifact | N |
| --- | --- |
| Earthenware construction tile | 252 |
| Container glass | |
| Colorless bottle glass | 8 |
| Aqua bottle glass | 1 |
| Green bottle glass | 3 |
| Brown bottle glass | 3 |
| Opaque "black" bottle glass | 1 |
| Glass tableware | |
| Aqua pressed drinking glass rim | 1 |
| Flat glass | |
| Colorless window glass | 4 |
| Clothing | |
| Pressed steel buckle | 1 |
| Fastener | |
| Industrial wire nail | 2 |
| Industrial bolt | 1 |
| Forged nail | 1 |
| Lithic | |
| Tan chert flake | 6 |

*Source:* Jamieson 1996:198–204.

**Table 8.** Hacienda Yanuncay Grande: Ceramic Artifacts

| Type | N | MNV | % of MNV |
|------|---|-----|----------|
| Coarse earthenware | | | |
|   Plain | 60 | 2 | 6.1 |
|   Red slipped | 14 | 3 | 9.1 |
|   Thick red slipped | 49 | 1 | 3.0 |
|   Tan slipped | 1 | 1 | 3.0 |
|   Brown slipped | 2 | 1 | 3.0 |
| Fine earthenware | | | |
|   Plain | 25 | 1 | 3.0 |
|   Slipped | 2 | 1 | 3.0 |
|   Green lead glazed | 1 | 1 | 3.0 |
|   Majolica | 40 | 20 | 60.6 |
| Stoneware | | | |
|   Mottled green on yellow glaze | 2 | 1 | 3.0 |
|   Refined white earthenware | 1 | 1 | 3.0 |
| Total | 197 | 33 | 100.0 |

Source: Jamieson 1996:198–204.

the buildings, and ceramics. The ceramics were once again largely split between fine earthenware majolicas and coarse earthenware plain and slipped vessels.

Republican-period artifacts included a scattering of refined white earthenwares, and a certain amount of molded glass from both drinking glasses and bottles. The recovery of a single black glass liquor bottle base dating to the 1850 to 1870 period suggests that by that date industrially produced goods were being consumed at the hacienda Yanuncay Grande.

It is interesting to note that not a single sherd of pearlware was recovered from the excavations at Yanuncay. This may be a significant difference from Cachaulo, showing that Yanuncay was occupied in the 1780 to 1820 period by people not as able to afford imported ceramics. In Greg Smith's (1991) excavations of colonial winery sites in the Moquegua Valley of Peru four rural properties were reported on in detail, and all four included small quantities of pearlware in the excavated assemblage.

The colonial documentary record unfortunately cannot be tied directly to this house, as no convenient nearby landmarks set it apart. Research focusing on the valley of the Yanuncay River, however, gives us some idea of what properties in the vicinity were like in the colonial period. The notarial sales documents available for the Yanuncay Valley (Jamieson 1996:206) show that both Indians and vecinos of Cuenca owned properties in Yanuncay in the colonial period.

Yanuncay properties were considerably smaller than the properties of the Machangara Valley, and considerably less valuable. No extensive inventories were included in these documents, but when material culture is listed, only agricultural tools are inventoried. This is an interesting fact when we compare this information to the list of archaeological materials recovered at Yanuncay. There are no imported luxury goods such as glassware or pearlware ceramics from the colonial period, suggesting that Yanuncay houses in the colonial period were probably furnished with the locally produced majolicas, a selection of coarse earthenwares, and not much else. Here we see a clear class difference between Cachaulo and Yanuncay at the end of the colonial period.

## SUMMARY OF RURAL EXCAVATIONS

No intact colonial midden deposits or features were encountered at either Cachaulo or Yanuncay. This could be explained in several ways. The first, and perhaps most likely, explanation is that the test pitting was in no way comprehensive, so there is the distinct possibility that middens dating to the colonial period are present somewhere on both properties and were simply missed. Another possibility is that throughout the colonial era refuse may have been distributed in "sheet deposits" over the surface rather than in distinct middens. If refuse material is tossed into corrals and gardens for fertilizer or animal feed, then remains may be fairly spread out around the buildings.

The third possibility is that the volume of refuse was quite small. This may have been the case if the site was not occupied as a full-time domestic residence. The architecture of both sites, as discussed in Chapter 4, tends to suggest that these were elite properties in the eighteenth century. The adobe structures may have functioned on a day-to-day basis only as tool storage areas and animal corrals, with only occasional occupation by the property owner, whose main house would have been in the city. This brings up the interesting question of where tribute laborers, the *mayordomo* (estate manager), and other inhabitants of the property were living. Colonial descriptions of large agricultural estates indicate that their houses were built of insubstantial wattle and daub and were probably in the vicinity of the standing adobe structures. In order to locate such insubstantial structures a much more extensive archaeological survey would have to be undertaken. Wattle and daub houses dotted the rural landscape in the colonial period and housed the vast majority of the rural poor. The large adobe structures at Cachaulo and Yanuncay represent administrative centers for the few elite landowners whose principal residences were in the city.

The excavation of rural structures from the Spanish colonial period in the New World has been limited, but some comparisons are possible. Several colonial rural estancias have been excavated in the southwestern United States, all of them built to supply agricultural products to local missions, and all inhabited by Native Americans.

Land grants outside the mission system began in areas such as Alta California in the 1770s, but large numbers of rural settlers began to arrive in California only after Mexico became independent in 1822 (Greenwood 1989:452–454). In Los Angeles County, California, the *casa de campo* of Patricio Ontiveros, occupied from 1815–35, has been excavated. This has provided information about life on a secular cattle ranch. The majority of the diet was comprised of beef; some sheep, pig, chicken, and domestic fowl were also present, with a small amount of fish. Most of the pottery was made right on the property using a local clay source, with rare sherds of large food storage vessels imported from Mexico. Glass and metal objects were very scarce. The overwhelming dominance of locally produced ceramics at this site is in sharp contrast to the assemblage from an 1830s to 1860s rural California farmstead, where the vast majority of ceramics were industrially produced European white earthenwares, and glass and metal imports were much more common (Greenwood 1989).

The Rancho de las Cabras, in what is now Texas, was a Franciscan mission ranch supplying cattle to Mission San Antonio de Valero from about 1750 to 1790. The ranch was fortified with a 2.5 meter high stone wall with two bastions, and included a chapel and several residence rooms for the Native American families that ran the ranch. It was a large operation with over one thousand cattle and three thousand sheep. The material culture of these Native American ranchers included ceramics, of which about three-quarters were Native-made local coarse earthenwares, with some lead-glazed and majolica wares from Mexico, and a few sherds of French faience and oriental porcelain. Faunal remains showed a mixed diet of Old World domestic cattle, sheep, goats, and chickens, as well as bones of a wide variety of local wild species, both hunted and fished. Stone tools were still commonly made and used by Natives at the ranch (Fox 1989). Thus, in what is now the southwestern United States, rural Spanish colonial sites appear to have been largely self-sufficient, relying on local coarse earthenwares made by the Native Americans who worked the ranches. The quantity of majolica used was quite small, probably because it was imported from distant Mexican ceramic centers. This contrasts with rural Cuenca sites, where local majolicas made in town were readily available. In the southwestern United States the introduction of European white earthenwares began in the 1830s and later, when Mexican independence and U.S. expansion brought new trade networks. This is in sharp contrast to the Andean situation, where the late-eighteenth-century Bourbon period brought importation of English creamwares and pearlwares, found in at least some elite rural Andean sites.

I am unaware of any other published descriptions of archaeological excavations at rural Andean domestic sites. The closest comparative sample is Greg Smith's (1991) shovel testing at 28 winery sites and more extensive excavation at four of these sites, in the Moquegua Valley of Peru. The program of shovel testing revealed an artifact assemblage similar to the two rural Cuenca sites. Smith's Moquegua site assemblages were dominated by coarse earthenwares, the mean percentage of which for all the sites combined was 46% of the artifact count. Glassware was the next most common artifact category, making up 20% of each site assemblage on average. This was closely followed by "other European pottery," including all pearlware and whitewares, which made up 14% of the Moquegua assemblage on average (Smith 1991:194).

Imported majolicas made up a small percentage of the Moquegua excavated materials, and by far the most common imported majolica was from Panama. There were also very occasional occurrences of Mexican Valle ware, French faience, and Delft tin-glazed wares, as well as Spanish Sevilla ware (Smith 1991:271–307). None of these imported materials were found at rural sites in Cuenca, perhaps because the properties were economically less affluent, perhaps because of the geographic isolation of the Cuenca sites, or perhaps simply because the sample of ceramics was not large enough to include these rare items.

Faunal materials from the indigenous village of Torata Alta in the Moquegua Valley, dating to the sixteenth century, showed an overwhelming reliance on camelids, with some use of European caprines and pigs, and a surprisingly small sample of guinea pig. In contrast, the wineries in the valley showed a reliance on cattle, although camelids were also an important part of the diet. Caprines and pigs were also consumed at the rural wineries. Wild *Cervidae* (deer) remains were recovered from only one of the wineries and were not present at Torata Alta, confirming the association of deer with the colonial elite (deFrance 1996).

Mary Van Buren has recently begun work in historical archaeology at Potosí, Bolivia. Excavation near Potosí at the hot baths of Tarapaya may be considered rural excavations (Van Buren 1996), but this was an elite site where the wealthy residents of seventeenth-century Potosí would go for relaxation and for health reasons. It is, therefore, not really comparable to the rural elite agricultural production properties surrounding Cuenca. At Tarapaya around 10% of the recovered colonial ceramics were glazed wares, with a few of these being Panamanian majolicas (Van Buren 1996).

Overall the two rural Cuenca sites show less artifact diversity in both the excavated materials and the documentary record than do the urban sites excavated in Cuenca. Elite tablewares such as glass, Panamanian majolicas (for the seventeenth century), and English pearlware (for the late eighteenth century) are all more rare at these rural sites than they are in the city. It would seem that despite the probable ownership of these two rural sites by elite vecinos of Cuenca, the emphasis was on agricultural production and not on displays of wealth in the form of tablewares. The chapel at Cachaulo is the only clear exception to this.

## URBAN EXCAVATIONS

In order to compare the colonial period material culture of urban and rural domestic sites, excavation was conducted within the city of Cuenca from November 1993 to February 1994. These excavations included a single unit at the site of the Inka center of Pumapungo directly southeast of the colonial core of the city, and several excavation units at a site in the urban core, near the main plaza of Cuenca. The locations of these excavations are given in Figure 3.

Previous research on urban Spanish colonial domestic sites has revealed several factors of urban discard patterns that are of relevance to the archaeologist. The first is that throughout the Spanish colonial world refuse on urban sites was usually discarded within the individual lot where it was generated, either along the back wall of the compound or in large depressions in the ground (Deagan 1995c:428). The maintenance of discrete property boundaries in the discard patterns is very useful for the archaeologist when attempting to match archaeological contexts to the documentary record, and I have assumed that large-scale movement of refuse between city lots did not occur in colonial Cuenca.

In urban contexts most refuse disposal tended to be around the kitchens, and kitchens were usually set back from the street. "Sheet deposits" seem to predominate and are easily disturbed by later architectural and garden remodeling (Deagan 1983:247–251). The majority of artifacts recovered from sealed contexts are found in pits and abandoned wells behind the kitchens (Deagan 1983:269). This pattern of discard is certainly true in Cuenca, as can be seen below.

## PUMAPUNGO

The archaeological remains of the core of the Incaic city of Tomebamba were discovered by Max Uhle in 1919 (Uhle 1983 [1923]). These have since been developed as an archaeological park by the Ecuadorian Central Bank. A large museum now stands on the site, and further extensive excavations were carried out on the site in the 1980s under the direction of Jaime Idrovo Urigüen (1984).

At the invitation of Leonardo Aguirre, the Tomebamba site archaeologist at the Central Bank Museum, I was able to excavate a single 1 × 1 meter unit to the north of the Incaic *kallanka*, or long hall, originally excavated by Uhle. The excavations under the direction of Aguirre were undertaken to reveal the foundation of the kallanka as part of a public interpretation program. The unit I excavated was designated "Kallankas 2N25E" under the grid system used by the museum, in an area known to contain significant amounts of historic period material.

The unit was excavated with the assistance of museum excavators. The stratigraphy of this unit consisted of a surface layer of twentieth-century debris capping a 40-centimeter thick layer of dark organic loam. The loam had a large number of artifacts of very mixed date. A wire nail recovered from this layer shows the deposit postdates 1900. The layer sloped away from the kallanka building foundation immediately to the south and appeared to be redeposited. It could be backdirt from Uhle's 1919 excavations, in which the kallanka was clearly delineated (Uhle 1983 [1923]). There were a large number of artifacts in the soil (Table 9), but Uhle's emphasis was probably on collecting only whole vessels and artifacts of interest, so the majority of sherds may have remained in the backdirt. If the layer is not associated with Uhle's excavation activities, it is probable that this deposit is the result of other Republican period redeposition and mixing from agricultural or construction activities.

There were a significant number of Incaic polychrome sherds. A single porcelain rim sherd from this context is evidence of colonial occupation. It is a typical Chinese Imari style bowl rim, dating between 1695 to 1750 (Deagan 1987:100–101; Godden 1979:172; Howard and Ayers 1978:137–138). A single pearlware sherd shows some occupation of the site in the 1780s to 1830s (Miller 1980:16).

The minimal faunal material included two identifiable fragments: cow (*Bos taurus*) and a cervid, very likely a white-tailed deer (*Odocoileus virginianus*). It is unfortunate that the deer remains cannot be said to be either prehistoric or historic in date.

Most of the ceramics were coarse earthenwares, with a much wider variety of slip colors than at the rural house excavations. The majority of these are probably prehistoric in date. Local fine earthenware majolicas were much less prevalent in this context than at the rural houses, probably because the large numbers of prehistoric ceramics in the context skews the sherd count away from the colonial and Republican period ceramics.

**Table 9.** Pumapungo 2N25E Level 2: Artifacts

| Type | N | MNV | % of MNV |
|---|---|---|---|
| Coarse earthenware | | | |
| Plain | 183 | 9 | 13.6 |
| Red slipped | 54 | 12 | 18.2 |
| Thick red slipped | 9 | 5 | 7.6 |
| Brown slipped | 2 | 1 | 1.5 |
| Gray slipped | 3 | 1 | 1.5 |
| Orange slipped | 10 | 6 | 9.1 |
| Black slipped | 6 | 3 | 4.5 |
| Cream slipped | 7 | 2 | 3.0 |
| Polychrome (Inkaic) | 22 | 14 | 21.2 |
| Fine earthenware | | | |
| Plain | 9 | 1 | 1.5 |
| Green lead glazed | 1 | 1 | 1.5 |
| Majolica | 12 | 6 | 9.1 |
| Brown slipped | 4 | 2 | 3.0 |
| Chinese export porcelain | | | |
| Blue underglaze, overglaze red paint and gilding | 1 | 1 | 1.5 |
| Pearlware | | | |
| Plain | 1 | 1 | 1.5 |
| Stoneware | | | |
| Light green with dark green spattering | 4 | 1 | 1.5 |
| Earthenware construction tile | 29 | – | – |
| Green bottle glass | 1 | – | – |
| Industrial wire nail | 1 | – | – |
| Unidentifiable iron fragment | 5 | – | – |
| Burnt daub | 6 | – | – |
| Flake, unidentified material | 3 | – | – |

*Source:* Jamieson 1996:216–217.

Notarial documents for the Pumapungo area included one large document that gives some picture of the neighborhood in the colonial period. The document is from a legal case resulting from the death of Don Diego Patino de Narvaes, priest for the San Blas parish of Cuenca, who owned six hectares of land in Pumapungo. He died in the 1660s, and from 1696 to 1702 a legal case was fought over ownership of the six hectares in Pumapungo (ANH/C C96.106, f1r–f98v). Juan de Velasco claimed to be the son and rightful heir of Patino de Narvaes. Velasco stated that from the 1660s to the 1690s he had personally, and with Indian workmen, removed a large number of rocks from the property. They had flattened the ground, which had been very hilly, and built walls to plant maize, all of which had been at great cost. It seems clear that this work was to remove the remains of the Incaic ruins, which would have made cultivation difficult. Velasco had also built a house on the property, with a thatch roof.

Patino de Narvaes's personal possessions when he died included ceramics described as two *"limetas preciosas de la china"* (pretty china vases/flasks), one *"porcelana grande de la china"* (large china porcelain vessel), and *"tinajas y botijas."* The tinajas (large earthenware jars with a flat base and wide mouth) and botijas (olive jars, with round bases and very narrow necks) are both storage vessels for liquids or other substances, the tinajas often being used for drinking water. These goods were inventoried at his house in the San Blas parish, where he was the priest, and not at his Pumapungo property. The Pumapungo property was said to have only cattle, plows, and sheep.

It is of interest that Chinese porcelain is mentioned in Velasco's San Blas house. The *limetas* are "squat, long-necked flasks" (Lister and Lister 1987:165), in this case probably a vase, while the "porcelana" is not identified, but may be a large bowl. The role of porcelain as an elite tableware in the colonial Spanish world is well known, but the presence of the Chinese Imari sherd in an area of rural garden plots in the late 1600s is unusual. Perhaps it came from a dish that the property owner had passed on to his rural workers after it became damaged.

## THE CENTRAL DRUGSTORE:
## 9-20 AND 9-38 CALLE BOLÍVAR

Half a block northwest of the main plaza of Cuenca (Figure 26), on a city block of closely spaced walled courtyard houses, a series of four test excavations were carried out to recover a sample of urban colonial material. This location is two city blocks directly east of the Tres Patios house described in Chapter 3. Two test pits were placed in each of two adjacent rear yards at 9-20 and 9-38 Calle Bolívar. This block was directly north of the Jesuit church and school during the colonial period, in one of the most elite neighborhoods of colonial Cuenca.

In the garden of number 9-38 a 60 × 60 centimeter test pit was dug to bedrock at 55 centimeters BS; all cultural layers were mixed with twentieth-century materials. The second excavation in this yard was a 1 × 1-meter unit that contained an intact clay tile floor at 50 centimeters BS. Sealed stratigraphy below this floor was Republican in date, with no intact colonial contexts.

In the garden immediately northeast of this one, at the back of 9-20 Calle Bolívar, a third test pit measuring 1 x 1 meter was excavated. It contained an intact cobble floor at 66 centimeters BS, but artifacts sealed under this floor were Republican in date. At 96 centimeters BS bedrock was encountered. In the northwest corner of the test pit a midden deposit

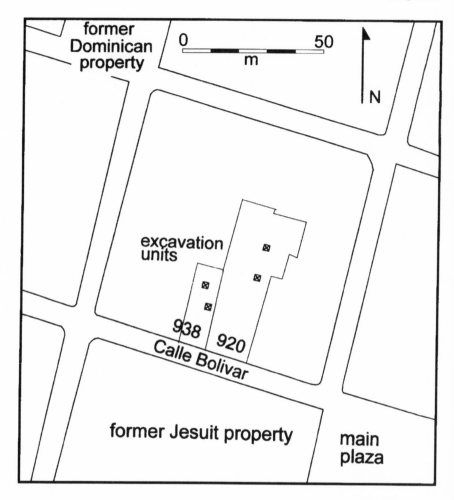

**Figure 26.** Location of central drugstore excavation, 9-20 and 9-38 Calle Bolívar.

was encountered containing 15 coarse earthenware sherds, all from a single cooking vessel. The shape of the vessel could be reconstructed (Figure 27) and has a distinctly Inka shape. No other artifacts were found in this small feature.

The presence of the hearth-blackened vessel is interesting in that it suggests Inka occupation of this property prior to the Spanish occupation. This is tantalizing evidence, as the extent of the Inka remains underlying the city is still unclear. Typical Inka masonry blocks can be seen in many

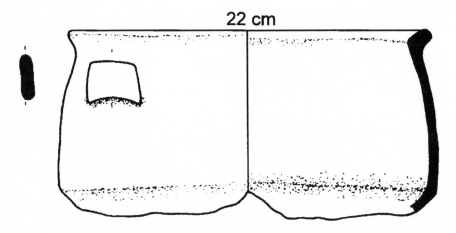

**Figure 27.** 9-20 Calle Bolívar: Inka vessel.

of the colonial and Republican period buildings in the city core. Further excavation could reveal Inka domestic occupations underlying the colonial core of the city itself.

Apart from this single piece of evidence of Inka occupation, all other artifacts from these three test pits came from contexts disturbed since the colonial period. The artifacts from these contexts (Tables 10, 11, and 12) reveal a mix of materials from the seventeenth to twentieth centuries. Wire nails and plastics were mixed with nineteenth-century refined white earthenwares and colonial period material.

A brass military button recovered from this context has a stamped design portraying the sun rising over the Andes, with the slogan "DEL PERU INDEPENDIENTE" around the perimeter. It is a one-piece brass button with attached eye, typical of the 1780 to 1830 period (Noël Hume 1970:90–91; Olsen 1963:552). Specialized buttons for military uniforms were introduced in Europe in the 1770s, and Latin American armies during the Wars of Independence adopted these all-important symbols of pride (Albert and Adams 1951:46–48). Most of the buttons used on early nineteenth-century Latin American military uniforms were manufactured in Britain. The only other archaeologically recovered military buttons that I have seen reported from South America come from the fort of San Rafael del Diamante in Argentina, which was occupied from 1805 to 1900. These have Argentinean Republican military insignia, and on the back are marked "Smith & Wright–Birmingham" and "P. Tait & Co.–Limerick" (Lagiglia 1983a:147).

A sherd of "marbled" or "finger-painted" pearlware is a type of dipped

**Table 10.** 9-20 and 9-38 Calle Bolívar:
Nonceramic Artifacts from Mixed Contents

| Artifact | N |
|---|---|
| Earthenware construction tile | 1,194 |
| Container glass | |
| Colorless bottle glass | 9 |
| Aqua bottle glass | 6 |
| Green bottle glass | 2 |
| Dark green bottle glass | 1 |
| Dark brown bottle glass | 1 |
| Glass tableware | |
| Colorless wheel-engraved tumbler | 2 |
| Colorless pressed glass | 1 |
| Flat glass | |
| Colorless window glass | 2 |
| Fastener | |
| Wire nail | 16 |
| Screw | 4 |
| Nails, unidentified | 4 |
| Clothing | |
| Sewing needle, steel | 1 |
| White glass button | 1 |
| Copper chain link | 1 |
| Military uniform button | 1 |
| Leather | |
| Clippings | 10 |
| Sole of shoe | 1 |
| Lithic | |
| Flake, unidentified material | 2 |

*Source:* Jamieson 1996:224–250.

**Table 11.** 9-20 and 9-38 Calle Bolívar:
Faunal Remains from Mixed Contexts

| Taxon | NISP |
|---|---|
| UID mammal | 137 |
| UID large mammal | 8 |
| UID medium mammal | 1 |
| UID large rodent | 1 |
| *Cavia porcellus* (guinea pig) | 1 |
| *Sus scrofa* (pig) | 1 |
| *Bos taurus* (cow) | 3 |
| *Caprine* (sheep/goat) | 3 |
| *Equus* spp. (horse/donkey) | 1 |
| *Gallus gallus* (chicken) | 2 |
| UID fish | 1 |
| UID vertebrate | 3 |

*Source:* Jamieson 1996:229–244.

**Table 12.** 9-20 and 9-38 Calle Bolívar: Ceramic Artifacts from Mixed Contexts

| Type | N | MNV | % of MNV |
|---|---|---|---|
| Coarse earthenware | | | |
| Plain | 161 | 4 | 3.5 |
| Red slipped | 61 | 9 | 7.8 |
| Thick red slipped | 71 | 13 | 11.3 |
| Orange slipped | 3 | 2 | 1.7 |
| Brown slipped | 14 | 3 | 2.6 |
| Black slipped | 12 | 3 | 2.6 |
| Polychrome slipped (Incaic) | 3 | 2 | 1.7 |
| Majolica | 1 | 1 | 1.9 |
| Fine earthenware | | | |
| Plain | 107 | 9 | 7.8 |
| Red slipped | 12 | 4 | 3.5 |
| Thick red slipped | 33 | 4 | 3.5 |
| Brown slipped | 8 | 3 | 2.6 |
| Cream slipped | 2 | 1 | 0.9 |
| Black slipped | 3 | 1 | 0.9 |
| Green lead glazed | 9 | 4 | 3.5 |
| Majolica | 149 | 28 | 24.3 |
| Panamanian earthenware | | | |
| Green lead glazed | 3 | 1 | 0.9 |
| Majolica | 13 | 4 | 3.5 |
| Pearlware | | | |
| Plain | 4 | 2 | 1.7 |
| Marbled | 1 | 1 | 0.9 |
| Refined white earthenware | | | |
| Plain | 9 | 2 | 1.7 |
| Transfer printed | 7 | 5 | 4.3 |
| Colored glaze | 2 | 2 | 1.7 |
| Decal (rose pattern) | 1 | 1 | 0.9 |
| Porcelain | | | |
| Plain | 2 | 1 | 0.9 |
| Blue underglaze | 1 | 1 | 0.9 |
| Gilded ext. rim band | 1 | 1 | 0.9 |
| Stoneware | | | |
| Green glaze with brown flecks | 2 | 1 | 0.9 |
| Total | 700 | 115 | 100.0 |

*Source:* Jamieson 1996:224–245.

ware, dated between 1795 and 1835 (Miller 1980:6; Noël Hume 1970:132). A fragment of gilded porcelain has the rim band very evenly applied and is therefore probably transfer-printed gilding, a process patented in 1815, but most popular after 1850 (Lueger 1981:138).

A single fragment of tumbler rim was found. This is from a Bohemian-style soda-glass tumbler with wheel-engraved decoration, similar to examples from the 1724 Guadeloupe wreck, as well as early to mid-eighteenth-century sites in Florida. Such tumblers were manufactured throughout Western Europe in the eighteenth century, using German technology, and were also made at Puebla in Mexico (Deagan 1987:146; Jones and Sullivan 1989:56; McNally 1982:47).

Sherds of Panamanian earthenwares are examples of the majolica industry at Panama la Vieja, on the Pacific coast of what is now Panama. These ceramics are thought to date to the period between 1519 and 1671 (Deagan 1987:29; Fairbanks 1972:160; Lister and Lister 1987:340 n. 82; Long 1964:104). These ceramics have been reported previously in Ecuador (Goggin 1968:48) and will be discussed in detail in Chapter 6.

One sherd of Chinese export porcelain was collected from the surface of the garden. This had an interior design with blue "outline wash" style underglaze typical of Kraakporcelain exported from China in the 1550 to 1700 period (Deagan 1987:98–99; Howard and Ayers 1978:53–63).

## THE CENTRAL DRUGSTORE:
## THE COLONIAL CONTEXT

A final 1 × 1-meter excavation was placed near the corner of the rear garden of 9-20 Calle Bolívar. The cultural stratigraphy of this excavation was much deeper than in the other urban excavations. To a depth of 146 centimeters BS this unit revealed several layers of architectural debris, consisting of adobe brick and clay roof tile fragments mixed with other debris. The presence of wire nails in all of these layers shows them to be twentieth-century deposits, although colonial period artifacts are mixed throughout the stratigraphy (Tables 13, 14, and 15).

The ceramics recovered (Table 13) show that this context is very mixed, with Panamanian majolicas (pre-1671), pearlware (1779–c. 1820), and both hand-painted (1840–70) and transfer printed (1830–60) refined white earthenwares (Majewski and O'Brien 1987; Miller 1980). The non-ceramic artifacts (Table 14) include an iron key with a heart-shaped handle.

At 146 centimeters BS a hard-packed earth surface was encountered. Several large flat plaster fragments were lying face down on this surface, suggesting that this is the bottom of the architectural destruction debris.

The faunal assemblage from the Republican levels (Table 15) was of particular interest. The most common identified species was sheep or goat, closely followed by cow and chicken. There were also guinea pig, dog, and rabbit remains present. This is an interesting contrast to the colonial levels in this unit, which had less species diversity and no rodents present at all. With the movement of the elite out of the downtown core of Cuenca

Excavations 149

**Table 13.** 9-20 Calle Bolívar, Unit 2: Ceramic Artifacts
from Mixed Contexts

| Type | N | MNV | % of MNV |
|---|---|---|---|
| Coarse earthenware | | | |
| Plain | 186 | 7 | 6.2 |
| Red slipped | 47 | 8 | 7.1 |
| Thick red slipped | 107 | 14 | 12.4 |
| Brown slipped | 9 | 2 | 1.8 |
| Black slipped | 35 | 6 | 5.3 |
| Polychrome slipped (Inkaic) | 2 | 1 | 0.9 |
| Majolica | 4 | 3 | 2.7 |
| Fine earthenware | | | |
| Plain | 52 | 5 | 4.4 |
| Red slipped | 3 | 1 | 0.9 |
| Thick red slipped | 6 | 2 | 2.4 |
| Cream slipped | 1 | 1 | 0.9 |
| Brown slipped | 1 | 1 | 0.9 |
| Green lead glazed | 20 | 3 | 2.7 |
| Majolica | 121 | 39 | 34.5 |
| Panamanian earthenware | | | |
| Plain | 5 | 1 | 0.9 |
| White slipped | 1 | 1 | 0.9 |
| Green lead glazed | 1 | 1 | 0.9 |
| Majolica | 5 | 4 | 3.5 |
| Olive jar | | | |
| White slipped | 2 | 1 | 0.9 |
| Pearlware | | | |
| Plain | 5 | 2 | 1.8 |
| Refined white earthenware | | | |
| Plain | 8 | 2 | 1.8 |
| Underglaze handpainted | 3 | 3 | 2.7 |
| Gilded rim, blue overglaze | 1 | 1 | 0.9 |
| Transfer print | 1 | 1 | 0.9 |
| Porcelain | | | |
| Plain | 5 | 2 | 1.8 |
| Stoneware | | | |
| Green glaze with brown spatter | 1 | 1 | 0.9 |
| Total | 634 | 113 | 100.0 |

*Source:* Jamieson 1996:240-245.

in the twentieth century, houses on this block were divided into smaller units. The presence of guinea pig and rabbit in the Republican period diet may be indicative of the shift of this block from colonial and early Republican elite houses to late Republican accommodations for urban native and mestizo workers.

From 146 to 199 centimeters BS a midden deposit consisting of a

**Table 14.** 9-20 Calle Bolívar, Unit 2: Nonceramic
Artifacts from Mixed Contexts

| Artifact | N |
|---|---|
| Earthenware construction tile | 1,262 |
| Container glass | |
|   Colorless bottle glass | 10 |
|   Aqua bottle glass | 4 |
|   Green bottle glass | 1 |
|   Light purple bottle glass base | 1 |
| Table glass | |
|   Colorless molded tumbler base | 1 |
|   Colorless wheel-engraved tumbler rim | 1 |
|   Colorless hand-blown wineglass stem | 1 |
|   Flat glass | 21 |
| Fasteners | |
|   Wire nail | 17 |
|   Forged nail | 1 |
|   Nail, unidentified | 1 |
| Hardware | |
|   Forged door hinge | 1 |
|   Iron padlock key | 1 |
| Other metal | |
|   Unidentified iron fragments | 17 |
| Lithics | |
|   Basalt flake | 1 |

*Source:* Jamieson 1996:238–248.

**Table 15.** 9-20 Calle Bolívar, Unit 2:
Faunal Remains from Mixed Contexts

| Taxon | NISP |
|---|---|
| UID mammal | 242 |
| UID large mammal | 13 |
| UID medium mammal | 12 |
| UID large rodent | 1 |
| *Cavia porcellus* (guinea pig) | 4 |
| *Lagomorph* (rabbit) | 1 |
| *Canidae* (dog, probably domestic) | 1 |
| *Sus scrofa* (pig) | 1 |
| *Bos taurus* (cow) | 18 |
| *Caprine* (sheep/goat) | 35 |
| UID bird | 4 |
| *Gallus gallus* (chicken) | 10 |
| UID fish | 2 |
| UID vertebrate | 22 |

Source: Jamieson 1996:238–244.

black organic loam with a large number of artifacts was encountered. This layer was resting on sterile clay subsoil. The deposit contained large fragments of mammal bone, including a complete horn core and a whole scapula from a cow (*Bos taurus*) and large ceramic fragments. None of the bones appeared to be articulated with any of the others; the layer was a midden made up largely of butchering refuse. Because of the large number of bone fragments the faunal analysis will be treated separately below. The lack of industrially produced artifacts shows that this is an intact sealed context predating 1780.

There is only one small locally produced majolica sherd in this context, which may be intrusive to the level through trampling. The olive jar fragments recovered, although unfortunately without any rim sherds, are consistent with seventeenth-century olive jar styles. The white slip exterior and the fact that none of the sherds have any green glaze applied are consistent with a seventeenth-century date (Marken 1994:133). The presence of Panamanian majolicas without any local Cuenca majolicas is also indicative of a context predating 1671 (Deagan 1987:29; Long 1964:104).

This context dates sometime within the 1557 to 1671 period, and is the only sealed seventeenth-century context excavated in Cuenca. There is an almost complete lack of nonceramic material culture (Table 16) with the exception of a large iron knife or spear blade, which was highly corroded. The depth of the deposit suggests that a small *arroyo*, or creek bed, existed here when the site was first occupied by the Spanish and was used as a discard area for household refuse. The mixture of large ceramic sherds and whole large animal bones indicates that this refuse is in a primary context.

The ceramics recovered (Table 17) show the overwhelming reliance on locally produced coarse earthenwares, the majority either plain or red slipped. All the remaining ceramics were imported, with olive jars from Spain that were no doubt imported to Cuenca containing wine, olive oil, or other agricultural products.

**Table 16.** 9-20 Calle Bolívar:
Nonceramic Artifacts from
Colonial Midden

| Artifact | N |
|---|---|
| Earthenware construction tile | 22 |
| Tools | |
|    Iron knife | 1 |
| Other metal | |
|    Unidentified iron fragments | 2 |

*Source:* Jamieson 1996:246.

**Table 17.** 9-20 Calle Bolívar:
Ceramic Artifacts from Colonial Midden

| Type | N | MNV | % of MNV |
|---|---|---|---|
| Coarse earthenware | | | |
| Plain | 79 | 3 | 11.5 |
| Red slipped | 23 | 8 | 30.8 |
| Thick red slipped | 10 | 4 | 15.4 |
| Cream slipped | 2 | 1 | 3.8 |
| Brown slipped | 2 | 1 | 3.8 |
| Black slipped | 2 | 1 | 3.8 |
| Polychrome slipped (Incaic?) | 1 | 1 | 3.8 |
| Fine earthenware | | | |
| Majolica | 1 | 1 | 3.8 |
| Panamanian earthenware | | | |
| Green lead glazed | 1 | 1 | 3.8 |
| Majolica | 5 | 3 | 11.5 |
| Olive jar | | | |
| Plain | 8 | 1 | 3.8 |
| White slipped exterior | 11 | 1 | 3.8 |
| Total | 145 | 26 | 100.0 |

*Source:* Jamieson 1996:246-247.

Majolica tableware was from Panama la Vieja, the major port for goods going to and from the Pacific coast of South America at the time. Panamanian majolicas are a good chronological indicator of contexts predating 1671 in the Andes, and this Cuenca context can be used to give an idea of the local coarse earthenware forms produced in Cuenca in the early colonial period.

The context is comparable to an intact midden at the Locumbilla winery in the Moquegua Valley of Peru (Smith 1991:313–314). A volcanic ash lens deposited in 1600 sealed the Moquegua material. The context was a domestic assemblage with the only imported artifacts being Panamanian majolicas.

The recovery of a quantity of animal bone from the midden in Cuenca (Tables 18 and 19) allows us to compare the faunal assemblage to similar assemblages from other colonial period Spanish sites in the New World. The remains from this context show a preponderance of caprines, followed by cow, and small amounts of pig and chicken. There were also two fragments of cervid maxilla recovered, probably from white-tailed deer (*Odocoileus virginianus*). There were no native Andean domesticates, such as guinea pig or llama, recovered from these levels. The presence of deer once again shows that this was a major hunted species around Cuenca, and that it made a contribution to the elite colonial diet. It is likely that

**Table 18.** 9-20 Calle Bolívar:
Faunal Remains from Colonial Midden

| Taxon | NISP | MNI |
|---|---|---|
| UID mammal | 145 | – |
| UID medium mammal | 6 | – |
| UID large mammal | 6 | – |
| *Artiodactyl* | 2 | – |
| *Cervidae* (deer) | 2 | 1 |
| *Sus scrofa* (pig) | 2 | 1 |
| *Bos taurus* (cow) | 10 | 1 |
| *Caprine* (sheep/goat) | 33 | 2 |
| *Gallus gallus* (chicken) | 2 | 1 |
| UID vertebrate | 5 | – |

*Source:* Jamieson 1996:250.

the occupants of 9-38 Calle Bolívar either went out on leisure hunting parties themselves, or that they hired hunters to kill deer for them (Reitz and Cumbaa 1983:183).

The domesticates from this context reflect an almost stereotypical range of Spanish preferences in livestock. Sheep were the most numerous animals in Iberia and the most common meat sold from the sixteenth to eighteenth centuries. Cattle were also important as a source of meat, hides, and tallow. Pigs and goats were less abundant and were raised in small numbers on small holdings rather than in large herds (Reitz and Cumbaa 1983:155–156; Reitz and McEwan 1995:295).

The faunal sample from this context is not large, but it does merit comparison to other Spanish colonial samples. A faunal collection from the colonial levels of the Osambela house in Lima, Peru, included an overwhelming (66%) preponderance of caprines, most of them juveniles. Domestic fowl was the next most popular species (10%), followed by cow (9%) and pig (7%). Camelids, deer, fish, viscacha (*Lagidium peruanum*), guinea pig, and domestic dog were also represented, but none made up more than 2% percent of the sample (Flores Espinoza et al. 1981:95).

At two domestic sites in Puerto Real, Haiti, the sixteenth-century remains included pigs as the most heavily exploited domestic animal, followed by cow, caprine, and chickens. A small but significant secondary source of meat was the pond turtle, a common local wild species (Ewen 1991:134–140; Reitz and McEwan 1995:310, 312–314). A third residence in Puerto Real, Locus 39, had an unusually high proportion of cattle bone, and the cattle bone elements show a high proportion of lower limb bones, as well as huge quantities of smashed unidentifiable bone (Deagan and Reitz 1995:275). Both of these factors suggest that this may have been a

**Table 19.** Mammal Elements Identified,
9-20 Calle Bolívar, Colonial Midden

| Element | Caprine | Cow | Deer | Pig | Artiodactyl |
|---|---|---|---|---|---|
| Head | | | | | |
| Cranial | 1 | – | – | – | – |
| Horn core | – | 2 | – | – | – |
| Maxilla | – | – | 1 | – | – |
| Mandible | 1 | – | – | – | – |
| Teeth | | | | | |
| Mandible molars | 7 | – | – | – | – |
| Maxilla molars | 5 | – | – | – | – |
| Premolars | 3 | – | – | – | – |
| Incisors | – | 2 | – | – | – |
| Vertebrae | | | | | |
| Cervical | – | 2 | – | – | – |
| Thoracic | 3 | – | – | – | – |
| Lumbar | 1 | – | – | – | – |
| Sacral | 1 | – | – | – | – |
| Ribs | | | | | |
| Forequarters | | | | | |
| Scapula | 2 | 2 | – | – | – |
| Radius | 1 | 1 | – | – | – |
| Ulna | 1 | – | – | – | – |
| Hindquarters | | | | | |
| Innominate | – | – | – | 1 | – |
| Femur | 1 | – | – | – | – |
| Feet | | | | | |
| Astragalus | – | – | – | 1 | – |
| Metatarsal | 1 | – | – | – | – |
| Tarsal | – | 1 | – | – | – |
| Phalanx | 1 | – | – | – | 2 |
| Total | 29 | 10 | 2 | 2 | 2 |

*Source:* Jamieson 1996:251.

specialized tallow and/or glue production site. The lack of cranial bones suggests the cattle were butchered elsewhere and their heads removed (Deagan and Reitz 1995:280). This site also included 27 double-pointed iron awls, two iron wedge fragments, and 2 iron knife blade fragments, proposed to be tools used in hide or tallow processing (Deagan and Reitz 1995:270–271). This cattle-processing activity is only 50 meters south of the central plaza of Puerto Real, which did not conform to Spanish colonial edicts against placing slaughterhouses in the town center (Deagan and Reitz 1995:283).

The Franciscan convent in Santo Domingo, Dominican Republic, was excavated in the 1960s, and faunal analysis of this late-sixteenth- to mideighteenth-century materials show a dominance of caprines (12.5% of minimum number of individuals), with other domesticates also present, and a large variety of wild species, mostly fish (Reitz and Scarry 1985:37).

Six houses at St. Augustine, Florida, have been excavated and contained faunal remains from the sixteenth century. These show a heavy reliance on a mix of cattle and pigs, but with very significant contributions from both wild deer and estuarine resources such as fish, tortoises, and sharks (Reitz and Scarry 1985:68). The eighteenth-century contexts excavated at St. Augustine also represent six separate households. The faunal sample from the eighteenth century was similar to that from the sixteenth-century households. The dominant species in terms of biomass in all eighteenth-century contexts was cow, followed by pig, then deer, and then fish. Caprines were rare and only found at three of the six houses (Reitz and Cumbaa 1983:176–77). In terms of status differences between the six eighteenth-century sites, the elite houses were larger consumers of both Spanish domestic animals and terrestrial wild game, while poorer households relied to a greater extent on aquatic species, mostly local estuarine fish and turtles (Reitz and Cumbaa 1983:176–177).

The lack of caprines was noticeable in all time periods for Spanish colonial St. Augustine, both when compared to Spanish ideals for domestic livestock production and when compared to the Cuenca sample. The failure of sheep and goat production at St. Augustine throughout the Spanish colonial period is now thought to be due to a combination of environmental factors. These include the presence of predators, parasites, and sandy, forested conditions, all of which affect the viability of sheep more than cattle or pigs (Reitz and Cumbaa 1983:183).

It would seem that highland Cuenca, more so than other Spanish colonial regions, was able to support an animal economy similar to the Spanish model, with all the standard domestic animals, and an overwhelming reliance on sheep. Sheep and goats do not do as well in lowland tropical settings and are much better suited to hilly semiarid regions with plenty of access to grass and frequent watering (Reitz and McEwan 1995:293). The highland regions around Cuenca were and are ideal for sheep raising and these animals dominate lists of colonial stock in the notarial records of the region.

## URBAN EXCAVATIONS SUMMARY

The excavations on Calle Bolívar are located on the city block directly north of the location of the colonial Jesuit church complex. Notarial documents show that this was one of the elite city blocks of colonial Cuenca.

Prices for property on the block in the mid- to late seventeenth century ranged from 600 to 2,300 pesos, and for the first half of the eighteenth century, despite the subdivision of the block into smaller lots, prices still ranged from 400 to 1,900 pesos (Jamieson 1996:253). Several inventories give an idea of the colonial material culture in this area.

The 1664 inventory of Doña Luisa Maldonado de San Juan, whose house was on the block where excavations took place, gives us an interesting picture of midseventeenth-century elite material culture in Cuenca. Her tableware included 19 pieces of silver tableware, 3 pieces of gold-plated silver tableware, 4 "coconuts for drinking chocolate from the coast," and 9 *molinillos*, or frothing instruments, to froth the chocolate drink (Coe and Coe 1996:120; ANH/C C116.404a, f2r, 5v, and 10r). It is interesting that there is no listing of any ceramics in the Maldonado de San Juan household. The inventory is very thorough, at least in terms of the more expensive items; any imported porcelains would have been listed. There are three mirrors listed, but absolutely no glass tablewares.

The 1678 inventory of the house of Francisco de Rojas, located one block north of where the excavations were undertaken, includes 16 pieces of silver tableware and several pieces of furniture, but no ceramics or glassware were included (ANH/C L528, f561r).

The house owned by Luisa Maldonado de San Juan in 1664 was inventoried again in 1783 in the will of her grandniece, Michaela Maldonado de San Juan (ANH/C L549, f223r–226r). In the 1783 inventory only the larger pieces of furniture and the artworks are mentioned. There is no listing of silver tablewares, glass, ceramics, or any other personal possessions.

The documentary record creates an interesting comparison to the early seventeenth-century archaeological contexts. The excavations indicate that in elite houses such as the Maldonado de San Juan house, Panamanian majolicas were the main ceramic tableware in the early to mid-seventeenth century. These apparently did not warrant any mention in the inventory, perhaps because they were not all that expensive. The silver tablewares were emphasized, and silver was clearly an essential economic and status item in colonial Cuenca (Paniagua Pérez 1989).

The lack of porcelain and glassware in the inventories is an interesting occurrence and may be due to the lack of detail in these inventories. The emphasis was clearly on silver, furniture, jewelry, and artworks, the most valuable items in a household. Porcelain and glass have been recorded in other colonial Cuenca inventories, but it would appear that large quantities of glass and porcelain were never the rule in colonial Cuenca houses, even of the elite.

## COMPARISON TO OTHER NEW WORLD
## SPANISH SITES

In Ecuador there have been no previously published excavations of urban domestic sites dating to the colonial period. There has been, however, some colonial period archaeology done in Quito, all at religious sites. These excavations give a picture of the ceramic assemblages from that city.

The Santo Domingo monastery excavations in Quito revealed a selection of colonial ceramics for which raw sherd count percentages have been reported. These included an overwhelming abundance of coarse earthenwares, plain and slipped (73%), some green-on-cream majolicas (24%), a small number of blue-on-white majolicas (Probably Panama blue-on-white) (2%), and a small amount of porcelain (1%) (Buys 1992).

Excavations in several rooms of the San Francisco monastery in the center of Quito revealed two brick-lined ossuaries under chapels and several prehistoric burials, probably Inka. Colonial ceramics were recovered in these excavations, but have not been described in any detail (Teran 1989).

Ceramics recovered from burial fill under the floors of the Mercedarian monastery in Quito included a majority of majolica sherds with a pinkish background glaze and emerald green decoration, and also a greenish-yellow background glaze with maroon decoration. Many slipped and plain coarse earthenwares were recovered, along with several large fragments of olive jars, some with tar adhering to them. Two small ceramic fragments with "an opaque white glaze with blue decoration" were probably Panama blue-on-white (Díaz 1991:22–23).

Ceramics from below the floor of the colonial El Robo chapel in Quito were for the most part prehistoric. Historic majolicas were reported to all be cream glazed, with green, café, and light blue decoration. All are thought to have been made in Quito and are very similar to samples recovered from the San Francisco and Santo Domingo monastery excavations in Quito (Bolaños and Manosalvas 1989:11, 14).

Extensive excavation of a colonial site in Lima, Peru, in the late 1970s recovered a large artifact collection. This property, located two blocks west of the colonial central plaza of Lima, is called the Osambela house. It was a part of the Dominican monastery from the mid-sixteenth century until 1807, when it was sold to the Osambela family; it is, therefore, more of a colonial religious property than an example of colonial domestic use (Flores Espinoza et al. 1981:75, 93).

Ceramics recovered from the Osambela house included coarse earthenwares (Flores Espinoza et al. 1981:35–39), some of which were feldspar-inlaid ware (Deagan 1987:42; Flores Espinoza et al. 1981:36). Tin-glazed earthenwares included Panamanian wares with both greenish-white tin-glaze and green lead glaze, which were recovered from the earliest colonial levels (Flores Espinoza et al. 1981:40–42), and are probably identical to majolicas recovered from Cuenca. Other later varieties of majolicas included Panama polychromes, which may in fact have been manufactured in Lima (Flores Espinoza et al. 1981:50). Quantities of refined white earthenwares and porcelains were also recovered (Flores Espinoza et al. 1981:43), but were not identified by comparison to any literature on historic ceramics.

Two domestic lots were excavated within the abandoned Spanish colonial town of Puerto Real, Haiti, occupied from 1503 to 1579. One of the lots, Locus 33/35, was directly adjacent to the central plaza, while the other lot, Locus 19, was about one hundred meters northeast of the plaza, toward the periphery of the visible urban area (McEwan 1995:201). The two lots showed a very similar ceramic assemblage, with 47% and 56% of the assemblage made up of "non-European utilitarian wares," presumably of "aboriginal" origin (McEwan 1995:213). Utilitarian wares (unglazed and lead glazed) made in Spain accounted for 18% to 28% of the two assemblages, and 17% to 18% of the assemblages were made up of majolicas, all of them imported from Spain (Deagan 1995c:441). A much wider variety of glass, metal, and bone artifacts were recovered at Puerto Real (McEwan 1995:215–221) than in the Cuenca excavations, once again because of the limited nature of the Cuenca sample.

Excavations at St. Augustine, Florida, provide data on urban domestic sites from the mid- to late eighteenth-century Spanish colonial period. Extensive excavations at a *criollo* (creole) household revealed intact midden deposits from the eighteenth century. The income of the occupant at the time was 264 pesos per year (Deagan 1983:69). The large scale of these excavations meant that a much wider selection of artifacts were recovered than in the Cuenca excavations.

The majority (66%) of the ceramics were "aboriginal" in nature, a proportion comparable to the unglazed coarse earthenwares in Cuenca excavations. The majolicas from this site came in a variety of types, all imported from Spain or New Spain, and made up 12% of the sherd count. Olive jars from Spain were also present (5% of sherd count). A major difference from Cuenca is the presence of small quantities of imported wares (none more than 2% of sherd count) from European countries other than Spain. These included Delftware, Jackfield, salt-glaze stonewares, and scratch blue (Deagan 1983:77). The presence of these ceramics is related to St. Augustine's position near the northeastern limits of the

Spanish colonial world, with interaction with English colonies and access to shipping from the Caribbean. This is in sharp contrast to the isolation of Cuenca, which lasted until the freeing of trade within the empire in the 1780s and 1790s. The end of Crown restrictions on trade between Spain and all Spanish colonies led to a flood of European goods entering Andean South America (Burkholder and Johnson 1990:269–270). Apart from ceramics, the de Hita site revealed a large number of colonial glass artifacts, metal pieces, and bone artifacts (Deagan 1983:79). These may represent greater access to material goods by eighteenth-century inhabitants of St. Augustine, but the extreme rarity of such artifacts in Cuenca is probably just a factor of the lack of extensive excavations.

The lower status Maria de la Cruz site was a household on the periphery of St. Augustine and was occupied by a soldier from New Spain married to a Gaule Indian woman in the late eighteenth century (Deagan 1983:100). At this site 91% of the ceramics recovered were "aboriginal" coarse earthenwares and only 2% were majolicas. There were still small quantities of the various wares imported from other European countries (Deagan 1983:113).

In general, Deagan concludes that it is clear that both majolica and Spanish coarse earthenwares were much more common at sites of wealthier people, as was glass (Deagan 1983:240). Access to majolica in colonial St. Augustine was limited to imported wares, which may be one of the reasons that Deagan equates them largely with the elite. In Cuenca excavations have not been extensive enough to compare assemblages from different urban social classes, but the production of majolicas locally may have made them less of an elite ware in Cuenca than in towns like St. Augustine.

In conclusion, the number of urban domestic sites from the Spanish colonial period in the New World that have been excavated is still very small. In Ecuador the Cuenca excavations are the first that have been fully analyzed. There are still very basic questions to be answered, but some aspects of the material culture of the Andean colonial city can be clearly stated.

The first is that imported Panamanian ceramics fulfilled the role of elite tableware prior to 1671 and can be used as chronologically significant markers in archaeological contexts. There have so far been no occurrences of majolicas from Spain or Mexico in the Cuenca archaeological record, although this may be due to the small size of the excavated sample. In Cuenca Panamanian ceramics are so far only seen at urban sites. This was not the case for Moquegua, Peru (Smith 1991), or in Potosí, Bolivia (Van Buren 1996), where such ceramics are found at elite rural sites as well.

After the demise of Panama majolica production, it would seem that local majolica production in many Andean centers filled this role. Quito, Cuenca, and Lima all produced majolicas locally, but a comparative study of these ceramics must be made before identification of local wares can be simplified.

In all regions coarse earthenwares were the most common artifacts found, and, to varying degrees, involved the participation of Native potting traditions in their production. This production should be the focus of extensive further study, as these wares are important to our understanding of colonial ethnic interaction.

The role of material culture in colonial Cuenca will be discussed further, but in general at elite urban sites in Cuenca the material culture, in terms of glassware and imported ceramics, was much less diverse than at urban sites in the Spanish colonial Caribbean. Further studies of the material culture of the different neighborhoods of Cuenca could reveal much more about the relationship between economics, ethnicity, and the material culture of the Spanish colonial world in the Andes.

# The Domestic
# Material Culture
# of Colonial Cuenca

6

## DOMESTIC MATERIAL CULTURE
## IN THE SPANISH COLONIAL WORLD

The material goods owned by private citizens were an essential part of the process of colonialism in the Andes. Clothing, dishes, and furniture were not simply functional, but carried a multiplicity of meanings for colonial Cuencanos. Material culture naturalized relationships of domination in the colonial encounter. In her research at St. Augustine, Florida, and in other parts of the Caribbean Kathleen Deagan formulated a framework for looking at these colonial relationships, a framework within which many archaeologists of the Spanish colonial period now work. Deagan's basic premise is that "Conservatism in certain areas—most notably, those that were socially visible and associated with male activities—was coupled with Spanish-Indian acculturation and syncretism in other areas, especially those that were less socially visible and female dominated" (Deagan 1983:271). Deagan has masterfully placed material culture at the crux of an argument about gender and ethnic interactions in a "garrison town" in which most of the males were in the military. Very few women emigrated to the settlement, and so the vast majority of women came from the Indian communities living around the garrison (Deagan 1973). Her ideas have been extremely influential in Spanish colonial archaeology and have been expanded by Bonnie McEwan to include ethnically Spanish women. These women, as the wives of wealthy men, "worked in the home and maintained traditional standards," and thus "the archaeological correlates of Spanish women are associated mostly with their domestic responsibilities" (McEwan 1991:34). McEwan has portrayed these women as a group who through their domestic activities "lent prestige to their communities, set cultural standards, and, to a lesser degree, exercised financial power" (McEwan 1991:39). Rather than setting up such strict dichotomies between the roles of different class, gender, and ethnic groups, I would prefer to look at the multiple roles that items of domestic material culture played in colonial Cuenca. Household items were used in mediating between these groups, both as objects used to control social action and to resist European hegemony. What these objects signaled to the people who used them was as complex as the relationships between the people themselves.

To examine this further we must place these items within their historical context. This is a task that is not easily accomplished. Archaeological excavation and household inventories from Cuenca have revealed two very different pictures of the domestic material culture, both of which help to reveal the chronology of artifact change in colonial Cuenca and the distribution of artifacts among different classes and ethnic groups.

## THE NOTARIAL DOCUMENTS

The Archivo Nacional de Historia in Cuenca contains a large collection of documents dating from the late sixteenth century through to the Republican period, the majority of which are wills, land transactions, and property inventories recorded by notaries. I have used these to look at house descriptions and to identify the properties where archaeological excavations were undertaken. They are also wonderful sources for detailed descriptions of the contents of colonial houses.

North American scholars have realized since at least the mid-1960s the great utility of household inventories as sources for data on material culture (Beaudry 1980; Bowen 1975; Brown 1972; Cummings 1964). The inventories themselves were a form of discourse, a way of speaking about the world. In medieval Europe inventories of noble houses were common, but it is from the mid-sixteenth century onward that they suddenly became standard for the middle classes. They were a part of the state apparatus that led to an explosion of administrative documents in that period. Inventories were a form of "discipline" in that the local people, in their roles as officers of the church or state, did the inventories and thus themselves reinforced the commodification of portable wealth, an important step toward modern capitalism (Johnson 1996:111–112).

This resource has also been used in the study of the Spanish colonial period in the New World. It is unfortunate that the notarial archives of St. Augustine, Florida, with its 30-year history of archaeological research into the Spanish colonial period, have not been preserved for the period before 1783 (Deagan 1983:17). In other parts of the Spanish colonies, however, such notarial records have been used to good effect, including Mexico (Boyd-Bowman 1972, 1973; Gasco 1992; Lavrin and Couturier 1979) and Argentina (Porro et al. 1982; Porro Girardi 1995). Within Ecuador Joanne Rappaport (1990a) used the wills of colonial caciques (ethnic leaders) to reveal uniquely Andean symbols used by Native leaders well into the colonial period. Several researchers have used notarial documents to look at the role of material culture in the lives of Native Andean women in colonial Ecuador (Caillavet 1982; Salomon 1988; Truhan 1991). There has, however, been little use of notarial documents to look at aspects of colonialism outside Native ethnohistory in Ecuador.

It is important to understand the many biases built into the use of household inventories. The first is that not all houses were inventoried. Inventories were much more common for elite houses than for the houses of the poor. Second, the individuals conducting the inventory may have had varying ability in describing the items they were seeing and widely varying value systems as to what they felt was important to record (Brown 1988:81; Porro Girardi 1995:92). Deliberate falsification, particularly of the value of inventoried objects, is also a possibility when dowries and wills were being contested (Porro Girardi 1995:92). The most important realization for the archaeologist is that only items considered to be of enough value to be "worth mentioning" were recorded.

Many of the items in daily use in a given house would never be recorded in an inventory, and it is in the archaeological record that some of these items of "little value" appear. The material recovered in excavations contrasts sharply with that recorded in colonial household inventories. Far from being an inconsistency in the relationship between what was documented and what turns up in excavation, the contrast between inventories and excavated materials can reveal much about the meaning of objects to the people who had used them.

## CLOTHING AND JEWELRY

The first category of objects that draws our attention in the colonial documents is the clothing and jewelry, descriptions of which go on for pages in the household inventories of elite members of society. This concern with personal apparel, particularly as a mark of ethnicity and status, is clear in the late-eighteenth-century paintings of daily life in the Carmelite convent refectory in Cuenca. Indians, mestizos, and vecinos were easily distinguished from one another by their dress as they undertook harvesting and hunting activities (Martínez Borrero 1983). In a time and place where the status differentiation in house size and decoration was not huge, wealth was expressed through portable possessions. Clothing and jewelry, instantly visible on the street or in the countryside, helped to define the wearer and was one of the most important categories of personal possessions.

For obvious reasons clothing is not frequently preserved in the archaeological record. In contrast to the minimal archaeological evidence, it is impossible to do justice to the rich documentary record describing colonial Cuenca clothing. A few examples can give some idea of the range of clothing owned by different members of colonial Cuenca society.

Pedro Ortiz Dávila, Crown prosecutor and court reporter of Cuenca in the late seventeenth century, had at his death a house on the main plaza with at least six rooms and extensive rural properties including over 2,000 head of cattle and the services of 49 mitayos (Native Andean forced laborers). The wardrobe in his house on the main plaza at the time of his death in 1672 was extensive and included

> a dressing gown of Cambray with Flanders lace and a belt of white silk with gold; ... six handkerchiefs, one of Rouen linen *de cofre*, embroidered with *amorada* [?] silk, another of lace, and four ordinary of flowered Rouen linen; six berets/soft caps embroidered with Rouen linen *de cofre*; five hats, two of black beaver felt, another of local black wool and another of white, and the other brown from Castile ... a waterproof cape of *chamelote*; a goatskin jacket from Flanders braided in gold with green satin and lined with green taffeta; six pairs of silk socks, one pair red and the other five black; ... three short white doublets/blouses; ... and three leather hats. (ANHC L520 f.611v–615r)

Cambray was a very delicate cloth made in Cambray, France, and used for expensive shirts, pillowcases, and so forth. The association of cambray cloth with high status was in fact codified in 1750 in the town of Cordoba (in what became Argentina), where the municipal council outlawed the use of cambray by *"mulata, india y negra"* (mixed race, Native Andean, or Black women). *"De cofre"* literally means "of the chest or strongbox" and refers to a very high quality of cloth (Porro et al. 1982:371, 448, 491). *Chamelote*, or camlet, was a cloth that may originally have been made of camelhair and silk, but during the Renaissance period it was more associated with angora goat wool mixed with silk, and it was known for its waterproofing abilities.

Ortiz Dávila's wardrobe contrasts sharply with that of Marcial Uruchima, a Native Andean who died in 1697 and whose entire listed wardrobe consisted of "an old piece of a cape of local cloth" and "a used skirt of local blue flannel" (ANH/C C.112.155 [1697]). Presumably the skirt belonged to a female relative, and any other clothing was simply not worth writing down. Uruchima's particular case should not be taken as an indication that being ethnically "Native" in colonial Cuenca brought a corollary of being poor. Uruchima may have been both, as were many other Native Andeans who had very few material indications of wealth, but in other cases distinctly "Native" clothing and jewelry were indicators of considerable economic and social power in Andean colonial society (Caillavet 1982; Cummins 1991; Rappaport 1990a; Truhan 1991).

Somewhere closer to Ortiz Dávila's station in life, but more of the middle class, was Sebastiana de Rojas, a doña (elite female) and vecina whose thatch house was outside the urban core of Cuenca. Her wardrobe at her death in 1683 consisted of

> an outfit of my use, the skirt of straw-colored silk stuff, with its hat of short black felt, another skirt of sky-blue camlet with its split black jacket with lace . . . a black outfit of silk stuff, skirt and jacket . . . three and a half *varas* of purple silk stuff, and four and a half *varas* of black velvet . . . a ruffled skirt with three gold bands of felt . . . an old hat . . . four *varas* of pink taffeta, three shirts of my use, the bodies of flowered Rouen linen and the sleeves of Brittany linen . . . some slips/petticoats of Rouen linen . . . and twenty *varas* of flowered Rouen linen which I have to make some shirts . . . ; a new shawl of good quality with part of point lace . . . another old muslin shawl . . . a brown skirt of *mamparado* [?] . . . a skirt of *cristal* from Holland . . . two petticoats of local baize, one purple and the other red with trim of *sevillanetas* [?]; . . . three Cambray head-scarves one with large Flanders lace and two with medium Flanders lace . . . and a handkerchief of Brittany linen and two others of Rouen linen and another two. (ANH/C L.528 f.44r–45r [1683]).

Cristal was a very thin white wool cloth with some gloss to it, made in several countries; in late eighteenth-century Buenos Aires it was exclusively white (Porro et al. 1982:457).

The association of fine clothing with wealth and status in late-seventeenth-century Cuenca is evident just from this small selection of inventories. The people who inventoried the wardrobe of a wealthy man like Ortiz Dávila spent time and effort identifying the types of cloth and describing the items of clothing in great detail. Much of the cloth was imported from European centers known for quality cloth making, and it is clear that elite Cuencanos could tell good quality from poor quality cloth. The minimal description and material poverty of Uruchima's wardrobe contrasted starkly with Ortiz Dávila's, while Rojas's wardrobe contains many items similar to Ortiz Dávila's, although in smaller quantities.

Along with clothing, jewelry was always inventoried in great detail. The jewelry of Luisa Maldonado de San Juan at the time of her death in 1664 contained considerable quantities of gold, silver, precious stones, and pearls (ANH/C C116.404a, f.1v, 4r–5v [1664]). For women in particular, considerable portions of their wealth were often invested in these highly visible and portable goods (McEwan 1991:35). Elite women's jewelry in the colonial Andes is known to have been used for economic transactions without the consent of a woman's husband (Borchart de Moreno 1992:358–359), or sometimes to purchase property for a husband who had been "cheated" of his own property inheritance (Wilson 1984:308). Thus, women's jewelry held a function as a public signal of status, but also as a rare form of material goods that could be controlled by a woman personally and used at her discretion.

Beyond a mere indication of wealth, personal apparel was one of the most important material manifestations of cultural identity in colonial Cuenca. Individuals moving through the spatial layout of the town and its buildings conveyed an array of signs through their bodily gestures and postures, and through their clothing and jewelry, from which the individual provided "a reading of himself when he is in the presence of others. Gender, age, class, state of health, ethnicity will all be conveyed, in the main unwittingly" (Goffman 1971:127). These visible symbols of cultural identity were important to the "reflexive monitoring of action" of people by other people in colonial Cuenca, which was an essential part of the process of people "decoding" others based on their appearance (Beaudry et al. 1991; Giddens 1984).

## FURNITURE

Clothing was of great utility in decoding others during meetings in public places, but an invitation into a colonial Cuenca house would have confronted the individual with an entirely new array of material culture, dominated by household furnishings. Largely built of wood and cloth, such furnishings are yet another form of material culture of great importance in the colonial period that does not survive archaeologically.

Household furnishings were far from a simple matter of functional convenience and were in fact viewed as an essential part of the colonizing process. During the Second (1567) and Third (1582) Councils of Lima dignitaries of the Catholic Church in the viceroyalty came together to formulate missionary strategies. They argued that an essential part of Christian conversion in the Andes was the use of tables and beds like those of Europe (MacCormack 1985:450 n. 26). Under the Toledan reforms one of the responsibilities of the municipal council of any Native town was to ensure that all houses in their jurisdiction were clean and that there were wooden bed frames for sleeping on (Chacón Zhapán 1990:63). Chairs and beds, as well as Christianity, were thus defining features of civilization to the sixteenth-century Spanish mind in the Andes.

The urban and rural houses of Luisa Maldonado de San Juan in 1664 give us a window on the furnishings of the midseventeenth-century elite. At Cachaulo the one-roomed thatch house contained only a small wooden desk or bureau and a stool, perhaps because the property was not a "residence" for permanent habitation, but only a place to meet with the agricultural laborers when the owners visited the property. In contrast Luisa's urban house contained 11 chairs, a desk/bureau, several large wooden chests, 9 religious paintings, 2 carpets, 2 copper braziers, and a stand for a ceramic water bottle. Neither beds nor tables were described in the inventory, although pillowcases and tablecloths are listed (ANH/C C116.404a, f.1v, 4r–5v [1664]). Other houses in the urban core were much simpler. The house of Francisco de Rojas, a vecino who lived two blocks north of the Maldonado de San Juan house, lists only a single wooden chest, a large desk, and bed canopy among the belongings worthy of mention in the household inventory (ANH/C L. 528 f. 561r [1697]).

The house of Pedro Ortiz Dávila on the main plaza contained considerably greater quantities of furniture and reflects the priorities of a family that may have been the wealthiest in Cuenca at the time. Two consecrated altars contained silver and expensive cloth fixtures as well as several religious statues. There were at least 26 paintings on canvas and 21 framed illustrations or prints. The power of the written word in Ortiz Dávila's life is expressed in the library of eight hundred books, the two wooden accounts desks, three writing desks, and four portable writing desks. Four wooden chests contained a large collection of cloth and other belongings. There were 71 chairs, 9 bureaus, and 4 cots. The description of the bed, however, receives the most attention, focusing on its sheets, pillowcases, canopies, and curtains, which were all made of silks, brocades, Chinese damasks, and the finest linens (ANH/C L. 520 ff. 610v–613v [1672]).

It was not until the early eighteenth century that inventories of the houses in the Todos Santos neighborhood, along the edge of the Tomebamba River, appear. Sergeant and vecino Baltazar Rodrigues Soriano lived in Todos Santos in a thatch-roof house on one solar of land in 1702. His inventoried furniture included ten paintings, six chairs, a wooden cot, a wooden bench, two bureaus, an *estrado* with rug, a writing desk and case for papers, a wooden cabinet for a drinking water jar, a cot with two "old and worn-out" mattresses and linens of local cotton and wool. An *estrado* was a low wooden piece of furniture usually covered in carpets or skins, used as both bed and couch. These were largely replaced by couches in wealthier Ecuadorian houses by the mideighteenth century (Benítez and Costa 1983:200; Jack Williams, personal communication 1995). Seventeen years later his son Francisco and his wife Maria Matute de Castro, both vecinos, had added a second room to the house and had reroofed it in tiles. Despite the architectural improvements it would appear that Francisco's family fortune had gone downhill slightly since his father's time, and the inventoried household furnishings included only three paintings, five chairs, a table, and a wooden bench (Jamieson 1996:267).

Perhaps more typical of the Todos Santos neighborhood was the house of Francisca Cusco, a Native Andean born in the city of Cuenca. The 1730 inventory of her tile-roofed one-room house is rare both because of the small value of her possessions and because prices are given for all the items. Francisca owned 35 pesos worth of clothing, and all of her other inventoried household items consisted of

> thirty-eight *frailejones* [a plant used for its resin] (1 peso, 4 reales); thirty wooden stakes (1 peso, 2 reales); two shelves (3 pesos); thirty-nine guinea pigs (2 pesos, 3 reales); seven chickens (7 reales); two sickles (1 peso, 4 reales); one old cape (1 peso, 4 reales); a back-strap loom of black wood (6 reales); a lock, and half of a machete (1 peso); a cow skin (2 pesos); one harness (2 reales); six ceramic vessels (2, pesos 4 reales); and two sieves (7 reales). (ANH/C C.116.072a [1730])

The household goods add up to a total of 20 pesos, or less than the value of Francisca Cusco's clothing. The great detail of the inventory leads us to believe that there was no furniture apart from the shelves and cow skin in the small residence. There is little doubt that this rare detailed inventory of someone living in considerable poverty represents innumerable other colonial residents of Cuenca whose properties went unrecorded.

Felipe Santos de Estoque and Juana del Castillo had a house in the urban core at the time of Felipe's death in 1709. The residence included a shop containing two desks and a set of balances for weighing goods, as well as a large selection of glassware, a variety of spices by the pound, nails and other hardware, several weapons, and even a chess set. The household furnishings are divided between two rooms, a tile-roofed room that contained an old wooden table and a wooden chest, and a thatch-roofed room that had ten paintings, a wooden cot with a woolen canopy, and an old mattress (ANH/C L. 533 f. 637v [1709]).

The rural Cachaulo property had been passed down in the Maldonado de San Juan family. By 1740 it was in the hands of Luisa's grand-nephew Alexandro Maldonado de San Juan (Jr.), and a complex of adobe-walled houses had been built to replace the flimsy wattle and daub buildings that had been present in the mid-seventeenth century. Most of the inventoried portable goods on the property were agricultural equipment, and it is clear that domestic items were still of minimal importance even at a large rural estancia like Cachaulo. The main house contained two tables, an estrado, a wooden cot, two benches, four chairs, and four stools. In the kitchen building there were two tables, a bench, and a bronze cooking brazier.

Of all the inventoried rooms, it is the wealth of material in the chapel that stands out. The chapel was richly furnished and contained several costly religious statues and paintings, in contrast to what is otherwise a very rustic-sounding farmstead (ANH/C L. 617 ff. 49v–50r [1740]).

In the urban core Luisa's grand-niece, Michaela Maldonado de San Juan, a vecina of Cuenca, bought property jointly with her husband on the Jesuit street in the 1770s. They "built one building with a double sloping roof, and one room with a single sloping roof," which were "roofed with tile, with one double room with a shop on the street." Michaela's belongings were listed as four tables, three benches, four chairs, a wooden cot with mattress and canopy, and some religious paintings (ANH/C L549 ff. 223r–226r [1783]). It would seem that Michaela, a widow like Luisa at the end of her life, was not nearly as wealthy as her great-aunt had been.

Finally, the house of Manuel Castro, a vecino who lived in the San Sebastián parish in the late eighteenth century, provides a very useful inventory because monetary values are given for each item. The house itself was valued at 1,450 pesos and the surrounding land at 200 pesos. The house contained a cabinet with iron lock (12 pesos), twelve unframed paintings (36 pesos), five framed paintings (10 pesos), a wooden statue of Christ (1 peso), four stools (8 pesos), five old chairs (7 pesos), two estrados (7 pesos, 6 reales), two large tables and one small table (2 pesos, 4 reales), a bronze brazier (8 pesos, 2 reales), a small rug (2 pesos, 4 reales), two wooden trunks (18 pesos), an altar with several statues of saints (7 pesos), a wooden cot (3 pesos) with pillows, cover, and sheets (total 2 pesos, 4 reales), a mattress (1 peso, 4 reales) a canopy of local cloth (20 pesos), and a harp (3 pesos) (ANH/C C. 97.541 [1778]).

The furnishings of colonial Cuenca houses fall into several categories. Chests and boxes were very common, often with locks, and were used to hold clothing, jewelry, linens, and other valuables. Religious paintings, statues, and in elite houses private altars attested to the religious devotion of the inhabitants. The large number of paintings in inventories of small houses suggests that the effect of the paintings must have been overwhelming when one entered a house.

Chairs, often specified as "with seats and backrests," are the first items listed in many inventories. Rural houses, even of elite landowners, frequently did not contain them, while the house of Pedro Ortiz Dávila had 71 and Luisa Maldonado de San Juan had 11. Other researchers have noted that in the seventeenth-century English colonies in North America (Deetz 1977:121–122) and in early modern Europe itself there was a growth over time in the number of chairs seen in households. These are in part associated with status, as chairs were viewed as symbols of authority in medieval Europe, in opposition to simple benches or wooden crates. In the sixteenth-century drawings of Guaman Poma de Ayala (1956 [1615]) elite members of the colonial establishment are often seen seated in a chair at the head of a table. It is clear from the Cuenca inventories that in houses such as Ortiz Dávila's it was important to have enough chairs (presumably lining the walls of the main room of the house when not in use) so that very important guests at social events could be seated in one. The chairs of colonial Cuenca resonated with the growth of individualism in the early modern world, as benches were replaced by chairs in everyday use in the elite house (Johnson 1996:171–172).

Beds are often not listed, and in Manuel Castro's inventory the value of his wooden bed is only three pesos. The cloth canopy that covered it was worth 20 pesos, and it is in these values that we can see why bed linens are often listed when the bed itself is not. The great expense invested in imported and richly worked bed linens such as those of Pedro Ortiz Dávila complicates Kathleen Deagan's assertion that items of great value were placed in highly visible areas of the house. The curtained four-poster bed was an elite medieval piece of furniture. It had a functional purpose of trapping heat in rooms where windows often did not even have shutters (Pounds 1989:198), but bed linens were for much more than warmth. In Europe the social customs surrounding the bed changed throughout the Renaissance. In some cases people received guests while still in bed, and opulent bedding was a form of public display of wealth. Over the course of the Renaissance in Europe beds in elite houses were moved into bedrooms, places where the bed, and often the chests containing many of the household valuables, were sequestered from all except the owners of the house (Ranum 1989:217–220).

Tables were often not listed and appear to have generally been of minimal financial value, as with Manuel Castro's tables, three of which were only worth a total of 2 pesos and 4 reales. Tablecloths on the other hand were usually listed in detail. In the case of Pedro Ortiz Dávila's house there were 8 tablecloths of *alemanisco* with 12 serviettes, 4 table-cloths of blue and white cotton, and 3 tablecloths of local colored wool (ANH/C L. 520 ff. 611v–612r [1672]). *Alemanisco* was originally made in Germany as its name implies, but later came to be an "ordinary quality" cloth made in various places, used commonly in late-eighteenth-century Latin America for tablecloth and serviette sets (Porro et al. 1982:438). The household of Luisa Maldonado de San Juan had one tablecloth of alemanisco from Castile, with three serviettes (ANH/C C.116.404a f.4r [1664]). Table-cloths lead us toward a discussion of the articles used for cooking and tablewares, a subject that will take up the rest of this chapter.

## TABLEWARES

The growth in both number and variety of tablewares in the English colonies of North America was related to the growth of an ideology of individualism. This topic has become one of great interest to archaeologists in their attempt to reveal the relationship between ideology and material culture in the colonial New World (Beaudry et al. 1988; Deetz 1972; Stone 1988 [1977]).

Ceramic sherd dominate the excavated materials from domestic contexts in Cuenca, as is common on Spanish colonial sites throughout the Americas (Deagan 1995e:440). It is important not to divorce these pieces from their cultural context, and for this reason the ceramics must be considered in comparison to the documentary record in order to give a broader picture of their role in the household. The idea that "the rich will invariably possess lots of pretty pots" ignores the cultural role of ceramics in the colonial world, as is shown in English colonial contexts where pewter was the main tableware in most households and ceramics received little mention (Beaudry et al. 1988:54–55). In some areas of the Spanish colonies pewter played an important role in colonial tablewares (Gasco 1992), but in the Andes it was silver that was the focus of expenditure.

The inventories of colonial houses show that as in many other Andean cities, silver tableware was the most important expression of the elite status of a household. Such items were easily portable, could be displayed to visitors during meals, and perhaps most importantly could be given a clear financial value based on their weight (Porro et al. 1982:17). Silver vessels were produced in Cuenca from at least the 1560s, with the earliest apprenticeship documents for the teaching of silver-smithing dating to the 1590s. Silver workers were considered some of the most important artisans in the city and held considerable status. The main area for such production in the colonial period was the street one block north of the main plaza and adjacent to the *casa de fundición* (Royal smelting house), where silver ore was processed for taxation (Paniagua Pérez 1989).

The ability to display silver tablewares during meals was an important part of social relations. The display of tablewares has been of considerable concern to archaeologists of the Spanish colonies, and Deagan has proposed that such socially visible items would be "conservative" and Spanish in their style and can also be associated with males (Deagan 1983:271). The "Spanish" style, or at least a clear European influence on the decoration of such wares, is evident in the silver items that have survived from the colonial period. These display the geometry and decorative styles advocated in Renaissance pattern books by Vignola, Bramante, and particularly Serlio (Paniagua Pérez 1989:143). These pattern books were intended for the design of architecture and were influential in the decoration of building facades in the audiencia of Quito. Both the architectural facades and the silver tableware of elite Cuenca houses may thus have expressed a "conservatism" of design in imitating the pattern books of Europe, which would have been an important factor in reinforcing colonial social relationships through material culture.

This conservatism is not the entire picture of the symbolic role of silver tableware in the Cuenca household. In several of the late-seventeenth-century inventories there is an entry marked as a silver *totuma* (a large gourd cup/bowl) (Alcedo 1967 [1786]:367) and in the late eighteenth century inventories of several examples of *mates* (gourd vessels for tea) encased in silver filigree with silver straws are listed (Jamieson 1996:273). The gourd vessel known as a *mate*, and the *yerba de mate*, or "Paraguay tea," that was served in the gourd, both came from the province of Mate in Paraguay. This was a popular colonial drink throughout the Andes, served at all hours. The social distinctions drawn from the tea ceremony of mate is clear. "There is no house, poor or rich, where there is not always *mate* on the table, and it is nothing short of amazing to see the luxury spent by women on *mate* utensils" (Alcedo 1967 [1786]:330). "People of distinction" used a *bombilla*, or tea straw, with a filter that was made of silver or gold (Alcedo 1967 [1786]:274).

Ten "coconuts for drinking chocolate from the coast," along with nine chocolate frothing sticks, are listed in Luisa Maldonado de San Juan's urban house (Jamieson 1996:273). Chocolate or cacao (*Theobroma cacao*), a Mesoamerican domesticate, was reported growing wild on the Ecuadorian coast at the time of the Spanish conquest and was being cultivated on the Ecuadorian coast and on the eastern Andean slopes by the 1570s. By 1617 cacao was being grown on a large scale on the coast and exported from Guayaquil to Peru and to New Spain, even though export to New Spain was technically illegal after 1634 (Estrella 1988:263; Jiménez de la Espada 1965, 2:338, León Borja and Nagy 1964:4-8).

Bernabe Cobo (1964 [1653]:258) described the great popularity of chocolate as a drink that was served to guests in the seventeenth-century Andes. In the house of Pedro Ortiz Dávila chocolate was grated on a silver grater and served from a "silver pot with lid." In the Maldonado de San Juan house the chocolate was served out of coconuts (Jamieson 1996:274). Coconuts in medieval Europe were extremely rare and were mounted in precious metals like silver to use as goblets, reliquaries, and other types of containers. By the 1520s, however, the coconut could be bought cheaply in Europe and the New World (Levenson 1991:128-129). The practice of mounting items like gourds and coconuts in silver was common in seventeenth-century Cuenca, and Ortiz Dávila also owned a *caracol*, or seashell set in silver (ANHC L.520 f. 610v). This, combined with the serving of herbal mate and chocolate at the elite table when guests were entertained, suggests that tablewares were not entirely about social conservatism on the part of Spaniards. Tablewares also represented the appropriation of

New World objects and social customs, and their introduction into the daily practice of seventeenth-century households.

Another aspect of the silver tablewares of Cuenca was their role in the Renaissance ideology of individualism. Several inventories listed multiple small silver plates (Jamieson 1996: 274). As with pewter in the late seventeenth-century English colonies (Beaudry et al. 1988:56), silver plates in the Andes appear to have been one of the first uses of individual tablewares for each guest.

Personal cutlery was another important indicator of this growth of individualism. By the late eighteenth century in Buenos Aires the place setting on a table usually consisted of a plate, fork, and spoon, while a "complete" place setting was more rare, and included a knife (Porro et al. 1982:27). Not everyone, even among the elite, used complete place settings in the period; some people thought that the fork was a bit affected, and that the fingers served quite well even at a polite dinner table (Porro et al. 1982:26). In the inventories from Cuenca there is no mention of individual place settings, even in the late eighteenth century. In the most elite house, that of Pedro Ortiz Dávila, there are 25 silver spoons, 15 silver forks, and a boxed set of 7 knives listed. This is far from sufficient cutlery to serve as individual sets for each guest who might have sat on Ortiz Dávila's 71 chairs. The occurrence of such sets in the late seventeenth century is interesting, but this is the only inventory with more than three of any given piece of cutlery. We can only conclude that such individual cutlery may have been standard for the most elite sector of colonial Andean society even in the seventeenth century, but even in wealthy Cuenca households it was not considered necessary.

Imported glass was another important part of elite consumption in seventeenth-century Cuenca, but may not have been a part of the tableware at meals. Pedro Ortiz Dávila owned three large glass bottles with silver mouths for making wine, and in his study he kept a set of 11 glasses, and a set of 2 large glass bottles in a locked box. Sebastiana de Rojas had six glass bottles in her house, two of which were in a box designed to hold them (Jamieson 1996:275). The lack of drinking glasses in any of the other inventories suggests that, as in the English colonies up until the 1690s (Beaudry et al. 1988:56), most elite households had only a few drinking vessels that would have been used communally by guests. This is a practice which continues into the present in many Andean rural households.

An inventory of a retail shop from 1709 gives a picture of the glassware available to Cuencanos by the beginning of the eighteenth century. This included regular drinking glasses; cruets or handled bottles, large and small squat flasks, canisters or jars, flasks, and large jars. By the late eighteenth century drinking glasses and glass bottles had gained much more popularity and were present even in more modest homes in Cuenca (Jamieson 1996:275).

All colonial period glassware was handblown, and although industrially produced glass postdating Independence was common in excavations, handblown glass of possible colonial date was extremely rare in Cuenca archaeological contexts. There was no handblown glass recovered from any rural contexts, and no glassware has so far been noted in colonial inventories of rural houses. This suggests that imported glassware was limited to urban households in the colonial period. A small fragment of a handblown colorless stemmed drinking glass was recovered from an urban context. Two handblown glass tumbler rims were recovered from urban excavations, one of them a Bohemian-style soda-glass tumbler with wheel-engraved decoration (Jones and Sullivan 1989:56). Such wheel-engraved tumblers were common throughout the Spanish empire in the early to mid-eighteenth century and were made in Western Europe as well as at Puebla in Mexico (Deagan 1987:146; McNally 1982:47). As early as 1672 Pedro Ortiz Dávila had glassware from Lima in his house (ANHC L.520 f.612v). Glass "from Lima" was actually manufactured in the Ica Valley of Peru. Glass production in Ica was in place by the first decades of the seventeenth century on several wine haciendas that had imported specialized slaves from Seville who knew the art of glass-making. At first sand for glass had to be imported from Panama. By 1746 all of the Ica glassworks had been bought up by one man, and in 1752 the Jesuits bought out the monopoly. The Crown in turn took over the monopoly at the time of the Jesuit expulsion in 1767. In 1803 the Ica glassworks finally closed (Ramos 1989).

# CERAMICS

Ceramics are rarely mentioned in inventories from colonial houses in Cuenca, and yet ceramics dominated both the rural and urban excavated artifact assemblages, as is the case at most Spanish colonial archaeological sites. The classification of ceramics recovered from Spanish colonial archaeological sites by North American archaeologists has relied on a typological approach in which "The types have traditionally been based upon combinations of attributes of paste group and color, surface treatment and decorative motifs" (Deagan 1987:25–26). Within the tin-glazed earthenwares, or majolicas, the group categories in standard use are based on John Goggin's (1968) magisterial summary of Caribbean basin majolicas. The usual practice within each "type is to then briefly list the vessel forms that are present for that 'type'" (Ewen 1991:60–68). This system is useful in providing an idea of trade patterns and source regions for ceramics on Caribbean sites, where wide varieties of majolicas from Europe and the Americas are often encountered within one context.

I have followed this methodology to a certain extent, having divided the excavated ceramics from Cuenca initially into paste groups. Vessel shape and decoration, particularly for the locally produced Cuenca majolicas, are described in order to study the uses of different vessels and their role within the colonial household. It is very useful to look at the "emic" or "folk" classifications of the ceramics that were used in the colonial Andes in order to look at the role of ceramics in the colonial Cuenca household. The comparison of ceramic terms in notarial records to the excavated materials can be a useful exercise for revealing the relationships between social relations, ideology, and ceramic material culture.

There are several aspects of the use of ceramics in Spanish colonial households that have been previously considered by archaeologists. There is a general belief, as outlined above, that socially visible areas of the household, such as the ceramics used on the dining table, demonstrated a "conservative" maintenance of Spanish values through material culture. Cooking wares were more associated with less visible areas of Spanish-Indian "acculturation" and "syncretism" (Deagan 1983:271; Ewen 1991:105). There are also gender-based arguments, as outlined above, suggesting that the "socially conservative" tablewares in many communities were associated with males and with elite Spanish women when they were present, while cooking wares were the domain of female Native people (Deagan 1983:271; McEwan 1991:34, 39). In order to look at how these relationships can be revealed through the ceramics of colonial Cuenca, we must understand how Cuencanos perceived different categories of ceramics.

In the colonial Andes there was a basic division of ceramics into *barro* or *barro de la tierra*, referring to earthenwares, and *loza*, referring to fine imported wares. Loza was a very general category, and could refer to *loza de China*, or porcelain, but also to finely made majolica earthenwares, usually imported from Europe. Beginning in the late eighteenth century loza could also refer to the refined white earthenwares made in the industrial factories of Europe (Porro et al. 1982:16). I have divided my analysis into much finer-grained paste groups, and I will begin with the coarse earthenwares that would have made up the barro of colonial Cuenca.

## Unglazed Earthenwares

Locally produced and unglazed coarse earthenwares, often termed "colono-ware" by Spanish colonial archaeologists, usually make up the largest part of the ceramic assemblage at Spanish colonial sites. These unglazed sherds are generally thought to represent cooking vessels. In sixteenth-century contexts at Puerto Real, Haiti, over 60% of the ceramics were plain coarse earthenwares, and the majority of these were bowl forms with external hearth blackening. In seventeenth-century contexts at St. Augustine, Florida, 41% to 66% of the ceramics were found to have been made by local Native American potters to supply the kitchens of the town (Ewen 1991; King 1984; Smith 1995).

The presence of Native American ceramics in such large quantities on Spanish colonial sites, and the absence of Spanish ceramic forms associated with cooking vessels, has been taken as evidence that the cooking vessels of the Spanish New World were dominated by Native American forms (McEwan 1992:104). The inventories of houses in colonial Cuenca suggest another reason for the absence of Spanish-style ceramic cooking vessels; the use of metal vessels, including copper and bronze braziers, *peroles* (half-sphere shaped vessels for frying), *sartenes* (frying pans), and *ollas* (pots). All of these vessels were commonly used for cooking food in the colonial Cuenca house (Jamieson 1996:281). The use of metal cooking vessels was also common in sixteenth-century Spain (McEwan 1992:97), but easier access to metals in the Andes may have made metal cooking vessels the norm in many colonial Andean households.

Metal vessels played a significant role in cooking, but unglazed coarse earthenwares were also common in the colonial house and were present in every excavated context in Cuenca. Such ceramics were of little economic value in the colonial Andes and were, therefore, very rarely mentioned in household inventories. The only mention of such ceramics from Cuenca found so far is the inventory of Francisca Cusco, a Native Andean woman who lived in the Todos Santos neighborhood. Her 1730 inventory included five ceramic vessels, two of them *guallos* (?) valued at 1 real each, and three ollas, or wide-mouthed jars. (I use the term olla throughout this chapter to refer to any independent-restricted vessel.)

Excavations revealed considerable quantities of unglazed ceramics at all of the domestic sites in the Cuenca region. At the rural sites unglazed earthenware sherds made up 64% of the assemblage. These sherds were plain (36%), red slipped (20%), or slipped in other colors such as tan, orange, and brown through black (9%). Vessel forms included ollas (Figure 28) with rim diameters ranging widely from 2 to 18 centimeters. *Plato hondo*, literally meaning deep plate, forms had rim diameters tightly clustered at 16 to 18 centimeters. The rim is a simple unrestricted form with an exterior thickened lip, and straight to slightly incurved walls, often with a sharp interior angle close to the point where the rim meets the base. *Lebrillo* forms, a simple unrestricted vessel with an exterior thickened lip, had rim diameters of 12 to 24 centimeters. The vessel walls are less steeply flared than the plato hondo and are straight. The ollas were largely made of coarse earthenwares with visible temper, while both the plato hondo and the lebrillo form were wheel-thrown, and usually made of a more compact earthenware with finer temper.

From the excavation unit at the Inka and colonial site of Pumapungo 68% of the sherds were unglazed, but most of these (49% of the collection) were very likely prehistoric. Those thought to be colonial in date included lebrillo and olla forms, unglazed or with monochrome slips.

At the urban sites unglazed sherds made up the majority (71%) of the collection. Many of these were undecorated (40% of the collection), while decoration included red slip (25%) and other monochrome slips in cream, gray, orange, brown, or black (7%). Unglazed forms included ollas with

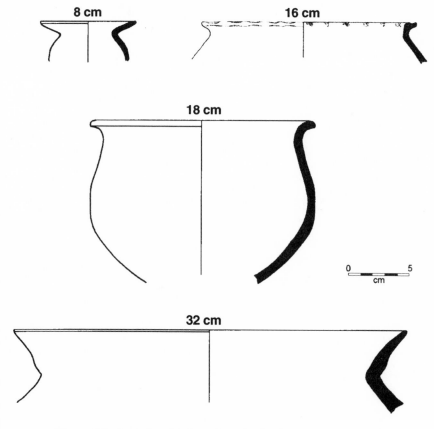

**Figure 28.** Examples of independent restricted vessel form, or olla.

rim diameters of 3 to 32 centimeters. Two *pocillos* had rim diameters of 6 and 8 centimeters. I have used the term *pocillo* to refer to straight-sided or slightly everted rims with exterior thickened lips and small (<10 cm) rim diameters (Figure 29). *Pozuelo,* or *pocillo,* was the Mexican term for a small, handleless cup with a ring foot, a vessel form introduced from China (Lister and Lister 1976:75). A single plato hondo rim and one bowl rim with a thickened exterior lip and a rim diameter of 30 centimeters were also encountered. Unglazed bowls (Figure 30) most commonly had square lips, although some had plain rims and one had a thickened exterior rim.

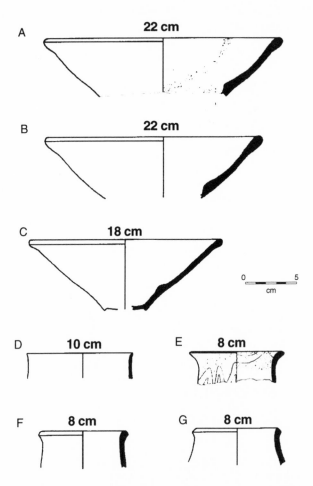

**Figure 29.** Examples of the plato hondo form (A to C) and the pocillo form (D to G).

**Figure 30.** Unglazed seventeenth-century bowls.

Within this collection of urban ceramics the unglazed sherds from the only sealed colonial context provide a unique opportunity to look at a seventeenth-century Cuenca ceramic sample. Apart from the Inkaic material described above, the unglazed locally made sherds within this sample included no examples of the finer-grade wheel-turned earthenwares, suggesting that this paste was not produced in Cuenca in the seventeenth century. All the remaining unglazed ceramics were coarse earthenwares, most of them plain, but some with red or brown slip. Forms included bowls with square or plain lips (Figures 30 and 31) with rim diameters of 16 to 30 centimeters, and ollas with rim diameters of 8 to 22 centimeters (Figure 28).

These excavated collections show that two different industries of unglazed ceramics existed in colonial Cuenca. The first were the finer wheel-thrown earthenwares. The traditional Spanish plato and lebrillo forms were commonly made of this paste. These vessel forms were more commonly majolica glazed, as described below, but were occasionally seen unglazed. Such vessels were introduced by the Spanish and were probably manufactured within the town of Cuenca. The lack of these vessels in the seventeenth-century urban context suggests that they were introduced into Cuenca sometime after the late seventeenth century.

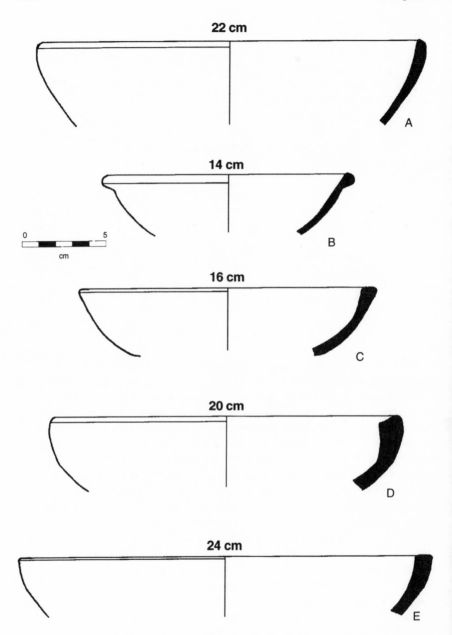

**Figure 31.** Examples of bowl forms.

The majority of the unglazed colonial ceramics were executed in coarse earthenware paste and consisted in large part of the ubiquitous olla of the Spanish colonial world. These were hand-formed rather than wheel-turned and were the "colono-ware" of the Andes, made in rural villages by Native Andean potters who continued the pre-Hispanic art of hand-crafted Andean ceramics.

These Native Andean unglazed ceramics fulfilled several roles in the colonial household. The most important was their use as cooking vessels. Taking all of the unglazed and unslipped ceramics recovered from all excavations as a group, 41% of the sherds show evidence of hearth blackening. In contrast 18% of the slipped sherds recovered were hearth blackened. This difference between unslipped and slipped ceramics is reinforced when we examine the unglazed sherds recovered from the only sealed seventeenth-century urban context. Plain sherds of coarse earthenwares dominated the ceramics from this context, and over half of them were hearth blackened. This suggests that when metal vessels were not used, plain unslipped coarse earthenwares were important cooking vessels. From the archaeological evidence plain coarse earthenwares, the majority of them in the form of independent restricted jars, made up the majority of the cooking vessels in the colonial Cuenca household.

Red-slipped coarse earthenwares made up 15% of the total sherds from the seventeenth-century context, and only a few were hearth blackened. Most of the slipped sherds found on Cuenca sites were red-slipped, and red-slipped coarse earthenwares were usually found in abundance in excavated colonial period ceramic collections throughout the Andes. Excavations at the Santo Domingo monastery and other colonial sites in Quito revealed earthenwares with a red, highly polished slip (Buys and Camino 1991). Similar "thick, dark red, lustrous slip" is reported for excavated colonial contexts at the Osambela house in Lima, Peru. The vessel forms were small and undecorated narrow-necked bottles, and small jars with flat bases (Flores Espinoza et al. 1981:37). These small vessels sound similar to vessels recovered in Cuenca. Winery excavations in the Moquegua Valley in southern Peru also included red-slipped earthenwares, most of them "diminutive bowls, cups or vases," but these made up a very small proportion of the overall ceramic assemblage (Smith 1991:262, 272–304). The most common category of ceramics excavated at the town of Santa Fe la Vieja in Argentina, occupied from 1573 to 1670, were slipped in a "ruddy chestnut red, waxy red, or chestnut" (Ceruti 1983b:497). The vessel forms from Santa Fe la Vieja included "local" convex- or conical-shaped bases, but the majority of these red slipped vessels were "European forms," including deep plates, pitchers, and large and small jars. In most cases these were not made on a potter's wheel. Ceruti (1983b:498) reports that similar red slipped material with indigenous manufacturing techniques predominated on several excavated Jesuit mission sites dating from the mid-sixteenth to mid-seventeenth centuries in Brazil. "Lustrous red-slipped finewares" were also recovered in considerable quantities in several contexts in Pacific ports and trade centers in Panama, and eighteenth-century reports of the importation of "Peruvian" ceramics into Panama suggests that these red-slipped wares were imported into Panama from Andean production centers (Rovira 1984:290).

Similarities in paste and vessel form between the plain coarse earthenwares and the slipped earthenwares excavated in Cuenca suggest that they were both made using similar technologies. Native Andeans in villages throughout the region manufactured ceramics. In the Native Andean village of Azogues (25 km north of Cuenca) in the late sixteenth century there was Native Andean ceramic production of "large jars, jars, pots, pitchers and other vessels" for both Spanish and Native Andean markets (Gallegos 1965 [1582]:278). The ceramic production in Azogues was said to date to Inka times, when the Inka moved ceramic specialists there. In the eighteenth century the Native Andean villages of Pujilí and Saquisilí, west of the town of Latacunga, were famous for the production of "large jars, jars, pitchers, etc.," which were exported throughout the province of Quito. Ceramics are still made in Pujilí today (Juan and Ulloa 1978 [1748]:1:423; Litto 1976:100–103). An inventory from the Todos Santos neighborhood in Cuenca from 1702 included "a wooden stand for jars with two jars from Pujilí" (ANHC L.533 f.111v). Despite the two hundred kilometer distance from Cuenca to Pujilí, the ceramics of the village were exported to Cuenca in the eighteenth century.

What role did these slipped wares play in the colonial household? The standard Andean drinking water storage vessel in the eighteenth century was the *tinaja de barro encarnado*, or large earthenware jar with red decoration (Alcedo 1967 [1786]:364). These water storage vessels are listed in several colonial urban houses, usually in wooden cabinets. A tinaja was placed in the bottom section of the cabinet, and two pumice stone filters were placed in the upper section. Water flowed through the stones for filtration and was stored in the large pottery jar in the bottom section for drinking. This was common in households throughout the colonial Andes (Porro et al. 1982:236), and an illustration of one is provided by Edward Whymper (1892:95). Olaf Holm (1970:268) reports that they were still used in the twentieth century on the Ecuadorian coast.

Large ceramic vessels were used for a variety of other purposes in the colonial period, including the use of large tinajas to catch the syrup from sugar cane processing at lowland sugar plantations. Holm described and illustrated a wide variety of large colonial jars and pitchers in Ecuadorian museum collections with a "thick, dark red slip, like oxblood, and thick enough to frequently be crazed" (1970:276, my translation). Many of the examples that Holm described are housed in the Central Bank Museum in Cuenca (Idrovo Urigüen 1990:26–36).

Vessels similar to the red-slipped "diminutive bowls, cups or vases" reported by Smith (1991:262) at the Moquegua winery sites have also been recovered from Cuenca in the form of thin-walled (<4 mm) sherds and a few small-diameter rims. These vessels may have served various functions as kitchen and/or tablewares in the colonial household.

In general, coarse unglazed earthenwares make up a large proportion of the ceramic vessels used in colonial Cuenca, and their use was not restricted to cooking vessels. Excavated data from Cuenca are too limited to state whether significant differences in the use of such unglazed wares occurred between Native Andean or Spanish households, and whether wealth was a significant factor in differential use of such Native Andean ceramic products. A significant proportion of red-slipped coarse earthenware bowls and other vessels were recovered from the only sealed seventeenth-century context excavated so far. The location of this context just off the main plaza of Cuenca suggests that in the seventeenth-century the elite of the city used such vessels extensively.

The entire question of the use of unglazed ceramics created by Native potters is very different in Cuenca than in the St. Augustine situation. The ceramic production of towns such as Pujilí and Azogues was in the hands of Native Andean potters, but they were creating vessels that were sold in public markets throughout the audiencia and were thus supplying goods to the formal economy. Some of the unglazed coarse earthenware vessels excavated at elite houses in Cuenca may have been produced in the villages of the native Andean mitayos who cooked with them. A large percentage of these "colono-wares" were, however, a part of the formal economy, transported over long distances and used by people, whether African slaves, Native mitayos, or creole vecinos, who held a very different social position in the colonial world than the manufacturers of the vessels.

## Olive Jars (Botijas) and Tinajas

The Mediterranean tradition of the amphora was carried throughout the Spanish Empire, with the use of thick-walled and roughly made ceramic vessels with very narrow necks and round or pointed bottoms. These are now known to North American researchers as "olive jars" because olive oil was one of the main products transported in them (Goggin 1960). These vessels were used to store and transport a vast variety of liquid and solid materials, including wine, cane alcohol, olive oil, grease, and water (Alcedo

184                                                                    Chapter 6

1967 [1786]:275; Porro et al. 1982:135). In the Spanish colonies the vessels
were known as *botijas, botijas peruleras,* and *botijuelas.* Olive jar sherds are
found on sites throughout the Spanish colonies, and the changes in their
sizes and shapes have been used to provide chronological markers for
Spanish colonial archaeology (Deagan 1987:30–35; Goggin 1960; Marken
1994:49). In general the sherds are recovered in more abundance from
seventeenth-century contexts (Deagan 1987:31), such as the domestic contexts of St. Augustine, Florida, where 21% to 42% of the seventeenth-
century assemblage was made up of olive jar sherds (King 1984:77). In
eighteenth-century contexts at St. Augustine only 4% to 7% of the assemblage was made up of olive jar sherds (Deagan 1983:77). Sixteenth-century
contexts at Puerto Real in Haiti had between 10% and 18% of the ceramic
collection made up of olive jar sherds (Deagan 1995c:441).

Closely associated with the botija was the tinaja. The term tinaja
refers to any large jar with a much wider mouth than the botija. Both
vessel forms were produced in Spain with an identical paste (Marken
1994:182–183), making the differentiation of body sherds between botijas
and tinajas impossible. The paste of olive jars made in Spain is quite
distinctive, and excavations in Cuenca recovered only 21 olive jar sherds
with the typical Spanish paste. Two of these sherds were redeposited in
later contexts, but all 19 other sherds were in the sealed seventeenth-
century urban context, making up 14% of the ceramics from this layer.
Eleven of the sherds had a white "film" on the exterior, a typical feature
of Spanish olive jars that may not be a deliberately applied slip, but a
chemical change from the firing process (Deagan 1987:30–35; James
1988:51). Ten of the sherds had a plain exterior surface. The predomi-
nance of the sherds in the seventeenth-century context demonstrates that
they were commonly imported to Cuenca at that time, but they are entirely absent in later contexts.

An extensive collection of olive jars is housed in the Central Bank
Museum in Cuenca (Idrovo Urigüen 1990:31–33), but the majority of these
vessels are made of a coarse earthenware paste very different from the
typical paste used in Spain for olive jar production. This has been previously noted, with the suggestion that the vessels may have come from
Peru (Buys 1992). Over 200,000 bottles of wine were exported annually in
the 1630s from southern Peruvian ports like Pisco, Nasca, and Ica through
the port of Lima, to send to Panama, Nicaragua, Quito, Loja, Cuenca, and
other provinces (Holm 1970:271; Vázquez de Espinosa 1969 [1630]:310).
The wine was stored and transported in olive jars, which were manufactured in kilns associated with the wineries throughout the colonial period.
Olive jars were manufactured in the wine-growing southern valleys of
Peru from at least the early seventeenth century if not earlier, and the

kilns used to fire these large vessels are still visible on the landscape (Rice 1994; Rice and Van Beck 1993). Olive jars manufactured on the winery properties were one of the most common finds at the Moquegua winery excavations in Peru (Smith 1991:96-97). They had a coarse, reddish-brown paste (Smith 1991:268) very different from the paste of the botijas manufactured in Spain and consistent with the paste of the olive jars in the Central Bank Museum in Cuenca. It seems likely that large quantities of olive jars from the southern Peruvian wine regions were transported to Cuenca from the seventeenth century onward, but the excavated seventeenth-century Cuenca examples were from Spain.

In colonial Cuenca the tinaja and botija were closely associated and were used for the storage and transport of a variety of liquids. At colonial lowland cane alcohol distilleries near Cuenca botijas were used to store the finished cane alcohol, while tinajas were used to collect the cane syrup from which the alcohol was distilled. Sebastiana de Rojas had four tinajas and four botijas in her house in Cuenca in 1683 for the purpose of making chicha (ANHC L.528 f.43v). The brewing of chicha, or corn beer, was a universal practice usually associated with women in the pre-Hispanic Andes (Rowe 1946:292) and remains common in rural areas today. In the eighteenth-century Andes chicha was defined as the "common drink of Indians and people of color, made of various fruits" (Alcedo 1967 [1786]:290). This raises an interesting question about the relationship between ethnicity and ceramics, in the sense that purely Spanish style botijas and tinajas may very well have been used for a uniquely Andean practice in the colonial household. It is also interesting to note that Sebastiana de Rojas, whose will the ceramics appeared in, was a vecina and she willed the pots (along with a house) to Maria de Mendoza, also identified as a vecina. There is little doubt that the majority of vecinos in seventeenth-century Cuenca were in some sense ethnically mestizo, and these women were passing on a practice from their Andean ancestors, although they used what are described as Spanish-style ceramics for the brewing.

## Cuenca Lead-Glazed Ceramics

Ceramics with lead glazes were produced both in Spain and at New World sites throughout the history of the Spanish colonies. This process involved dipping bisque-fired pots into a mixture of pulverized quartz sand, clay, and crushed lead oxide for clear lead glaze, and adding copper, iron, or manganese for green, amber, or brown hues (Lister and Lister 1987:54-55). Several of the early colonial lead-glazed ceramic types from the Caribbean basin have been defined in detail, but the characteristics and production areas among the many Spanish colonial lead-glazed wares are still poorly identified (Deagan 1987:47–53; Marken 1994:194–198). In the Andean region lead-glazed pieces have been reported from Moquegua, Peru, with brown, green, and clear glazes, usually in the form of small bowls and ollas (Smith 1991:258–259).

Lead-glazed ceramics at the two rural sites near Cuenca made up 4% of the rural ceramic collection. All rural lead-glazed ceramics were executed on the finer earthenware paste, and glaze colors included brown, green, and clear. Lead-glazed sherds were rare (1% of total sherds) at Pumapungo, but appeared in both brown and green.

Lead-glazed sherds made up 5% of the ceramic assemblage recovered from the urban contexts. Of these the majority were on fine earthenware wheel-turned vessels and included brown, green, dark green, and clear glazes. A few coarse earthenware with brown or dark green lead glazes were recovered. Lead-glazed vessels from the urban contexts included ollas, a plain lipped bowl, and a pocillo. One rim sherd with green lead-glazed interior and gray slipped exterior appears to be an example of the Spanish bacín vessel form, or chamber pot. The bacín has vertical walls with a sharply everted rim. This is the typical form of the Spanish chamber pot, a form that was frequently glazed in utilitarian green lead glaze (Deagan 1987:48–50; Lister and Lister 1976:22; Marken 1994:161).

Most of the lead-glazed sherds were executed on the finer earthenware paste and were wheel-thrown. The paste is identical to that of the local majolica sherds described below, suggesting that ceramic specialists within the city of Cuenca made these vessels. The lead-glazed sherds from all excavated contexts included only 20% with hearth blackening. This suggests that some lead-glazed vessels were used for cooking, while most were not. The vessel forms are widely varying considering the small size of the ceramic sample, suggesting that lead-glazed ceramics fulfilled a wide variety of roles in the colonial Cuenca house.

## Majolica Importation to the Andes

The production of tin-glazed ceramics was developed in Europe in the thirteenth century, with the addition of tin oxide to lead glazes, creating an opaque white glaze. Mineral solutions painted on top of the tin glaze before firing would fuse into the glaze, creating polychrome glazed ceramics, which in the Spanish world became known as majolicas (Lister and Lister 1974:17–18). Majolica ceramics were one of the elite tablewares of the Spanish colonial world, and a wide variety of majolica ceramics were imported to the Spanish New World colonies from Spain and Italy (Deagan 1987:53–71). Several production centers for majolica were also set up throughout Mexico and Central America during the Spanish colonial period (Deagan 1987:71–93).

In the Andes it is rare to encounter European or Mexican majolica sherds in excavated contexts. One document for Mexican majolica made in Puebla for export to Peru is known, in which Puebla wares were exported in exchange for raw tin (Goggin 1968:215), but this is only a single transaction. In excavations at the Moquegua wineries a tiny percentage of the excavated ceramics consisted of Valle, faience, and Sevilla wares from Europe and Mexico (Smith 1991:252–322). The "minor role" of Old World ceramics in the Moquegua assemblage was noted as "dramatically different" from the importance of Old World majolicas in Caribbean basin colonial sites (Smith 1991:307).

The only production center outside the Andean region that provided large quantities of majolica ceramics to the Andean colonies was Panama. This was because Panama, as part of the viceroyalty of Peru, could legally provide locally produced goods for other cities in the viceroyalty. Trade in locally produced products between the viceroyalty of New Spain and that of Peru was illegal throughout most of the colonial period (Lister and Lister 1987:340 n.82). The town of Panama la Vieja ("Old Panama"), on the Pacific coast of what is now the nation of Panama, was founded in 1519. Ceramic production in this location began sometime in the mid- to late-sixteenth century and ended abruptly in 1671 when the English privateer Henry Morgan sacked and burned the city (Lister and Lister 1974:44–47; Long 1964:104; Deagan 1987:24).

John Goggin and George Long excavated two kilns and three domestic contexts at Panama la Vieja in the early 1960s and have defined the distinctive colonial ceramics produced there (Long 1964). Green lead-glazed sherds were produced at Panama la Vieja from the late sixteenth century onward and can be recognized by the "distinctive Panama paste, which is a dark brick red containing mineral temper" (Deagan 1987:48, 91). From approximately 1575 to 1650 "Panama Plain" majolicas were produced using this same paste. These consisted of a "thick enamel, which has a greenish tint, variable thickness, and tendency to exhibit numerous imperfections, including crazing, pinholing, crawling, and bare spots" (Deagan 1987:92). "Panama Blue on White," built from the same paste, has "a pale cobalt blue on an off-white background enamel" (Deagan 1987:92), while "Panama Polychromes" consisted of the same paste, with a white to pale green background glaze and decoration in black, green, and blue (Long 1964:107). The polychromes were concentrated in the upper levels of the site and are therefore thought to date to the latter part of the occupation of the city, perhaps 1600–71. The presence of several pieces of "Panama plain" and "blue-on-white" on the 1622 *Nuestra Señors de Atocha* wreck in the Florida Keys (Marken 1994:231–232), and the absence of Panama polychrome suggests that Panama polychromes may not yet have been available as late as the 1620s. With the sacking of the city in 1671 the population was moved to the current location of Panama City. Excavations there have revealed typical Panama majolicas in a 1670s context, which were replaced by French faience in the later seventeenth-century contexts, confirming that the Panamanian majolica industry ended in the 1670s with the destruction of Panama la Vieja (Rovira 1984:286–287).

Panama majolicas have been found in various colonial contexts in Andean South America. Panama polychrome sherds were first recognized in South American contexts by John Goggin based on sherds recovered by G.H.S. Bushnell and Edwin Ferdon on the Santa Elena peninsula in Ecuador (Goggin 1968:48). The early colonial levels excavated at the Casa de Osambela in Lima had majolicas with a reddish fine paste and no visible temper, with white to greenish-white tin-glaze covering the entire vessel, and another group with the same paste and green lead-glaze covering the vessel. Vessel forms were most popularly plates with annular ring bases, small curved-walled bowls, deep plates with concave bases, and small bowls with angular sides (escudillas) (Flores Espinoza et al. 1981:40–42). At the Santo Domingo monastery excavations in Quito blue-on-white majolicas with a thick glaze and a dark paste were recovered (Buys and Camino 1991). This is very likely Panama blue-on-white, although they were not identified as such.

The only problem in positively identifying sherds made in Panama is that some or all of them may in fact have been produced in Lima, Peru. John Goggin (1968:165) first suggested this possibility, as majolica is known from documents to have been produced in Lima with a distinctive red paste. The excavations of the Osambela house in Lima uncovered considerable quantities of this majolica. In personally comparing these ceramics to a surface collection from Panama la Vieja, Isabel Flores Espinoza et al. (1981:52) state that the polychrome majolicas from Lima are "exactly the same" as the Panamanian sherds "except in the color of the paste." Unfortunately, they do not describe how the pastes differ. With the current published evidence it seems likely that similar polychrome majolicas were produced in Lima and Panama la Vieja in the seventeenth century, but that the pastes were somewhat different.

Some attempt has been made to use physical techniques to discover the sources of Panamanian and South American majolica ceramics. A dozen samples of Panama polychrome recovered from several sites in Panama have been analyzed using gamma-ray-induced thermoluminescence, and all had a consistent thermoluminescence curve that was distinct from samples from Puebla, Mexico, and Spain (Vaz and Cruxent 1978:290). Neutron activation analysis has been used to compare majolica sherds from Panama la Vieja, Cuzco, Peru, and Quito, Ecuador. The results showed that each of the three locations had a distinct signature, suggesting that each set of sherds was from a separate clay source (Olin et al. 1978:224–227). None of the sherds in any of these physical studies is from a well-dated excavated context in the Andes, which makes it difficult to characterize how representative they are. In order to undertake a serious study of majolica trade for western South America in the Spanish colonial period, a large sample of excavated sherds from various colonial centers in Panama and western South America needs to be assembled for physical comparison of the pastes.

In the Cuenca excavations a total of 33 sherds composed of the typical Panama paste were recovered (Figure 32). These sherds were found only at the two urban sites. The highest concentration of these sherds was in the sealed seventeenth-century context, where they made up 4% of the ceramic assemblage. No locally made Cuenca majolicas occurred in this context, and the Panama majolica sherds present are the key evidence that these levels are indeed a sealed seventeenth-century context. The restriction of Panamanian ceramics to the urban sites confirms that they were high status items and therefore only present at the urban houses of the elite.

The recovered Panamanian majolica sherds included five plain body sherds and one body sherd with a thin cream slip or wash on the exterior.

**Figure 32.** Panamanian majolica sherds.

Lead-glazed Panamanian wares included one body sherd with brown lead glaze, and four sherds with green lead glaze one of which may be a pocillo rim. The 21 tin-glazed Panamanian sherds with typical thick cream to greenish-cream colored glaze of "Panama Plain" (Deagan 1987:92) included six independent restricted rim sherds. There were also four sherds with Panama blue-on-white glaze, two of which were independent restricted rim sherds. None of the Panamanian rim sherds were large enough to reconstruct vessel forms.

Panamanian majolicas were probably only used in elite urban houses, and the expense of shipping them from Panama and transporting them overland to Cuenca must have given them a higher economic value than locally produced wares. These vessels were used entirely as tablewares and items for display in more public rooms. The lack of locally produced majolicas in the seventeenth-century-excavated context suggests that Panamanian majolicas were the only tin-glazed wares available in early colonial Cuenca. It is possible, as Florence and Robert Lister suggest (1974:47–48), that the end of majolica production at Panama la Vieja in 1671 was the impetus for the expansion of local majolica manufacturing centers in the Andes. Majolica was already being produced in centers such as Quito, however, before Panama production ended (Buys 1992:32).

## Andean Majolicas

The production centers for colonial period majolicas in the Andes are very poorly understood by archaeologists. Florence and Robert Lister (1974:47–48) suggest that the earliest Andean majolica production occurred in the mid-eighteenth century, but it is now known that the Jesuits in Quito had set up a majolica production facility by 1635 (Buys 1992:32). The recovery of majolica sherds in association with Inka vessels and a late sixteenth-century coin in the vicinity of Quito suggests an even earlier date for initial majolica production in Quito (Fournier Garcia 1989:63). The most common majolicas recovered in excavations at the Santo Domingo monastery in Quito had a cream to greenish-cream background glaze with green decoration, the glazes being thin and poorly applied. Vessel forms included the plato hondo, bowl, lebrillo, and olla (Buys and Camino 1991).

The extensive excavation of wineries in the Moquegua Valley revealed two distinct majolica types. "Más Allá Polychrome" is described as a majolica with "cream to pale bluish-green" background glaze, and green and "purple to black" decoration. The paste was "fine-grained and dense, typically reddish-brown in color, with occasional calcite-like inclusions (less than 0.5 mm in diameter) and small voids." Vessel forms were most commonly plates and bowls, with some jars, cups, and a candleholder

(Smith 1991:253). "Escapalaque Polychrome" has a yellow background glaze on the same paste, with better coverage than the "Más Allá" background glaze. "Escapalaque" has black and green decoration over the yellow glaze, and vessel forms are "primarily bowls and plates, with one example of a brimmed plate and one tile fragment" (Smith 1991:256). Both of these types were only recovered from contexts dating after 1600 and were common by the late eighteenth century. Their initial date of introduction is, however, unclear.

## Cuenca Majolica

The date of the introduction of majolica ceramic production in Cuenca is still unknown. The earliest reference to a neighborhood where glazed ceramics were manufactured in Cuenca is from 1858, when Manuel Villavicencio described the Cuenca potter's district: "The main street continues through the pottery workshops, which produce the best *loza de barro* (glazed earthenware) in the republic for their delicacy, durability, glaze and manufacture" (1858:429, my translation). This production took place in both the San Sebastián parish and in the neighboring village of Sayausí (Villavicencio 1858:433). Ceramic production in San Sebastián continued well into the twentieth century in a neighborhood that became known as the Convención del 45 (Convention of the 45), named for the ceramicists union. It is only in the last twenty years that this neighborhood has ceased to be a focus of ceramic production (González Aguirre 1991:34; Idrovo Urigüen 1990:29). I have been unable to locate documentary evidence for majolica production in Cuenca in the colonial period, although Florence and Robert Lister (1974:47–48) suggest that such production began in Cuenca by the mid-eighteenth century.

Majolica sherds were recovered from all of the domestic excavations in Cuenca. At rural sites the most common glaze was a thin and unevenly applied cream-colored background glaze, with green and/or brown decoration (19% of the overall rural ceramics) (Figure 33). Vessel forms for the cream-colored glaze included plato hondo forms, bowls with plain rims, and ollas. The plato hondo was one of the most common majolica vessel forms in the Spanish colonial world. It came in a variety of forms, and the examples recovered in Cuenca (Figure 29) are annular ring-based and fairly deep, generally similar in form to the "small deep-brimmed plates" illustrated by John Goggin (1968:153, 162, 168). The plato hondo was intimately associated with tablewares in the Spanish colonial world (Ewen 1991:105). It represented the "growing custom of individual rather than communal dishes and served as an all-purpose eating vessel for liquids as well as solid foods" (Lister and Lister 1976:72).

**Figure 33.** Cuenca majolicas and Chinese export porcelain.

There were six lebrillo forms (Figure 29) recovered from rural contexts. These were small vessels, with rim diameters ranging from 16 to 22 centimeters. Their small size suggests the vessels may have been used as individual tablewares, similar to the recovered plato hondo vessels, rather than serving the function of washing or cooking basins, which would have generally been larger.

There were several majolica pocillos found at the rural sites, with 8-centimeter rim diameters. The shape of the pocillo was an imitation of Chinese porcelain teacups, and in Mexico is associated with the consumption of chocolate drinks (Lister and Lister 1976:73, 1987:236; Marken 1994:225-236).

Tin glaze was at a premium in the Cuenca majolica industry, and the glazes were not only thin and unevenly applied, but were usually only applied to one side of the vessel. In general open forms, such as unrestricted bowls, the plato hondo, and pocillo forms, were decorated only on the interior, while ollas and pitchers were glazed on the exterior of the body and the rim interiors. At the rural sites 63% of tin-glazed sherds were glazed on the interior only. This confirms the evidence from the rim forms in showing that open serving and tableware vessels dominated the cream-glazed majolica ceramic collection from the rural sites.

A second group of majolicas at the rural sites (3% of the rural collection) had a thicker, more evenly applied background glaze in a yellow through mustard color, with green and/or brown decoration. Diagnostic sherds with yellow glaze included two annular ring bases; unfortunately no rims were recovered. The vast majority of the yellow majolica sherds were only glazed on the interior, proving that most vessels were unrestricted tablewares.

Locally produced majolicas with a cream background glaze and green/ brown decoration made up 14% of the overall ceramic collection at the urban sites. The sample included 20 annular ring bases, 5 of which had measurable base diameters ranging from 6 to 7 centimeters, and were thus probably from plato hondo vessels. One of these was decorated on the interior with a corn plant executed in green and brown glaze on a cream glazed background. Two annular ring bases had diameters of 4 centimeters, suggesting they came from pocillo vessel forms. Rim forms included olla rims ranging in rim diameter from 12 to 18 centimeters, and bowl rims ranging from 16 to 22 centimeters in diameter. One large bowl rim with a square lip had a diameter of 38 centimeters. Large serving bowls, common in the Spanish colonies, were known as *poncheros* (punchbowls) (Marken 1994:149–150, 157–158). Other forms included plato hondo rims with diameters of 16 centimeters and lebrillo rims with diameters of 16 to 22 centimeters. Of the cream glazed majolicas at urban sites, 72% were interior glazed and thus represent open serving vessels or tablewares.

Local majolicas with yellow background glaze and green/brown decoration made up 2% of the urban ceramic collection. Vessel forms included only olla rims with rim diameters ranging from 12 to 16 centimeters. The urban yellow glazed majolicas were overwhelmingly glazed on the interior only, and were thus open serving vessels.

It is difficult to find documentary evidence of the role of the locally produced majolicas in the colonial Cuenca household. The lack of any mention of glazed ceramics in documentary sources reviewed so far gives the impression that they had very little economic value. In other areas of the Spanish colonial world majolica ceramics were used as tablewares and serving vessels, to be displayed conspicuously during meals. The occurrence of hearth blackening on Cuenca majolicas may shed some light on their role. At rural sites 20% of majolicas glazed only on the interior were hearth blackened, while only 5% of the majolicas with exterior glaze or glaze on both interior and exterior showed hearth blackening. At the urban sites this difference is even more striking, with 26% of interior glazed majolicas hearth blackened and only 3% of majolicas glazed on the exterior or both sides hearth blackened. This confirms that the main role of the majolicas was as tablewares, although unrestricted vessels were on occasion used as cooking vessels.

## Chinese Export Porcelain

The Manila galleon trade brought large quantities of Chinese porcelain to the Pacific coast of the Americas from 1573 onward (Deagan 1987:96), and porcelain on sixteenth-century Spanish colonial sites is an indication of the elite status of the occupants of the site (South 1988:36–37). By the eighteenth century, however, porcelains had been greatly devalued on the world market (Braudel 1981:186), with the result that eighteenth-century household inventories from places such as Soconusco, Mexico, list porcelains of equal or lesser value than some locally produced earthenwares (Gasco 1992:85). The minimal quantities of porcelain (always less than 1% of the ceramic assemblage) in eighteenth-century domestic contexts excavated at St. Augustine, Florida, does not in any way correlate to the economic status of households (Deagan 1983:236).

The main route for porcelains to reach Cuenca was through Guayaquil. Throughout the colonial period ships from Guayaquil carried cacao north to the Pacific ports of New Spain and returned with various products, including ceramics, perfumes, and spices from the Manila trade (Montufar y Fraso 1992 [1754]:362). Trade between the viceroyalties was generally frowned upon by the Crown, and the government of the audiencia of Quito in the seventeenth century was particularly concerned that trade with Acapulco would bring in silks and taffetas, which would destroy the Andean markets for domestic Quito textiles. Trade with New Spain was severely regulated, and it is very likely that porcelains would have been a part of the ongoing battle between legislation and smuggling in the Pacific coast trade (Phelan 1967:68).

Very little porcelain has been reported from archaeological contexts in Andean South America, although at Chucuito, Peru, on Lake Titicaca, "Sherds of Chinese porcelains . . . were encountered in rather surprising numbers" (Tschopik 1950:204). No details on the porcelains recovered in these excavations were given. Excavations at the wineries in the Moquegua Valley recovered "a handful of tiny fragments" of porcelain (Smith 1991:93). At the elite Osambela house in Lima, Peru, porcelain plates and "small cups," both with annular ring bases, were recovered, although no quantification of these artifacts is given. The blue decoration is described as "birds, flowers, and conventional designs" arranged "in horizontal bands bordered above and below with one or two parallel lines" (Flores Espinoza et al. 1981:43). Although these porcelains were not identified by the researchers and no illustrations of the vessels were published, the description is consistent with Ming "Kraakporcelain" vessels, commonly exported to the Spanish colonies between 1570 and 1640 (Deagan 1987:97-98). Excavations at the Santo Domingo monastery in Quito recovered only five sherds of porcelain, all of them underglaze blue-on-white, and identified as possibly seventeenth-century Ming wares (Buys 1992; Buys and Camino 1991).

Porcelain is mentioned in several Cuenca household inventories. In the late seventeenth century Sebastiana de Rojas had one porcelain plate in her house outside the city core. Diego Patino de Narvaes had two "*limetas preciosas de la china*" (precious China bottles/vases) and one "*porcelana grande de la china*" (large China porcelain) in his house in San Blas parish. In the mid- to late eighteenth-century porcelain still appears only as scattered pieces in household inventories. Captain Esteban Saenz de Viteri owned one porcelain *posuelo* (cup) at his urban house in 1746. Maria Avila, a vecina and widow, had two porcelain *jícaras* (cups) at her house outside the city core in 1781, and Juana Arcentales, an unmarried woman, had two *pozuelitos* (small cups) at her house in an unknown location in 1791 (Jamieson 1996:312).

In late eighteenth-century Buenos Aires pocillos were common in many houses and could be made of European *loza* (majolicas or refined white earthenwares), but the best quality *pocillos* were specified as "*china*" (porcelain), with a value of 6 reales (Porro et al. 1982:215). The *jícara* was a pre-Hispanic Mesoamerican term for a gourd used for drinking chocolate, but in the colonial period it became associated with the small handleless Chinese cups used for drinking chocolate and was synonymous with *pozuelo* (Lister and Lister 1976:54). In the eighteenth-century Andes, it is clear that the definition of the jícara was tied to its function as a chocolate cup (Alcedo 1967 [1786]:371) more than to its shape or material. In late-eighteenth-century Buenos Aires it has been suggested that the jícara was a small handleless cup for drinking chocolate or tea, while the pocillo was a coffee cup, which sometimes had a handle (Porro et al. 1982:215).

I am unaware of any colonial period porcelains held in museums in Cuenca, with the possible exception of a large blue underglaze *tibor,* or "ginger jar," housed in the Cuenca Municipal Museum, which I have been unable to date. The only other piece of Chinese export porcelain I know of in the museums of Cuenca is a teapot, in typical "Canton" or "Rose Medallion" overglaze enamels, introduced around 1820 and popular into the 1850s (Crossman 1927:165; Godden 1979:159, 191, 298). It is a reminder of the new international trade networks that Cuenca became a part of after the Ecuadorian Wars of Independence rather than an artifact of the colonial past.

Only three export porcelain sherds were recovered from Cuenca.

Two sherds from the urban core were decorated in underglaze blue Kraakporcelain style, dating the sherds to the 1550 to 1640 period (Figure 33) (Curtis 1988:24; Deagan 1987:98). Finally, a single rim sherd from a Chinese Imari bowl, with underglaze blue and overglaze red and gold paint, dating to the 1695 to 1750 period, was found at Pumapungo (Deagan 1987:100).

In the English colonies of North America seventeenth-century tables were dominated by heterogeneous collections of pewter and ceramics, but this situation changed in the eighteenth century as matched sets of teawares, often in porcelain, were introduced, first to urban households and then among the rural "gentry" (Stone 1988 [1977]:71–72). In Cuenca the situation was rather different. Porcelains remained a rarity in inventories into the late eighteenth century, although some houses had one or two pieces. In the late eighteenth century these pieces appear to have most commonly been small cups, used for serving chocolate. Such cups were not held in large matched sets, however, and remained rare throughout the colonial period.

## Industrial Imports

The first English refined white earthenwares introduced into the Andes were creamwares and pearlwares, common in the English colonies from the 1770s until the end of the 1820s (Miller 1980; Noël Hume 1970:128–132). The recognition and analysis of refined white earthenwares at Andean historic sites is still very much in its infancy, but excavations at the wineries in the Moquegua Valley of Peru have revealed small quantities of pearlware ceramics at most of the sites (Smith 1991:268–305).

In Cuenca excavations only one sherd of creamware was recovered, a plain body sherd from the urban excavations. Pearlware was slightly more common, with seven plain white sherds recovered from the urban sites, including one saucer rim sherd. A single decorated pearlware sherd, with "dipped" exterior decoration in a marbled pattern (Miller 1980:6; Noël Hume 1970:132) was recovered from the urban excavations. At Pumapungo only one pearlware sherd was recovered, and two plain pearlware body sherds were recovered at Cachaulo.

What does this pearlware represent? Imported goods were rare in late-eighteenth- and early-nineteenth-century Cuenca (Palomeque 1990:24), but the opening of the Cape Horn sea route and the Bourbon relaxation of commercial trade restrictions allowed Andeans larger access to European imports (Brading 1984:431). English domination of the world ceramic trade by the end of the eighteenth century was one of the initial results of the Industrial Revolution, as the marketing of mass-produced ceramics devastated many local pottery industries worldwide (Miller 1980:1), reaching as far as the rural Andes.

But did the importation of pearlwares accompany an ideology of individualism, such as James Deetz (1972) postulated for the late eighteenth-century English colonies? In Plymouth individual matching sets of ceramics suddenly dominated the late eighteenth-century table, along with all of the associated ideas of whitewares as symbolic of power, conspicuous consumption, and pomp (Deetz 1988:223; Yentsch 1991:213–221). The minimal archaeological excavation completed so far is not sufficient to give any clear indication of the popularity of English refined white earthenwares in Cuenca in the final years of the colonial period, but there is no mention of such ceramics in household inventories. Cuenca in the late eighteenth century appears not to have been penetrated by large numbers of industrially produced ceramics. Such ceramics, and the ideology that went with them, do appear to have been present in the metropolis of Buenos Aires 20 years later. There the plate was the most indispensable item in the tablewares of the elite, and the secretary of the viceroy in 1810 owned 1,108 "French flinty white plates with blue borders," presumably used for state dinners (Porro et al. 1982:20–21).

It is not until after 1850, with the emergent export economy of the new Republic, that the elite of Cuenca began to import large quantities of consumer goods, including foreign "metalwork, glass, ceramics, textiles and furniture" (Palomeque 1990:56). The opening of the Panama Canal in 1900 brought many more industrially produced goods to Ecuador, including ceramics. It is at the beginning of the twentieth century that the domestic material culture that accompanied the Industrial Revolution was introduced to Ecuadorian elite houses, including indoor plumbing and electric lighting (Holm 1970:265; Rippy 1944:78–81).

A wide variety of industrially produced ceramics were imported to Cuenca in the Republican era. A set of six soft-paste porcelain plates, manufactured by Criel and Montereau in France, are held in the municipal museum. They are decorative pieces and date between 1819 and 1895 (Haggar 1960:119–120; Kovel and Kovel 1986:53).

From the 1820s onward refined white earthenwares made in Europe dominated the world ceramics trade (Miller 1980:2). In Cuenca refined white earthenwares must have remained relatively rare through the nineteenth century. Only 1.3% of sherds recovered from the two rural sites, less than 1% of the Pumapungo ceramics, and 1.5% of the urban ceramic collection were refined white earthenwares. This suggests that locally-made earthenwares continued to dominate the nineteenth-century Cuenca table, with imported European whitewares as rare accent pieces.

Complete stamped or hand-painted whiteware vessels are present in both private and museum collections in Cuenca. Both stamped and hand-painted examples of refined white earthenwares are present in local museum collections, dating from the 1840s through 1890s. Stamped whiteware vessels in North America are proposed to have come mainly from factories in Scotland (Collard 1984:145–146; Finlayson 1972:4–7), but very similar vessels were manufactured in various European countries including England, France, and Belgium (Finlayson 1972:7; Lueger 1981:128).

Two hand-painted whiteware bowls in private collections in Cuenca provide maker's marks that give some evidence of where the whitewares imported into Cuenca were coming from. One hand-painted annular base bowl is stamped "J. VILLEARD & CIE.," while a second is stamped on the bottom "J. Wendard/Bourdeaux." Refined white earthenwares with hand-painted bands from the San Jerónimo convent in Mexico City have been identified by Patricia Fournier from maker's marks as products of the "Maastricht" factory in Holland, which began production in 1836 (Fournier Garcia and Silva T. 1989:92). Early nineteenth-century excavated ceramics in Panama City, Panama, included "Villeard" and "Bourdeaux" maker's marks (Rovira 1984:293–294). From all of these examples it would appear that the Latin American markets of the early Republican period were supplied extensively with hand-painted and "stamped" whitewares from factories in continental Europe, in contrast to the English and Scottish production, which was exported to North American markets.

Three transfer-printed refined white earthenware plates are held in Cuenca's Municipal Museum, all dating to the period from 1850 to 1890, and all having been manufactured in England. All of the whitewares from both the excavated contexts and the museum collections are evidence of the new world markets that were set up after the Ecuadorian Wars of Independence and that brought both continental European and English ceramics into the Cuenca region in the mid- to late nineteenth century.

# Conclusions | 7

## COLONIAL CATEGORIES

It is an inherent part of colonialism to create dichotomous definitions of reality, such as the ethnic and class division between Indio (Indian) and vecino (citizen) in colonial Cuenca. Definitions of ethnicity in particular underwent profound reformulation in the colonial encounter. The term "Spaniard," signifying a member of a nation that did not exist in the fifteenth century, was created in the midst of Spanish imperial expansion. The term "Indian" signified an ethnicity created in the colonial encounter from a vast diversity of New World populations (Silverblatt 1995). Finally, the term "African" represented peoples from a vast variety of ethnic groups on the African continent brought together by the common experience of slavery in the Spanish colonies. These terms do not do justice to the diverse encounters between myriad ethnic groups that Spanish colonialism brought about.

The contested relations between those of different gender and ethnic categories were also an important factor in the creation and use of material culture. In colonial St. Augustine Kathleen Deagan has portrayed a relationship involving Native women who married "white" criollo and peninsular soldiers and merchants. In their households the kitchen was dominated by Native material culture, and white males of Spanish descent controlled all of the more public areas (Deagan 1983:263–271). Deagan's model has also been influential in interpreting the extensive excavations at the colonial town of Puerto Real in present-day Haiti (Deagan 1995d; Ewen 1991). St. Augustine was a garrison town, and in the majority of its households this pattern probably fit quite well. The situation in Cuenca, where people of many social situations lived in a variety of circumstances, was quite different from a town like St. Augustine.

Instead of the early "crystallization" of Spanish and Native cultures into a new, and static, Spanish colonial pattern (Foster 1960), we need to look at the history of Spanish colonialism as an ongoing struggle between many groups over the exercise of social power (Paynter‘ and McGuire 1991). Spanish colonialism in Cuenca and elsewhere was about the reformulation of ethnic groups and categories, and it was also about the growth of mercantile capitalism through the commodification of material goods.

The writing of household inventories, the assignation of monetary values to household goods, and the growing separation between the public and private spheres were all a part of the penetration of mercantile capitalism into many facets of life in Cuenca as the colonial period progressed.

Rather than assuming that the categories used in colonial Cuenca to classify people were natural or immutable, we must instead examine how this particular system of meanings and values was related to colonial developments. It is important that as anthropologists we do not reify categories like Indio or vecino, which were created in the colonial culture itself. Instead, we need to examine how such categories developed and were confirmed through the daily practices of people in colonial society. Many of the encounters that occurred were infused with unequal relationships of power, and these can be explored through the material culture of these encounters. Rather than examining how static Iberian or Native Andean "traditions" were preserved or dominated in colonial Cuenca, we must instead realize that the history of the colonizer and that of the colonized cannot be disentangled (Wolf 1982).

The material world was an important part of this colonial discourse, helping to create and maintain multiple social categories in the minds of the colonizer and colonized alike. The worldview of each member of colonial Cuenca society was both reinforced and changed by his or her daily experiences of the cultural landscape and the material objects they used. As people went about their daily affairs in Cuenca, they incorporated and reproduced the overall institutions of Spanish colonialism (Giddens 1984:19). Daily life and its routines constrained people within particular social structures, and yet they could choose to either reproduce the existing structure or to change it, each time they performed a task (Giddens 1984:50). Through observing one another undertaking daily tasks, the people of Cuenca monitored their own actions and the actions of others. Thus, the built forms and material culture of colonial Cuenca are mute testimony to a web of changing social relations, played out in daily behaviour, and visible to us through the physical remains and documentary descriptions left behind. Through the combination of archaeology, architectural history, and documentary research, it is possible to reveal many aspects of these social relations.

# THE URBAN

The Spanish foundation of Cuenca is the first example of this relationship, and it is an example that endures until today in the plan of the city. Cuenca was founded on the ruins of an Inka center, which itself was founded on a previous Cañari center. In this way the Spanish Empire appropriated a locally recognizable center of power, as had the Inka before them. On the edge of the ruins of the Inka center the Spanish laid out a typical sixteenth-century gridiron town plan, a plan that was not purely based on Renaissance European ideals, but that itself was a response to the European encounter with the New World (Low 1995). The gridiron town developed in the earliest years of New World colonization. It spread throughout the Spanish colonies as part of a dialectic between the practices of colonial Spaniards in founding cities (often in areas where indigenous built environments already existed) and the written code of the Council of the Indies on urban planning. In Cuenca as in other Spanish colonial cities this was the traza, literally "the plan," an area where geographic space was abstracted into a controllable grid, which theoretically radiated infinitely from the central plaza. Activities within the traza were regulated by the strict guidance of the town council, and within the traza only those admitted to the status of vecino had full rights.

    This level of abstract control did not extend as thoroughly to the houses of colonial Cuenca, as professional architects and written codes were largely absent from the design and construction of houses. Yet despite the absence of codified law, the interiors of the urban houses of colonial Cuenca were arranged, partially as microcosms of the ideal town plan, around central patios echoing the town plaza, and surrounded by porticoes, as the plaza should be. The blank-walled facades of urban houses, such as the Tres Patios, provided no views from the street of the activities within the house, and thus prevented surveillance of the interior from other members of colonial society. The interior arrangements of rooms provided the greatest impermeability to the private chambers of the houseowner's family, thus providing privacy for both their activities and for the commodities, such as jewelry and linens, which were generally stored in locked trunks in these private rooms. At the same time balconies accessible from these rooms provided elite families the ability to undertake surveillance of the street below and of the patios of the house. Such an arrangement, allowing an elite a privileged point to monitor the routine tasks that others were performing, is an important aspect of colonial built form (Giddens 1984:127–136). The streetscape exterior to the front of their house could be monitored from exterior balconies, while the domestic activities of the interior courtyard could be monitored from the interior second floor balconies. The arrangement of patios within the house allowed spatial separation, with the activities of Native Andean or African laborers in the house restricted to a second or third rear patio. This is a spatial arrangement echoing that found by Kathleen Deagan at St. Augustine, which contrasts the socially "visible" with the "invisible" (Deagan

1983:271). Inconspicuous rear entrances to alleyways allowed access for servants from the backs of houses, thus avoiding interference between the activities of house owners and servants. Deagan's model echoes that of Erving Goffman (1959, 1963), who used the analogy of the theater to suggest that people acted out their social roles in "front stage" areas, and dropped their social personae in "back stage" private spaces. In Cuenca the separation of domestic space, or the material culture used in it, does not seem to fit this model. I would rather consider all material culture as visible, but visible with particular meanings depending on the spatial and temporal context. Artifacts are always multivocal, in that they have different meanings to different people, and different meanings in different contexts (Beaudry et al. 1991).

Women in Cuenca were quite active in certain aspects of the public sphere. The primary association of women with domestic labor and men with monetarily supported labor, implying a strict division between the private world of the family and the public world of the formal economy, was not as clear-cut a separation in this preindustrial world. It is more a factor of the nineteenth-century Industrial Revolution (Yentsch 1991:198; Moore 1988). In many regions of colonial Latin America it was the family structure itself that dominated the economy, as "Through marriage and the family, individuals achieved what the formal business organizations and political parties of the time could not: a long-lasting association of power and money" (Balmori et al. 1984:17). Historians have realized for decades now that "The assumption that colonial women were mostly occupied in familial household activities should be altered" (Lavrin and Coutu-rier 1979:300).

The lack of separation between the domestic economy and the formal economy within the mercantile capitalism of the Spanish empire meant that houses were the center of considerable business activity, particularly in the tiendas, or rooms that fronted the street. Some families were themselves business empires, and this lack of separation between public and private was an important aspect of gender relations. It was common for elite women in the Spanish colonies to own urban houses, and they often used their personal possessions as commodities to gain power within the colonial system. This reflects Bonnie McEwan's formulation of the lives of elite women in the Spanish colonies as "associated mostly with their domestic responsibilities" (McEwan 1991:34). Yet the lack of separation between the domestic and the formal economies meant that elite women's role in society was more varied than this formulation suggests. From the 1540s onward men who began to gain roots in Peru sent back to Spain for female relatives, and from this point onward Spanish women emigrated to the Andes in large numbers (Lockhart 1994 [1968]:152). These women in the Andes frequently took active roles in their family's business affairs (Borchart de Moreno 1992). When widowed or abandoned (a not infrequent occurrence in a society where men frequently married women much younger than themselves) a widow could become an important economic force in her own right. In the case of Luisa Maldonado de San Juan in the late seventeenth century, as with many other widows, the death of her husband led to her movement into the formal economy, inheriting the control of a cloth importing business and allowing her to purchase rural agricultural properties. Luisa's case is a warning to us that we must not place women's role in the Spanish colonies as solely within the private sphere.

In Spain from the fifteenth to eighteenth centuries women often undertook artisanal work if their husbands were artisans, and they had the legal privilege to take over the family business if their husband was absent or dead. Women participated on their own in the informal economy, particularly in the areas of textile and food marketing. Economic participation in the formal economy took place through property ownership and transactions, but women were excluded from other aspects of the formal sector, such as membership in guilds (Perry 1990; Vicente 1996).

Rather than looking at the restriction of women to the domestic sphere as an inherent part of Spanish colonialism, it may be better to consider this segregation as part of the negotiation of power between the genders. As Carole Shammas has proposed, a proliferation of expensive tablewares can be tied to the increasing segregation of women in the home in the early modern world, but women were probably an active force in promoting such enhancements to the domestic environment (Shammas 1990:186–188).

The exercise of power in colonial Cuenca was manifest in the material culture that elite houses contained. An important part of elite interaction was a gradual growth in the segregation of space and an emphasis on an ideology of individualism. The material culture within the houses of the Cuenca colonial elite, including that of Luisa Maldonado de San Juan as well as those of even greater wealth such as Pedro Ortiz Dávila, included tablewares and furnishings that reinforced the growth of individualism in the mercantile capitalist economy. The use of individual chairs with backs for the family as well as guests and individual silver plates at the dining table are just two examples. These objects were associated with the increasing discipline involved in dining and hospitality. The elite followed more intricate behavioral rules at the table, which was a part of the increasing segmentation of mercantile capitalist society, differentiating the "polite" household from the lower classes. Communal dishes became increasingly frowned upon in elite circles throughout the Western world in the Renaissance. This was a change that both commodified the increasing number of objects used on the table and reinforced the ideology of strict discipline and "correct" behavior among all who sat at the elite table (Shackel 1992:209).

In the English colonies of North America the appearance of the "Georgian" ideals of symmetry and individual place settings at the elite table became relatively sudden late-eighteenth-century phenomena (Deetz 1977, 1988). This rapid transition in material culture is not seen in the Spanish colonial material assemblage (Deagan 1983:270). It is much more accurate to look at the growth of such an ideology in the Spanish colonial world as a long-term process starting at the beginning of the Renaissance (Braudel 1981; Johnson 1996). The segregation of the individual through material culture is evident from at least the seventeenth century onward in elite Cuenca houses and was clearly associated with elite status. Matching sets of chairs, plates, and silver cutlery were the items where it was most clearly expressed. The ritual of the dining table was a very important part of this negotiation of domestic relationships through material culture. In the best-preserved example of colonial domestic architecture in Cuenca, the Posadas house, it is the dining room that was positioned at the point of interaction between the public face of the front patio and the service area of the rear patio.

The material culture used during meals was a complex expression of colonial culture. Luisa Maldonado de San Juan provides a good case study for this phenomenon. Her collection of silver and gold-plated silver tablewares was extensive, but her role in owning and maintaining both a large rural agricultural property at Cachaulo and a merchant cloth business inherited from her husband meant that she was far from segregated within her urban house. Bonnie McEwan (1991:34) emphasizes the role of elite women of Spanish descent in the colonies in "maintaining traditional standards." Many of Luisa's possessions, including her eleven chairs for visitors, her silver tablewares, and her clothing and jewelry, did indeed emphasize her role in an emerging ideal of individualism in a far corner of the empire.

Yet the symbols of her elite status were not all from Iberia. Instead of replicating Iberian traditions in an attempt at "careful preservation of Spanish identification in the *visible* areas" (Dillehay and Deagan 1992:118), the symbols of elite status used in Cuenca houses were in many respects uniquely colonial, building an entirely new discourse, particularly through the rituals of dining. Silver tablewares themselves, much valued in Europe, were perhaps the most commodified items in colonial Cuenca, often listed first in inventories and given strict monetary values based on the weight of the silver they contained. Although restricted to a fairly wealthy elite, a silver production center like Cuenca had much greater access to such tablewares than would have been the case in an Iberian center.

It is in other tablewares, however, that the colonial appropriation of foodstuffs "exotic" to European traditions is most evident. Many of Luisa's practices were intimately entwined with the construction of a creole New World elite. The serving of hot drinks as a form of hospitality is just one example. Luisa served people chocolate, an appropriated symbol of Mesoamerican Native hospitality, in coconut cups. In the colonial period the serving of chocolate was a common form of elite Andean hospitality, often served from Chinese porcelain cups or in majolica cups designed to replicate the Asian examples. If chocolate was not served, Paraguayan tea was an acceptable alternative. Tea from Paraguay was made by elite "Spanish" women in Andean gourds encased in silver filigree and served with a silver straw to visitors. In this way the Cuenca elite were far from conservative in their mode of hospitality, and they had appropriated and combined symbols of hospitality from Europe, Asia, and the Americas.

Individual plates in the dining service of elite houses, whether silver plates for the urban elite or locally produced majolica plates at rural elite sites, expressed the individualism of an emerging capitalist society from the seventeenth century onward in Cuenca. This is not to suggest that dining habits in eighteenth-century Cuenca resembled those of North American elites of the same period. In the late-eighteenth-century painting of the Last Supper in the Carmelite convent in Cuenca, the place settings include a slice of bread, or trencher, in front of each person, along with a fork and spoon at each place. In the same series of paintings the "Communion of St. Theresa" shows each of the nuns eating from an individual white bowl, their trenchers of bread pushed aside, without cutlery and eating with their hands (Martínez Borrero 1983:148, 154). It looks as if the nuns had finished their main course and are eating a fruit or dessert course. Throughout the colonial period the domestic material culture of Cuenca never reached the levels of segregation that occurred in eighteenth-century North American place settings. It was only after the Wars of Independence that Cuenca elite houses were penetrated by the ideology expressed in individual sets of matching ceramics and flatware for all courses of the meal.

## THE EDGES OF THE TRAZA

The gridiron town plan of Cuenca created a traza, a defined abstract space in which the urban houses were aligned and regimented, but this is only a small part of the urban form of colonial Cuenca. The intended rationality and order of the gridiron was overlain on the existing cultural landscape at the time of Cuenca's founding. Beyond the traza on all sides were several other parishes, including San Blas to the east, San Sebastián to the west, and the Todos Santos neighborhood to the south. In this way the colonial city was an exercise in constantly redrawing boundaries between the colonizer and the colonized (Prakash 1995). The riverside location of Todos Santos meant that for the vecinos of Cuenca, the neighborhood was in every sense on the edge of the urban core. The riverside was essential as a source of the town's water, both for domestic use and for the mills, but the river's edge was also a place of immorality.

The urban poor were the main inhabitants of the mainly one-room houses of the Todos Santos neighborhood. The arrangement of these houses, with a single interior room and a single rear patio, was a house form that gave the inhabitants privacy from the street, but very little internal differentiation of space. This is reflected in the relatively shallow permeability diagrams for these houses. At the entrance to the Todos Santos houses the presence of front porticoes on the street created an area where the activities of the family during waking hours would be visible to people in the street. This arrangement both enabled community solidarity, by allowing interaction between neighbors, and created a situation of surveillance, in which the inhabitants of Todos Santos could monitor one another's activities. In Giddens's (1984) terms these are actually two aspects of the same process, in that the structure of the Todos Santos community could both enable community solidarity and simultaneously, through surveillance, constrain behaviors deemed inappropriate.

No excavations were undertaken in the Todos Santos neighborhood, which is unfortunate because the demographic structure of this neighborhood was so different from that of the urban core. Inventories such as that of Marcial Uruchima's provide a rare documentary glimpse of the material culture of urban poverty in colonial Cuenca. It is likely that excavation would provide a very different view of the material culture of the neighborhoods outside the urban core, particularly in terms of their use of ceramics.

When we look at women who were not of "Spanish" descent, the issue of ethnicity becomes another important factor in the negotiation of relationships using material culture. Elite women of Spanish descent were not the only female participants in the "public" formal economy. In the early colonial period Native Andean women who were part of the elite class of caciques had considerable access to, and power over, economic resources (Caillavet 1982; Rappaport 1990b; Truhan 1991). Poorer Native Andean women also frequently participated in the market economy, perhaps more frequently than their husbands did (Minchom 1989; Poloni 1992:291, 302).

At St. Augustine Native pottery was used in the kitchen, and as

Deagan (1974) states, this is a material manifestation of the restriction of Native women within the domestic sphere. The use of (probably Spanish made) botijas by Sebastiana de Rojas for brewing chicha, or Andean beer, is an example of the use of non-Native ceramics to create traditional Andean food. Women often brewed chicha and sold it in the public market, as with many other categories of goods. Women's use of Spanish imported ceramics to create the quintessentially Andean drink, and then to sell it in public markets, must make us question any strict line between Native and Spanish ethnic groups. Such an activity crossed the lines between the public and private spheres and also challenges the assignation of ceramic vessel forms to particular ethnic groups. It is the context that gave these artifacts meaning, and the negotiation of power in colonial Cuenca created contexts that were very complex.

Native Andeans were not restricted to the lowest of economic levels in the colonial economy, although there were certainly large numbers of Native Andeans who lived in extreme poverty in colonial Cuenca. In some cases, and particularly in the case of kurakas (Andean ethnic leaders), the perceived inheritance of pre-Hispanic political rights led to the negotiation of considerable power in the colonial world. I have not been able to explore the material culture or architecture of the families of kurakas in this book. This is unfortunate, as it is an area where the negotiation of power through the manipulation of material symbols would have involved important renegotiations of ethnic identity. My impression is that the urban houses of powerful local kurakas would have been located in the San Blas or San Sebastián parishes, near the plazas, but further reconstruction of colonial residence patterns from the archival documents would be necessary to confirm this. It is thus in these two other urban parishes, San Blas and San Sebastián, that future research could give significant results, in looking at groups of people in the colonial urban area very different from the elite of the colonial core or the urban poor of Todos Santos.

# THE RURAL

Towns such as Cuenca were centers of colonial power that relied in every sense on the rural lands that surrounded them. This strict dichotomy between "town" and "country," and the ideological and economic realities of "core" and "periphery" that it implied, was in itself a colonial adaptation of medieval European categorizations. The three rural elite houses that I have presented in this book, the Cachaulo, Challuabamba, and Yanuncay Grande houses, enclosed pieces of the Andean landscape, alienating this landscape from the symbolic values it held to Native Andean peoples living in the area. These rural houses enclosed the elite landowners in a microcosm of colonial urban architecture, with patios and porticoes cutting off the surrounding countryside and shifting the gaze of the inhabitants inward. These houses, and the walls and fences that accompanied them, set out abstract boundaries around agricultural fields alienated from Native Andean communities. They were architectural extensions of the colonial abstraction of space into the countryside. There is the feeling that these were "outposts," areas outside the traza, outside the "plan," and slightly dangerous. Women often owned urban property, but Luisa Maldonado de San Juan's ownership of Cachaulo in the late seventeenth century was made more tenable by her status as a widow. Elite women in the Spanish colonial world owned rural properties less frequently than did men, and the machinations of inheritance within the Maldonado de San Juan family soon brought Cachaulo back into the control of a male heir.

The lack of an extensive artifact collection from the archaeological excavations undertaken at these rural houses is very likely due to their role as rural outposts of elite urban families. These were domestic buildings, but in a sense they were not, in that the people who dwelled on these properties permanently, the mitayo laborers and the majordomo who supervised them, along with their families, lived in much more ephemeral architecture that has long ago disappeared from the landscape. The adobe buildings that have survived for us to examine are the symbolic remains of the urban elite's ownership of the rural landscape. They are places where urban landowners would visit, and perhaps occasionally sleep, but they were essentially designed for monitoring the agricultural production of the laborers who worked there.

The majolica ceramics recovered archaeologically at Cachaulo, although undated, are dominated by the plato hondo, a ceramic form associated with the growth of individualism. This is interesting, in that no rural inventories provide evidence of individual table settings. Perhaps these majolicas were the cheaper replacements for the individual silver plates used on elite urban tables. As such they were appropriate for the rural visits of an urban elite accustomed to individual place settings at the table in their daily practice, but not seeking to invest heavily in tablewares for a residence where influential visitors were not received.

The chapel of the Cachaulo house, although small in size, contained a considerable investment in material culture, both in the mural paintings that decorate the walls, and the material culture that is listed in the mideighteenth-century inventory. This emphasis on the chapel in rural estancia architecture was common in many areas of the Andes. The chapel holds the position of greatest privacy of any room at Cachaulo, a distinct arrangement in comparison to the urban houses, which suggests different priorities on the use of space in the rural context. The chapel was the point of interaction between the Maldonado de San Juan family and the rural laborers who worked the land at Cachaulo. The investment in the religious art in the Cachaulo chapel was a statement of the importance of religion within the colonial relationship of urban elites to rural Native Andeans.

The three rural houses that I have presented represent just one aspect of the encounter between the urban and the rural in the colonial Andes. The houses of Native Andeans, whether outside town life in the rural landscape, or in the Native reducción (resettlement) towns set up by the colonial administration, made up another important part of the Andean colonial world, one that I have unfortunately been unable to include here. The houses and material culture of rural Native Andeans is an area essential for future comparative research.

## THE THREAT OF MODERNIZATION

The threat posed by modern development to both the standing colonial architecture and the subsurface archaeological remains of colonial domestic occupations in Cuenca is profound. As neighborhoods abandoned to the urban poor by the elite in the nineteenth century are reclaimed as office and retail space in the late twentieth century, the old houses are torn down, and deep foundations for modern multistory buildings destroy the archaeological remains in the former house yards. Local government archaeologists and architectural historians working for the Instituto Nacional del Patrimonio Cultural and other organizations do what they can to save these important resources with limited money and limited legal recourse. The situation is grave, and yet it is not entirely bleak. The people of Cuenca have great pride in their past, and many individuals have put considerable effort into research and preservation, particularly of colonial architecture associated with the church. The restoration of the Yanuncay Grande house by the Instituto Nacional del Patrimonio Cultural is a good sign that these efforts are being extended to domestic architecture as well.

Beyond the immediate goals for the Cuenca area, architectural and archaeological remains of the colonial period throughout Ecuador, from high elevation mining boomtowns to coastal seaports essential to colonial trade, provide myriad opportunities for further research. Historical archaeology is still very new in Ecuador. The domestic architecture and material culture of the colonial period in the Andes is a field that has received little academic attention, and yet it provides one of the most eloquent records of the interactions among the many categories of people who made up the colonial Andean world. To understand Ecuador today we must understand its formation and transitions during the colonial period, and the research completed to date has only begun to scratch the surface.

# References

**Archival Sources:** Archivo Nacional de Historia/Cuenca (ANH/C). The archive is arranged in two different systems. Books (*libros*) are numbered and are referred to with an "L" designation followed by the folio numbers within the book (e.g., ANH/C L549f3v-7r). Loose documents have been placed in file folders (*carpetas*) which are referred to with a "C" designation followed by the number of that file (e.g., ANH/C C94.055).

Achig Subía, Lucas, 1980, La estructura administrativa de la Gobernación de Cuenca. *Revista del Archivo Nacional de Historia, Sección del Azuay* (Cuenca) 2:7-51.

Achig Subía, Lucas, and Diego Mora Castro, 1987, Exacción tributaria y motines indígenas en el Azuay: 1830-1895. *Revista del Archivo Nacional de Historia, Sección del Azuay* (Cuenca) 7:82-104.

Acosta, José de, 1894 [1590], *História natural y moral de las Indias*, Vol. q. Ramón Anglés, Madrid, Spain.

Agustín Landívar, Manuel, 1974, *Informe preliminar de la comision sobre las ruinas de Todos Santos.* Casa de la Cultura, Nucleo del Azuay, Cuenca.

Albert, Lillian Smith, and Jane Ford Adams, 1951, *The Button Sampler.* Gramercy Publishing, New York.

Alcedo, Antonio de, 1967 [1786], *Diccionario Geográfico de las Indias occidentales o América,* Vol. 4. Biblioteca de Autores Españoles, Vol. 208, edited by Ciriaco Perez-Bustamente. Ediciones Atlas, Madrid, Spain.

Alchon, Suzanne Austin, 1991, *Native Society and Disease in Colonial Ecuador.* Cambridge University Press, Cambridge, UK.

Alcina Franch, José, 1986, Los Indios Cañaris de la sierra sur del Ecuador. *Miscelánea Antropológica Ecuatoriana* (Guayaquil) 6:141-188.

Aldana Rivera, Susana, 1989, Esbozo de un eje de integración: el comercio Piura-Loja-Cuenca, Siglo XVIII tardio. *Revista del Archivo Nacional de Historia, Sección del Azuay* (Cuenca) 8:108-132.

Almeida, Napoleon, n.d., El sitio de Todos Santos de Cuenca. 4 pages. Manuscript on file, Museo Manuel Agustín Landívar, Casa de la Cultura, Nucleo del Azuay, Cuenca.

Anda Aguirre, Alfonso, 1960, *Zaruma en la colonia.* Casa de la Cultura Ecuatoriana, Quito, Ecuador.

Andrien, Kenneth J., 1994, The State and Dependancy in Late Colonial and Early Republican Ecuador. In *The Political Economy of Spanish America in the Age of Revolution, 1750-1850,* edited by Kenneth J. Andrien and Lyman L. Johnson, pp. 169-195. University of New Mexico Press, Albuquerque.

Andrien, Kenneth J., 1994, *The Kingdom of Quito, 1690-1830: The State and Regional Development.* Cambridge University Press, Cambridge, UK.

Angeles, Domingo de los, 1965 [1582], San Francisco de Pacha y San Bartolomé de Arocxapa. In *Relaciones Geográficas de Indias: Perú,* Vol. 2, edited by Marcos Jiménez de la Espada, pp. 270-271. Biblioteca de Autores Españoles, Madrid.

Anonymous, 1965 [1573], La cibdad de Sant Francisco del Quito. In *Relaciones Geográficas de Indias: Perú*, Vol. 2, edited by Marcos Jiménez de la Espada, pp. 205-230. Biblioteca de Autores Españoles, Madrid.

Anonymous, 1979 [before 1571] An Account of the Shrines of Ancient Cuzco, edited by John H. Rowe. *Ñawpa Pacha* 17:1-80.

Anonymous, 1992 [1605] Descripción de la gobernación de Guayaquil. In *Relaciones Histórico-Geográficas de la Audiencia de Quito, Tomo II.*, edited by Pilar Ponce Leiva, pp. 10-47. Consejo Superior de Estudios Historicos, Madrid, Spain.

Aprile-Gniset, Jacques, 1991, *La ciudad colombiana*. Banco Popular, Bogota, Colombia.

Arias Dávila, Pedro, 1965 [1582], Pacaibamba o Leoquina. In *Relaciones Geográficas de Indias: Perú*, Vol. 2, edited by Marcos Jiménez de la Espada, pp. 278-281. Biblioteca de Autores Españoles, Madrid.

Ayala Mora, Enrique, 1991, Ecuador since 1930. In *The Cambridge History of Latin America*, Vol. 8, edited by Leslie Bethell, pp. 687-725. Cambridge University Press, Cambridge, UK.

Balmori, Diana, Stuart F. Voss, and Miles Wortman, 1984, *Notable Family Networks in Latin America*. University of Chicago Press, Chicago.

Barrera, Isaac J., 1956, *Historiografia del Ecuador*. Instituto Panamericano de Geografia é Historia, Mexico, D.F.

Barthes, Roland, 1967 [1964], *Elements of Semiology*. Hill and Wang, New York.

Barton, Tamsyn, 1994, *Ancient Astrology*. Routledge, London, UK.

Batllori, Miguel, 1965, The Role of the Jesuit Exiles. In *The Origins of the Latin American Revolutions, 1808-1826*, edited by R. A. Humphreys and John Lynch. Alfred A. Knopf, New York.

Bayón, Damián, 1979, La casa colonial porteña vista por viajeros y memorialistas. *Actes du XLIIᵉ Congrès International des Américanistes* (Paris) 10:142-170.

Beals, Ralph, 1953, Acculturation. In *Anthropology Today*, edited by A. L. Kroeber, pp. 00-00. University of Chicago Press, Chicago.

Beaudry, Mary C., 1980, *"Or What Else You Please to Call It": Folk Semantic Domains in Early Virginia Probate Inventories*. Ph.D. dissertation, Brown University, Providence, RI.

Beaudry, Mary C., 1986, Words for Things: Linguistic Analysis of Probate Inventories. In *Documentary Archaeology in the New World*, edited by Mary C. Beaudry, pp. 43-50. Cambridge University Press, Cambridge, UK.

Beaudry, Mary C., Lauren J. Cook, and Stephen A. Mrozowski, 1987, Artifacts and Active Voices: Material Culture as Social Discourse. In *The Archaeology of Inequality*, edited by Randall H. McGuire and Robert Paynter, pp. 192-230. Blackwell, Cambridge, MA.

Beaudry, Mary C., Janet Long, Henry M. Miller, Fraser D. Neiman, and Gary Wheeler Store, 1988, A Vessel Typology for Early Chesapeake Ceramics. In *Documentary Archaeology and the New World*, pp. 51-67. Cambridge University Press, Cambridge, UK.

Beck, Colleen M., Eric E. Deeds, Sheila Pozorski, and Thomas Pozorski, 1983, Pajatambo: an Eighteenth Century Roadside Structure in Peru. *Historical Archaeology* 17:54-68.

Begoña, Ana de, 1986, *Arquitectura Doméstica en la Llanada de Alava, Siglos XVI, XVII y XVIII*. Diputación Foral de Alava, Vitoria, Spain.

Benítez, Sylvia, and Gaby Costa, 1983, La familia, la ciudad y la vida cotidiana en el período colonial. In *Nueva Historia del Ecuador*, Vol. 5, edited by Enrique Ayala Mora, pp. 187-230. Corporación Editora Nacional, Quito, Ecuador.

Bolaños, Monica, and Byron Camino, 1991, Prospección Arqueologica en el Observatorio Astronómico, Quito. Submitted to Instituto Naciónal de Patrimonio Cultural, Quito, Ecuador.

Bolaños Pantoja, Mónica, and Oscar Manosalvas Naranjo, 1989, Arqueología Historica–Caso: Capilla de el Robo–Quito. Submitted to Instituto Naciónal de Patrimonio Cultural, Quito, Ecuador.

Bonnet Medina, Percy, 1983, Trabajos Arqueologicos en la casa colonial "Los Marqueces de Valleumbroso." Manuscript on file, Instituto Naciónal de Cultura, Lima, Peru.

Borchart de Moreno, Christiana, 1992, La Imbecilidad y el Coraje: la participacion femenina en la economia colonial (Quito, 1780-1830). In *Mujeres de los Andes: condiciones de vida y salud*, edited by A. C. Defossez, D. Fassin, and M. Viveros, pp. 357-376. Instituto Frances de Estudios Andinos and Universidad Externado de Colombia.

Borregán, Alonso, 1948 [1597], *Crónica de la conquista del Perú*, edited by Rafael Loredo. Universidad de Sevilla, Seville, Spain.

Borrero Crespo, Maximiliano, 1962, *Orígenes Cuencanos*, Vol. 1. Universidad de Cuenca, Cuenca, Ecuador.

Bourdieu, Pierre, 1977 [1972], *Outline of a Theory of Practice*. Translated by Richard Nice. Cambridge University Press, Cambridge, UK.

Bowen, Joanne, 1975, Probate Inventories: An Evaluation from the Perspective of Zooarchaeology and Agricultural History at Mott Farm. *Historical Archaeology* 9:11-25.

Boyd-Bowman, Peter, 1972, Two Country Stores in XVIIth Century Mexico. *The Americas* 28(3):239-251.

Boyd-Bowman, Peter, 1973, Spanish and European Textiles in Sixteenth Century Mexico. *The Americas* 29(3):334-358.

Brading, D. A., 1984, Bourbon Spain and Its American Empire. In *The Cambridge History of Latin America*, Vol. 1, edited by Leslie Bethell, pp. 389-440. Cambridge University Press, Cambridge, UK.

Braudel, Fernand, 1981, *The Structures of Everyday Life*, Vol. 1, *Civilization and Capitalism, 15th-18th Century*. Harper and Row, New York.

Brown, Marley R., III, 1972, Ceramics from Plymouth, 1621-1800: The Documentary Record. In *Ceramics in America*, edited by Ian Quimby, pp. 41-74. Winterthur Museum, Wilmington, DE.

Brown, Marley, R., III, 1988, The behavioral Context of Probate Inventories: An Example from Plymouth Colony. In *Documentary Archaeology in the New World*, edited by Mary C. Beaudry, pp. 79-91. Cambridge University Press, Cambridge, UK.

Burkholder, Mark A., and Lyman L. Johnson, 1990, *Colonial Latin America*. Oxford University Press, Oxford, UK.

Bushnell, David, 1985, The Independence of Spanish South America. In *The Cambridge History of Latin America*, Vol. 3, edited by Leslie Bethell, pp. 95-156. Cambridge University Press, Cambridge, UK.

Buys, Jozef, 1992, La Cerámica Colonial. Paper presented at the Conference on Historical and Underwater Archaeology, Kingston, Jamaica.

Buys, Jozef, and Byron Camino, 1991, El Convento Santo Domingo de Quito: un caso de Arqueología histórica en el Ecuador. Paper Presented at the 47th International Congress of Americanists, New Orleans.

Cabello Valboa, Miguel, 1951 [1586], *Miscelánea antártica*. Universidad Nacional Mayor de San Marcos, Lima, Peru.

Cáceres Freyre, Julián, 1983, El Fuerte de San Blas del Pantano (Siglo XVII). In *Presencia hispánica en la Arqueología argentina*, Vol. 2, edited by Eldo Serafín Morresi and Ramón Gutiérrez, pp. 567-598. Universidad Nacional del Nordeste, Resistencia, Argentina.

Caillavet, Chantal, 1982, Caciques de Otavalo en el Siglo XVI: Don Alonso Maldonado y su esposa. *Miscelánea Antropológica Ecuatoriana* 2:38-55.

Calderón, Alfonso, 1985, *Saraguro Huasi: la Casa en la tierra del Maíz*. Banco Central del Ecuador, Quito, Ecuador.

Carbia, Rómulo D., 1926, *La civilizacion Hispano Americana del siglo XVIII en el Virreynato del Río de la Plata*. Instituto Nacional del Profesorado Secundario, Buenos Aires, Argentina.

Centro de Investigación y Cultura, 1991, *Cuenca Tradicional, 2ª Parte*. Coleccion Imagenes, Vol. 9, Banco Central del Ecuador, Cuenca.

Ceruti, Carlos N., 1983a, La Reducción de San Francisco Javier. In *Presencia hispánica en la Arqueología argentina*, Vol. 2, edited by Eldo Serafín Morresi and Ramón Gutiérrez, pp. 455–485. Universidad Nacional del Nordeste, Resistencia, Argentina.

Ceruti, Carlos N., 1983b, Evidencias del contacto hispano-indígena en la cerámica de Santa Fe La Vieja (Cayastá). In *Presencia hispánica en la Arqueología argentina*, Vol. 2, edited by Eldo Serafín Morresi and Ramón Gutiérrez, pp. 487–519. Universidad Nacional del Nordeste, Resistencia, Argentina.

Chacón Zhapán, Juan, 1982, *Libro Cuarto de Cabildos de la ciudad de Cuenca*. Archivo Histórico Municipal/Xerox del Ecuador, Cuenca, Ecuador.

Chacón Zhapán, Juan, 1990, *Historia del Corregimiento de Cuenca (1557–1777)*. Banco Central del Ecuador, Quito, Ecuador.

Cieza de León, Pedro de, 1965 [1553], *La Crónica del Perú*. 3rd ed. Colección Austral, Espasa-Calpe, Madrid, Spain.

Cieza de León, Pedro de, 1985 [before 1554], *Crónica del Perú: Segunda parte*, edited by Francesca Cantù. Pontificia Universidad Católica del Perú, Lima, Peru.

Claval, Paul, 1984, Reflections on the Cultural Geography of the European City. In *The City in Cultural Context*, edited by John Agnew, John Mercer and David Sopher, pp. 31–49. Allen and Unwin, Boston, MA.

Cobo, Bernabe, 1964 [1653], *Historia del Nuevo Mundo*, Vol. 1, edited by Marcos Jimenez del la Espada. Biblioteca de Autores Españoles, Vol. 91. Ed. Atlas, Madrid, Spain.

Coe, Sophie D., and Michael D. Coe, 1996, *The True History of Chocolate*. Thames and Hudson, New York.

Collard, Elizabeth, 1984, *Nineteenth-Century Pottery and Porcelain in Canada*. McGill-Queens University Press, Kingston, Ontario, Canada.

Cook, Noble David, 1982, *Demographic Collapse: Indian Peru 1520–1620*. Cambridge University Press, Cambridge, UK.

Cook, Noble David, 1990, Migration in Colonial Peru: An Overview. In *Migration in Colonial Spanish America*, edited by David J. Robinson, pp. 41–61. Cambridge University Press, New York.

Cordero Jaramillo, Leoncio, 1989, Hospitales de la época colonial. In *El Libro de Cuenca*, edited by Rigoberto Cordero y Leon, pp. 86–93. Editores y Publicistas, Cuenca, Ecuador.

Cornejo Garcia, Miguel, 1983, Asentamientos Hispanicos del Siglo XVIII en la Quebrada de Uripe, Valle de Moche. Manuscript on file, Instituto Naciónal de Cultura, Lima.

Corradine Angulo, Alberto, 1981, *Santa Cruz de Mompox: Estudio Morfologico y Reglamentario*. Corporacion Nacional de Turismo, Bogota, Colombia.

Couturier, Edith, 1985, Women and the Family in Eighteenth-Century Mexico: Law and Practice. *Journal of Family History* 10(3):294–304.

Crespo Toral, Hernán (Ed.), 1976, *Arte Ecuatoriano*. Vol. 2. Salvat Editores, Quito, Ecuador.

Crossman, Carl L., 1927, The Rose Medallion and Mandarin Patterns in China Trade Porcelain. In *Chinese Export Porcelain: An Historical Survey*, edited by Elinor Gordon, pp. 165–170. Universe Books, New York.

Crouch, Dora P., 1991, Roman Models for Spanish Colonization. In *Columbian Consequences* Vol. 3: *The Spanish Borderlands in Pan-American Perspective*, edited by David Hurst Thomas, pp. 21–35. Smithsonian Institution Press, Washington, DC.

Crouch, Dora P., Daniel J. Garr, and Axel I. Mundigo, 1982, *Spanish City Planning in North America*. MIT Press, Cambridge, MA.

Cummings, Abbott Lowell (Ed.), 1964, *Rural Household Inventories: Establishing the Names, Uses and Furnishings of Rooms in the Colonial New England Home, 1675–1775*. Society for the Preservation of New England Antiquities, Boston, MA.

Cummins, Thomas B. F., 1991, We Are the Other: Peruvian Portraits of Colonial *Kurakakuna*. In *Transatlantic Encounters: Europeans and Andeans in the Sixteenth Century*, edited by Kenneth J. Andrien and Rolena Adorno, pp. 203–231. University of California Press, Berkeley.

Curry, Patrick, 1989, *Prophesy and Power: Astrology in Early Modern England*. Princeton University Press, Princeton, NJ.

Curtis, Julia B., 1988, Perceptions of an Artifact: Chinese Porcelain in Colonial Tidewater Virginia. In *Documentary Archaeology in the New World*, edited by Mary C. Beaudry, pp. 20–31. Cambridge University Press, Cambridge, UK.

Deagan, Kathleen, 1974, *Sex, Status and Role in the Mestizaje of Spanish Colonial Florida*. Ph.D. dissertation, Department of Anthropology, University of Florida, Gainesville.

Deagan, Kathleen, 1981, Downtown Survey: The Discovery of Sixteenth-Century St. Augustine in an Urban Area. *American Antiquity* 46(3):626–633.

Deagan, Kathleen, 1984, Historical Archaeology in Peru. *Society for Historical Archaeology Newsletter* (Williamsburg, Virginia) 17(1):37.

Deagan, Kathleen, 1985, *The Archaeology of Sixteenth-Centruy St. Augustine*. Florida Anthropologist 38(1–2):6–38.

Deagan, Kathleen, 1987, *Artifacts of the Spanish Colonies of Florida and the Caribbean, 1500–1800*. Vol. 1: *Ceramics, Glassware and Beads*. Smithsonian Institution Press, Washington, DC.

Deagan, Kathleen, 1988, The Archaeology of the Spanish Contact Period in the Caribbean. *Journal of World Prehistory* 2(2):187–233.

Deagan, Kathleen, 1990, Sixteenth-Century Spanish-American Colonization in the Southeastern United States and the Caribbean. In *Columbian Consequences* Vol. 2: *Archaeological and Historical Perspectives on the Spanish Borderlands East*, edited by David Hurst Thomas, pp. 259–267. Smithsonian Institution Press, Washington, DC.

Deagan, Kathleen, 1995a, Introduction. In *Puerto Real: The Archaeology of a Sixteenth-Century Spanish Town in Hispaniola*, edited by Kathleen Deagan, pp. 1–6. University Press of Florida, Gainesville.

Deagan, Kathleen, 1995b, Historical Archaeology at Puerto Real. In *Puerto Real: The Archaeology of a Sixteenth-Century Spanish Town in Hispaniola*, edited by Kathleen Deagan, pp. 33–49. University Press of Florida, Gainesville.

Deagan, Kathleen, 1995c, After Columbus: The Sixteenth-Century Spanish-Caribbean Frontier. In *Puerto Real: The Archaeology of a Sixteenth-Century Spanish Town in Hispaniola*, edited by Kathleen Deagan, pp. 419–456. University Press of Florida, Gainesville.

Deagan, Kathleen, 1995d, *Puerto Real: The Archaeology of a Sixteenth-Century Spanish Town in Hispaniola*. University Press of Florida, Gainesville.

Deagan, Kathleen, 1997, Cross-Disciplinary Themes in the Recovery of the Colonial Middle Period. *Historical Archaeology* 31(1):4–8.

Deagan, Kathleen (Ed.), 1983, *Spanish St. Augustine: The Archaeology of a Colonial Creole Community*. Academic Press, New York.

Deagan, Kathleen, and Elizabeth J. Reitz, 1995, Merchants and Cattlemen: The Archaeology of a Commercial Structure at Puerto Real. In *Puerto Real: The Archaeology of a Sixteenth-Century Spanish Town in Hispaniola*, edited by Kathleen Deagan, pp. 419–456. University Press of Florida, Gainesville.

Deas, Malcolm, 1986, Colombia, Ecuador and Venezuela, c. 1880–1930. In *The Cambridge History of Latin America*, Vol. V, edited by Leslie Bethell, pp. 641–684. Cambridge University Press, Cambridge, UK.

Deas, Malcolm, 1987, Venezuela, Colombia and Ecuador. In *Spanish America after Independence, c. 1820–c. 1870*, edited by Leslie Bethell, pp. 207–238. Cambridge University Press, Cambridge, UK.

Deetz, James F., 1967, *Invitation to Archaeology*. Natural History Press, Garden City, NY.

Deetz, James F., 1972, Ceramics from Plymouth, 1620–1835: The Archaeological Evidence. In *Ceramics in America*, edited by Ian M. G. Quimby, pp. 15–40. University Press of Virginia, Charlottesville.

Deetz, James F., 1977a, *In Small Things Forgotten: The Archaeology of Early American Life*. Doubleday, New York.

Deetz, James F., 1977b, Material Culture and Archaeology—What's the Difference? In *Historical Archaeology and the Importance of Material Things*, edited by Leland Ferguson, pp. 9–12. Special Publication Series, No. 2, Society for Historical Archaeology.

Deetz, James F., 1988, Material Culture and Worldview in Colonial Anglo-America. In *The Recovery of Meaning: Historical Archaeology in the Eastern United States*, edited by Mark P. Leone and Parker B. Potter Jr., pp. 219–234. Smithsonian Institution Press, Washington, DC.

deFrance, Susan D., 1996, Iberian Foodways in the Moquegua and Torata Valleys of Southern Peru. *Historical Archaeology* 30(3):20–48.

Descola, Jean, 1962, *La vie quotidienne au Pérou au temps des espagnols, 1710–1820*. Hachette, Paris, France.

Díaz, Rita, 1991, Proyecto arqueológico "El Tejar." Submitted to Instituto Naciónal de Patrimonio Cultural, Quito, Ecuador.

Dillehay, Tom D., and Kathleen Deagan, 1992, Introduction to "Special Section": The Spanish Quest for Empire. *Antiquity* 66(250):115–119.

Dobyns, Henry (Ed.), 1982, *Spanish Colonial Frontier Research*. Spanish Borderlands Research Series, No. 1, Center for Anthropological Studies, Albuquerque, New Mexico.

Durkheim, Émile, 1965 [1915], *The Elementary Forms of the Religious Life*. University of Chicago Press, Chicago.

Durkheim, Émile, and Marcel Mauss, 1963 [1903], *Primitive Classification*. University of Chicago Press, Chicago.

Duviols, Pierre, 1986, *Cultura andina y represión. Procesos y visitas de idolatrías y hechicerías, Cajatambo siglo XVII*. Cuzco, Peru.

Early, James, 1994, *The Colonial Architecture of Mexico*. University of New Mexico Press, Albuquerque.

Equip Broida, 1983, La Viudez, ¿triste o feliz estado?, In *Las mujeres en las ciudades medievales*, edited by Cristina Segura Graíno, pp. 27–41. Universidad Autónoma de Madrid, Madrid, Spain.

Espinoza, Leonardo, Lucas Achig, and Rubén Martínez, 1982, La gobernación colonial de Cuenca: Formación social y producción mercantil simple. In *Ensayos sobre historia regional: la región centro sur*, edited by Claudio Cordero E., pp. 31–116. Instituto de Investigaciones Sociales de la Universidad de Cuenca, Cuenca, Ecuador.

Estrella, Eduardo, 1988, *El pan de América: etnohistoria de los alimentos aborígenes en el Ecuador*. 2nd ed. Ediciones Abya-Yala, Quito, Ecuador.

Ewen, Charles R., 1991, *From Spaniard to Creole: The Archaeology of Cultural Formation at Puerto Real, Haiti*. University of Alabama Press, Tuscaloosa.

Fairbanks, Charles H., 1972, The Cultural Significance of Spanish Ceramics. In *Ceramics in America*, edited by Ian M. G. Quimby, pp. 141–174. University Press of Virginia, Charlottesville.

Fairbanks, Charles H., 1975, Backyard Archaeology as a Research Strategy. *The Conference on Historic Sites Archaeology Papers* 11:133–139.

Farnsworth, Paul, 1986, Spanish California: The Final Frontier. *Journal of New World Archaeology* 6(4):34–46.

Fernández, Jorge, 1983, Arqueología de la Ciudad del Nombre de Jesús. In *Presencia hispánica en la Arqueología argentina*, Vol. 2, edited by Eldo Serafín Morresi and Ramón Gutiérrez, pp. 895–930. Universidad Nacional del Nordeste, Resistencia, Argentina.

Finlayson, R. W., 1972, *Portneuf Pottery and Other Early Wares*. Longman Canada Ltd., Don Mills, Ontario, Canada.

Fitting, James E., 1977, The Structure of Historical Archaeology and the Importance of Material Things. In *Historical Archaeology and the Importance of Material Things*, edited by Leland Ferguson, pp. 62–67. Special Publication Series, No. 2, Society for Historical Archaeology.

Flores Espinoza, Isabel, Ruben Garcia Soto, and Lorenzo Huertas V., 1981, *Investigación Arqueológica-Histórica de la Casa Osambela (o de Oquendo)–Lima*. Instituto Naciónal de Cultura, Lima, Peru.

Foster, George, 1960, *Culture and Conquest: The American Spanish Heritage*. Viking Fund Publications in Anthropology, No. 27, Wenner Gren Foundation, New York.

Foucault, Michel, 1975, *Discipline and Punish: The Birth of the Prison*. Translated by Alan Sheridan. Vintage Books, New York.

Foucault, Michel, 1980, *Power and Knowledge*. Pantheon, New York.

Foucault, Michel, 1984, *The Foucault Reader*, edited by Paul Rabinow. Pantheon Books, New York.

Fournier Garcia, Patricia, 1989, 20 Tiestos de mayolica procedentes de Ecuador. In *Tres estudios sobre cerámica histórica*, edited by Patricia Fournier Garcia, Maria de Lourdes Fournier, and Eduardo Silva T., pp. 62–66. Instituto Nacional de Antropología e Historia, Mexico City, Mexico.

Fournier Garcia, Patricia, and Eduardo Silva T., 1989, Cerámica ornamental asociado con arquitectura religiosa en Temoac, Morelos, Mexico. In *Tres estudios sobre cerámica histórica*, edited by Patricia Fournier Garcia, María de Lourdes Fournier, and Eduardo Silva T., pp. 67–93. Instituto Nacional de Antropología e Historia, Mexico City, Mexico.

Fournier Garcia, Patricia, and Fernando A. Miranda Flores, 1992, Historic Sites Archaeology in Mexico. *Historical Archaeology* 26(1):75–83.

Fox, Anne A., 1989, The Indians at Rancho de las Cabras. In *Columbian Consequences Vol. 1: Archaeological and Historical Perspectives on the Spanish Borderlands West*, edited by David Hurst Thomas, pp. 259–267. Smithsonian Institution Press, Washington, DC.

Frankl, Paul, 1969 [1914], *Principles of Architectural History: The Four Phases of Architectural Style, 1420–1900*. Translated by J. F. O'Gorman. MIT Press, Cambridge, MA.

Fraser, Valerie, 1990, *The Architecture of Conquest: Building in the Viceroyalty of Peru, 1535–1635*. Cambridge University Press, Cambridge, UK.

Gallegos, Gaspar de, 1965 [1582], Sant Francisco Pueleusi del Azogue. In *Relaciones Geográficas de Indias: Perú*, Vol. 2, edited by Marcos Jiménez de la Espada, pp. 274–278. Biblioteca de Autores Españoles, Madrid, Spain.

Gasco, Janine, 1992, Documentary and Archaeological Evidence for Household Differentiation in Colonial Soconusco, New Spain. In *Text-Aided Archaeology*, edited by Barbara J. Little, pp. 83–94. CRC Press, Boca Raton, FL.

Geertz, Clifford, 1973, *The Interpretation of Cultures*. Basic Books, New York.

Giddens, Anthony, 1979, *Central Problems in Social Theory*. University of California Press, Berkeley.

Giddens, Anthony, 1984 *The Constitution of Society: Outline of the Theory of Structuration*. Polity Press, Cambridge, UK.

Gil, D. Francisco, 1983 [1784], *Disertación física-médica para la preservación de los pueblos de las viruelas*, edited by David Marley. Colección documenta novae hispaniae, Vol. B-2. Rolston-Bain, Mexico, D.F.

Glassie, Henry, 1975, *Folk Housing in Middle Virginia: A Structural Analysis of Historic Artifacts*. University of Tennessee Press, Knoxville.

Glassie, Henry, 1990 Vernacular architecture and society. In *Vernacular Architecture: Paradigms of Environmental Response*, edited by Mete Turan, pp. 271–284. Avebury Press, Aldershot, UK.

Godden, Geoffrey A., 1979, *Oriental Export Market Porcelain and Its influence on European Wares*. Granada, London, UK.

Goffman, Erving, 1959, *The Presentation of Self in Everyday Life*. Doubleday, New York.

Goffman, Erving, 1963, *Behavior in Public Places*. Free Press, New York.

Goffman, Erving, 1971, *Relations in Public: Microstudies of the Public Order*. Basic Books, New York.

Goggin, John M., 1960, *The Spanish Olive Jar: An Introductory Study*. Yale University Publications in Anthropology, No. 62. Yale University, New Haven, CT.

Goggin, John M., 1968, *Spanish Majolica in the New World: Types of the Sixteenth to Eighteenth Centuries*. Yale University Publications in Anthropology, No. 73, New Haven, CT.

Goicoechea, Helga Nilda, 1983, Las Reducciones del Bermejo. In *Presencia hispánica en la Arqueología argentina*, Vol. 1, edited by Eldo Serafín Morresi and Ramón Gutiérrez, pp. 313–341. Universidad Nacional del Nordeste, Resistencia, Argentina.

Gómez, Juan, Juan Vélez Benavente, and Alvaro García, 1965 [1582], Cañaribamba. In *Relaciones Geográficas de Indias: Perú*, Vol. 2, edited by Marcos Jiménez de la Espada, pp. 281–285. Biblioteca de Autores Españoles, Madrid, Spain.

Gonzales Carre, Enrique, and José Cahuas Massa, 1983, Arqueología Historica en Ayacucho: Experiencias y Problemas. Manuscript on file, Instituto Naciónal de Cultura, Lima, Peru.

González Aguirre, Iván, 1987, Los orígens urbanos de Cuenca. *Revista del Archivo Nacional de Historia, Sección del Azuay* (Cuenca) 7:36–45.

González Aguirre, Iván, 1989, Los orígenes urbanos de Cuenca. In *Las Ciudades en la Historia*, edited by Eduardo Kingman Garces, pp. 207–229. Centro de Investigaciones CIUDAD, Quito, Ecuador.

González Aguirre, Iván, 1991, *Cuenca: Barrios de Tierra y Fuego*. Fundación Paul Rivet, Cuenca, Ecuador.

González Suárez, Federico, 1983 [1891], Antecedentes para la Fundación de la ciudad de Cuenca. In *Compilacion de Cronicas, Relatos y Descripciones de Cuenca y su Provincia, Segunda Parte*, edited by Luis A. León, pp. 23–26. Banco Central del Ecuador, Cuenca, Ecuador.

Goody, Jack, 1983, *The Development of the Family and Marriage in Europe*. Cambridge University Press, Cambridge, UK.

Goody, Jack (Ed.), 1971 [1958], *The Developmental Cycle in Domestic Groups*. Cambridge University Press, Cambridge, UK.

Gose, Peter, 1991, House Rethatching in an Andean Annual Cycle: Practice, Meaning and Contradiction. *American Ethnologist* 18(1):39-56.

Greenwood, Roberta S., 1989, The California Ranchero: Fact and Fancy. In *Columbian Consequences*, Vol. 1: *Archaeological and Historical Perspectives on the Spanish Borderlands West*, edited by David Hurst Thomas, pp. 451-465. Smithsonian Institution Press, Washington, DC.

Guaman Poma de Ayala, Felipe, 1956 [1615], *La Nueva crónica y buen gobierno*, edited by Luis Bustíos Gálvez. Editorial Cultura, Ministerio de Educación Publica del Perú, Lima, Peru.

Gutiérrez, Ramón, Paulo de Azevedo, Graciela M. Viñuales, Esterzilda de Azevedo, and Rodolfo Vallin, 1981, *La casa Cusqueña*. Universidad Nacional del Nordeste, Corrientes (?), Argentina.

Gutiérrez, Ramón, Cristina Esteras, and Alejandro Málaga, 1986a, *El Valle del Colca (Arequipa): Cinco Siglos de arquitectura y Urbanismo*. Libros de Hispanoamerica, Buenos Aires, Argentina.

Gutiérrez, Ramón, Carlos Pernaut, Graciela Viñuelas, Hernán Rodríguez Villegas, Rodolfo Vallin Magaña, Bertha Estela Benavides, Elizabeth Kuon Arce, and Jesús Lambarri, 1986b, *Arquitectura del Altiplano Peruano*. Libros de Hispanoamerica, Buenos Aires, Argentina.

Haggar, Reginald G., 1960, *The Concise Encyclopedia of Continental Pottery and Porcelain*. Andre Deutsch, London, UK.

Hall, Edward T., 1959, *The Silent Language*. Fawcett, Greenwich, CT.

Hall, Edward T., 1966, *The Hidden Dimension*. Anchor Books, Garden City, NY.

Harth-Terré, Emilio, and Márquez Abanto, 1962, Historia de la casa urbana virreinal en Lima. *Revista del Archivo Nacional del Perú* (Lima) 26(1):109-206.

Hillier, Bill, and Julienne Hanson, 1984, *The Social Logic of Space*. Cambridge University Press, New York.

Hobsbawm, E. J., and T. Ranger (Eds.), 1983, *The Invention of Tradition*. Cambridge University Press, Cambridge, UK.

Hodges, William H., and Eugene Lyon, 1995, A General History of Puerto Real. In *Puerto Real: The Archaeology of a Sixteenth-Century Spanish Town in Hispaniola*, edited by Kathleen Deagan, pp. 83-114. University Press of Florida, Gainesville.

Holm, Olaf, 1970, La Cerámica Colonial del Ecuador. *Boletín de la Academia Nacional de Historia* (Quito) 116:265-283.

Howard, David, and John Ayers, 1978, *China for the West: Chinese Porcelain and Other Decorative Arts for Export Illustrated from the Mottahedeh Collection*. Sotheby Parke Bernet, New York.

Hugh-Jones, Christine, 1977, *From the Milk River: Spatial and Temporal Processes in Northwest Amazonia*. Cambridge University Press, Cambridge, UK.

Hurst Thomas, David (Ed.), 1989, *Columbian Consequences*, Vol. 1: *Archaeological and Historical Perspectives on the Spanish Borderlands West*. Smithsonian Institution Press, Washington, DC.

Hurst Thomas, David (Ed.), 1990, *Columbian Consequences*, Vol. 2: *Archaeological and Historical Perspectives on the Spanish Borderlands East*. Smithsonian Institution Press, Washington, DC.

Hurst Thomas, David (Ed.), 1991, *Columbian Consequences*, Vol. 3: *The Spanish Borderlands in Pan-American Perspective*. Smithsonian Institution Press, Washington, DC.

Hyslop, John, 1990, *Inka Settlement Planning*. University of Texas Press, Austin.

Idrovo Urigüen, Jaime, 1984, *Prospection archeologique de la vallée de Cuenca, Ecuador (Secteur Sud; ou l'emplacement de la ville Inca de Tomebamba)*. 2 vols. Ph.D. disser-

220                                                            References

tation, Université de Paris I, Panteon Sorbonne, Paris, France.
Idrovo Urigüen, Jaime, 1986, Tomebamba: primera fase de conquista en Los Andes septentrionales. *Revista del Archivo Nacional de Historia, Sección del Azuay* (Cuenca) 6:49-70.
Idrovo Urigüen, Jaime, 1990, Siglos XVI y XVII: la desarticulación del mundo andino y sus efectos en al alfarería indígena del austro ecuatoriano. In *Cerámica colonial y vida cotidiana*, edited by Jaime Idrovo Urigüen and Alexandra Kennedy Troya, pp. 21-38. Fundación Paul Rivet, Cuenca, Ecuador.
Isbell, Billie Jean, 1978, *To Defend Ourselves: Ecology and Ritual in an Andean Village.* Waveland Press, Prospect Heights, IL.
Jácome, Nicanor, 1983, Economía y Sociedad en el siglo XVI. In *Nueva Historia del Ecuador*, vol. 3, edited by Enrique Ayala Mora, pp. 123-160. Corporación Editora Nacional, Quito.
James, Stephen R., 1988, A Reassessment of Chronological and Typological Framework of the Spanish Olive Jar. *Historical Archaeology* 22(1):43-66.
Jamieson, Ross W., 1996, *The Domestic Architecture and Material Culture of Colonial Cuenca, Ecuador, A.D. 1600-1800.* Ph.D. dissertation, Department of Archaeology, University of Calgary, Calgary, Canada.
Jiménez de la Espada, Marcos, 1965, *Relaciones Geográficas de Indias: Perú.* 3 vols. Biblioteca de Autores Españoles, Madrid, Spain.
Johnson, Matthew, 1996, *An Archaeology of Capitalism.* Blackwell, Oxford, UK.
Jones, Olive, and Catherine Sullivan, 1989, *The Parks Canada Glass Glossary.* Revised ed., Canadian Parks Service, Ottawa.
Juan, Jorge, and Antonio de Ulloa, 1978 [1748], *Relación Histórica del viaje a la América Meridional*, Vol. 1, edited by Jose P. Merino Navarro and Miguel M. Rodriguez San Vicente. Fundación Universitaria Española, Madrid, Spain.
King, Julia, 1984, Ceramic Variability in 17th Century St. Augustine, Florida. *Historical Archaeology* 18(2):75-82.
Kniffen, Fred B., 1965, Folk Housing: Key to Diffusion. *Annals of the Association of American Geographers* 55 (4):549-577.
Kovel, Ralph, and Terry Kovel, 1986, *Kovel's New Dictionary of Marks.* Crown Publishers, New York.
Kubler, George, 1948, *Mexican Architecture of the 16th Century.* New Haven, CT.
Kubler, George, and Martin Soria, 1959, *Art and Architecture in Spain and Portugal and Their American Dominions, 1500 to 1800.* Penguin Books, Baltimore, MD.
Lagiglia, Humberto, 1983a, Arqueología e Historia del Fuerte de San Rafael del Diamante. In *Presencia hispánica en la Arqueología argentina*, Vol. 1, edited by Eldo Serafín Morresi and Ramón Gutiérrez, pp. 89-190. Universidad Nacional del Nordeste, Resistencia, Argentina.
Lagiglia, Humberto, 1983b, Primeros Contactos hispano-indígenas en Mendoza. In *Presencia hispánica en la Arqueología argentina*, Vol. 1, edited by Eldo Serafín Morresi and Ramón Gutiérrez, pp. 191-201. Universidad Nacional del Nordeste, Resistencia, Argentina.
Landázuri Camacho, Carlos, 1983, De las Guerras Civiles a la Insurrección de las Alcabalas. In *Nueva Historia del Ecuador*, Vol. 3, edited by Enrique Ayala Mora, pp. 161-210. Corporación Editora Nacional, Quito.
Lavrin, Asunción, 1994, Lo femenino: Women in Colonial Historical Source. In *Coded Encounters: Writing, Gender and Ethnicity in Colonial Latin America*, edited by Francisoc Javier Cevallos-Candau, Jeffrey A. Cole, Nina M. Scott, and Nicomedes Suárez-Araúz, pp. 153-176. University of Massachusetts Press, Amherst.

Lavrin, Asunción, and Edith Couturier, 1979, Dowries and Wills: A View of Women's Socioeconomic Role in Colonial Guadalajara and Puebla, 1640–1790. *Hispanic American Historical Review* 59(2):280–304.

Lawrence, Denise L., and Setha M. Low, 1990, The Built Environment and Spatial Form. *Annual Review of Anthropology* 19:453–505.

Lefebvre, Henri, 1991, *The Production of Space*. Translated by Donald Nicholson-Smith. Blackwell, Oxford, UK.

León, Luis A., 1983, *Compilacion de Cronicas, Relatos y Descripciones de Cuenca y su Provincia*. 3 vols. Banco Central del Ecuador, Cuenca, Ecuador.

León Borja, Dora, and Ádám Szászdi Nagy, 1964, El Comercio del Cacao de Guayaquil. *Revista de Historia de América* 57–58:1–50.

Leone, Mark P., 1984, Interpreting Ideology in Historical Archaeology: Using the Rules of Perspective in the William Paca Garden in Annapolis, MD. In *Ideology, Power and Prehistory*, edited by Daniel Miller and Christopher Tilley, pp. 25–36. Cambridge University Press, Cambridge, UK.

Leone, Mark P., 1987, Rule by Ostentation: The Relationship between Space and Sight in Eighteenth-Century Landscape Architecture in Maryland. In *Method and Theory for Activity Area Research*, edited by Susan Kent, pp. 605–632. Columbia University Press, New York.

Leone, Mark P., and Parker B. Potter, Jr. (Eds.), 1988, *The Recovery of Meaning: Historical Archaeology in the Eastern United States*. Smithsonian Institution Press, Washington, DC.

Levenson, Jay A. (Ed.), 1991, *Circa 1492: Art in the Age of Exploration*. National Gallery of Art, Washington, DC.

Lévi-Strauss, Claude, 1963, *Structural Anthropology*. Translated by C. Jacobson. Doubleday Anchor Books, Garden City, NJ.

Lister, Florence C., and Robert H. Lister, 1974, Maiolica in Colonial Spanish America. *Historical Archaeology* 8:17–52.

Lister, Florence C., and Robert H. Lister, 1976, *A Descriptive Dictionary for 500 Years of Spanish-Tradition Ceramics (13th Through 18th Centuries)*. Special Publication, No. 1, Society for Historical Archaeology.

Lister, Florence C., and Robert H. Lister, 1987, *Andalusian Ceramics in Spain and New Spain: A Cultural Register from the Third Century B.C. to 1700*. University of Arizona Press, Tucson.

Litto, Gertrude, 1976, *South American Folk Pottery*. Watson-Guptill Publications, New York.

Lockhart, James, 1994 [1968], *Spanish Peru, 1532–1560: A Social History*. 2nd ed. University of Wisconsin Press, Madison.

Long, George A., 1964, Excavations at Panama Vieja. *Florida Anthropologist* 17 (2):104–109.

Low, Setha M., 1993, Cultural Meaning of the Plaza: The History of the Spanish-American Gridplan-Plaza Urban Design. In *The Cultural Meaning of Urban Space*, edited by Robert Rotenburg and Gary McDonogh, pp. 75–93. Bergin and Garvey, Westport, CT.

Low, Setha M., 1995, Indigenous Architecture and the Spanish American Plaza in Mesoamerica and the Caribbean. *American Anthropologist* 97(4):748–762.

Lueger, Richard, 1981, Ceramics from Yuquot, British Columbia. *History and Archaeology* 44:103–178. Parks Canada, Ottawa, Canada.

Luna Tamayo, Milton, 1987, Estado: regionalización y lucha política del Ecuador, 1800–1869. *Revista del Archivo Nacional de Historia, Sección del Azuay* (Cuenca) 7:105–130.

Lynch, John, 1986 [1973], *The Spanish-American Revolutions, 1806-1828.* Norton, New York.

MacCormack, Sabine, 1985, "The Heart Has Its Reasons": Predicaments of Missionary Christianity in Early Colonial Peru. *Hispanic American Historical Review* 65:443-466.

MacCormack, Sabine, 1991, *Religion in the Andes: Vision and Imagination in Early Colonial Peru.* Princeton University Press, Princeton, NJ.

MacLeod, Murdo J., 1984, Spain and America: The Atlantic Trade, 1492-1720. In *The Cambridge History of Latin America,* Vol. I, edited by Leslie Bethell, pp. 341-388. Cambridge University Press, Cambridge, UK.

Mahfouz, Afaf, and Ismail Serageldin, 1990, Women and Space in Muslim Societies. In *Expressions of Islam in Buildings,* edited by Hayat Salam, pp. 79-107. Aga Khan Trust for Culture, Jakarta, İndonesia.

Majewski, Teresita, and Michael J. O'Brien, 1987, The Use and Misuse of Nineteenth-Century English and American Ceramics in Archaeological Analysis. In *Advances in Archaeological Method and Theory,* Vol. 11, edited by Michael B. Schiffer, pp. 97-209. Academic Press, New York.

Manucy, Albert, 1978, *The Houses of St. Augustine, 1565-1821.* University Press of Florida, Gainesville.

Margolies, Luise, 1979, The Peasant Farmhouse: Continuity and Change in the Venezuelan Andes. *Actes du XLIIᴱ Congrès International des Américanistes (Paris)* 10:207-225.

Marken, Mitchell W., 1994, *Pottery from Spanish Shipwrecks, 1500-1800.* University Press of Florida, Gainesville.

Markman, Sidney David, 1966, *Colonial Architecture of Antigua Guatemala.*

Markman, Sidney David, 1979, Los estilos arquitectonicos y el paisaje urbano de Cuenca actual: Problemas de conservación de forma y de función. Submitted to Dr. Pedro Cordova, *alcalde* of Cuenca, July 6, 1979. Manuscript on file, Instituto Naciónal de Patrimonio Cultural, Cuenca, Ecuador.

Markman, Sidney David, 1984, *Architecture and Urbanization in Colonial Chiapas, Mexico.* American Philosophical Society, Philadelphia, PA.

Markus, Thomas A., 1993, *Buildings and Power: Freedom and Control in the Origin of Modern Building Types.* Routledge, London.

Marrinan, Rochelle, 1985, The Archaeology of the Spanish Missions of Florida: 1565-1704. In *Indians, Colonists, and Slaves,* edited by K. Johnson, J. Leader, and R. Wilson, pp. 241-252. Florida Journal of Anthropology Special Publication No. 4, Gainesville, FL.

Martínez Borrero, Juan, 1983, *La pintura popular del Carmen: identidad y cultura en el siglo XVIII.* Centro Interamericano de artesanías y artes populares, Cuenca, Ecuador.

Matienzo, Juan de, 1967 [1567], *Gobierno del Perú,* edited by Guillermo Lohmann Villena. L'Institut Français d'Études Andines, Paris, France and Lima, Peru.

McEwan, Bonnie G., 1988, *An Archaeological Perspective of Sixteenth Century Spanish Life in the Old World and the Americas.* Ph.D. dissertation, University of Florida, Gainesville. University Microfilms, Ann Arbor, Michigan.

McEwan, Bonnie G., 1991, The Archaeology of Women in the Spanish New World. *Historical Archaeology* 25(4):33-41.

McEwan, Bonnie G., 1992, The Role of Ceramics in Spain and Spanish America During the 16th Century. *Historical Archaeology* 26(1):92-108.

McEwan, Bonnie G., 1995, Spanish Precedents and Domestic Life at Puerto Real: The Archaeology of Two Spanish Homesites. In *Puerto Real: The Archaeology of a Six-*

*teenth-Century Spanish Town in Hispaniola,* edited by Kathleen Deagan, pp. 197–229. University Press of Florida, Gainesville.

McGuire, Randall H., 1992, *A Marxist Archaeology.* Academic Press, San Diego, CA.

McGuire, Randall H., and Robert Paynter (Eds.), 1991, *The Archaeology of Inequality.* Blackwell, Oxford, UK.

McNally, Paul, 1982, *Table Glass in Canada, 1700–1850.* History and Archaeology, Vol. 60, Parks Canada, Ottawa, Canada.

Menzel, Dorothy, and Francis A. Riddell, 1986, *Archaeological Investigations at Tambo Viejo, Acari Valley, Peru, 1954.* California Institute for Peruvian Studies, Sacramento, CA.

Merisalde y Santiesteban, Joaquín, 1992 [1765], Relación Histórica, Política, y Moral de la ciudad de Cuenca. Población y hermosura de su provincia. In *Relaciones Histórico-Geográficas de la Audiencia de Quito, Tomo II.,* edited by Pilar Ponce Leiva, pp. 369–412. Consejo Superior de Estudios Historicos, Madrid, Spain.

Mesa, José de, 1979, Arquitectura civil del Cuzco. La casa: evolución de tipologías y elementos. *Actes du XLII$^E$ Congrès International des Américanistes (Paris)* 10:249–272.

Miasta Gutierrez, Jaime, 1985, *Arqueología Historica en Huarochiri: Santo Domingo de Los Olleros, San José de Los Chorrillos y San Lorenzo de Quinti.* Universidad Nacional Mayor de San Marcos, Lima, Peru.

Miller, George L., 1980, Classification and Economic Scaling of 19th Century Ceramics. *Historical Archaeology* 14:1–40.

Miller, George L., and Catherine Sullivan, 1984, Machine-Made Glass Containers and the End of Production for Mouth-Blown Bottles. *Historical Archaeology* 18(2):83–96.

Minchom, Martin, 1989, La Economía Subterranea y el Mercado Urbano: Pulperas, "Indias Gateras" y "Recatones" del Quito Colonial (siglos XVI–XVII). In *Antropología del Ecuador,* edited by Segundo E. Moreno Yanez, pp. 197–209. Editores Abya-Yala, Quito, Ecuador.

Miño S., Lenin, n.d., Informe histórico preliminar sobre la Casa de la Hacienda: La Primavera. Manuscript on file, Instituto Naciónal de Patrimonio Cultural, Cuenca, Ecuador.

Montes de Oca, Vicente Pólit, 1983, Conquista del Perú, Quito y descubrimiento del río de las Amazonas. In *Nueva Historia del Ecuador,* vol. 3, edited by Enrique Ayala Mora, pp. 67–90. Corporación Editora Nacional, Quito.

Montufar y Fraso, Juan Pío, 1992 [1754], Razón que sobre el estado y gobernación política y militar de las provincias, ciudades y villas que contiene la jurisdicción de la Real Audiencia de Quito da . . . , In *Relaciones Histórico-Geográficas de la Audiencia de Quito, Tomo II.,* edited by Pilar Ponce Leiva, pp. 323–352. Consejo Superior de Estudios Historicos, Madrid, Spain.

Moore, Henrietta L., 1988, *Feminism and Anthropology.* Polity Press, Cambridge, UK.

Morgan, Lewis H., 1965 [1881], *Houses and House-Life of the American Aborigines.* University of Chicago Press, Chicago.

Morresi, Eldo Serafín, 1983a, Alternativa y camino válido para una presencia activa en la Investigación de Arqueología Histórica Argentina. In *Presencia hispánica en la Arqueología argentina,* Vol. 1, edited by Eldo Serafín Morresi and Ramón Gutiérrez, pp. 15–27. Universidad Nacional del Nordeste, Resistencia, Argentina.

Morresi, Eldo Serafín, 1983b, Muestrario de Material Arqueológico del Contacto Hispano-Indígena en le "Lugar Histórico" de Concepción del Bermejo. In *Presencia hispánica en la Arqueología argentina,* Vol. 1, edited by Eldo Serafín Morresi and Ramón Gutiérrez, pp. 393–426. Universidad Nacional del Nordeste, Resistencia, Argentina.

Morresi, Eldo Serafín, and Ramón Gutiérrez (Eds.), 1983 *Presencia hispánica en la Arqueología argentina*. 2 vols. Universidad Nacional del Nordeste, Resistencia, Argentina.

Moscoso C., Martha, 1989, Indígenas y ciudades en el siglo XVI. In *Las ciudades en la historia*, edited by Eduardo Kingman Garces, pp. 343-356. Centro de Investigaciones CIUDAD, Quito, Ecuador.

Municipio de Cuenca, n.d., *Plan de Desarrollo Urbano del Area Metropolitana de la Ciudad de Cuenca: Volumen XII, Diagnostico Definitivo, Aspectos Fisicos*. Municipio de Cuenca, Cuenca, Ecuador.

Muñoz Vega, Patricio, 1989, La arquitectura en la Provincia del Azuay. In *El Libro de Cuenca*, edited by Rigoberto Cordero y Leon, pp. 123-140. Editores y Publicistas, Cuenca, Ecuador.

Murra, John, 1963 [1944], The historic tribes of Ecuador. In *Handbook of South American Indians* Vol. 2: *The Andean Civilizations*, edited by Julian H. Steward, pp. 785-822. Cooper Square Publishers, New York.

Murra, John, 1972, El "control vertical" de un máximo de pisos ecológicos en la economía de las sociedades anidinas. In *Visita de la Provincia de Huánuco, por Inigo Ortiz de Zuniga*, Vol 2, pp. 427-476. Universidad Hermilio Valdizan, Huanuco, Peru.

Myers, Thomas P., 1990, *Sarayacu: Ethnohistorical and Archaeological Investigations of a Nineteenth-Century Franciscan Mission in the Peruvian Montaña*. University of Nebraska Press, Lincoln.

Nevett, Lisa, 1994, Separation or Seclusion? Towards an Archeaological Approach to Investigating Women in the Greek Household in the Fifth to Third Centuries B.C. In *Architecture and Order: Approaches to Social Space*, edited by Mike Parker Pearson and Colin Richards, pp. 98-112. Routledge, New York.

Newson, Linda, 1991, Old World Epidemics in Early Colonial Ecuador. In *"Secret Judgements of God": Old World Disease in Colonial Spanish America*, edited by Noble David Cook and W. George Lovell, pp. 84-112. University of Oklahoma Press, Norman.

Newson, Linda, 1995, *Life and Death in Early Colonial Ecuador*. University of Oklahoma Press, Norman.

Noël Hume, Ivor, 1970, *A Guide to Artifacts of Colonial America*. Alfred A. Knopf, New York.

Oberem, Udo, 1983, El período incaico en el Ecuador. In *Nueva Historia del Ecuador*, Vol. 2, edited by Enrique Ayala Mora, pp. 135-166. Corporación Editora Nacional, Quito.

Oberti R., Italo, 1983, La Casa de Mancio Sierra de Leguisamo y la arquitectonica Inca. Manuscript on file, Instituto Naciónal de Cultura, Lima, Peru.

Olin, Jacqueline S., Garman Harbottle, and Edward V. Sayre, 1978, Elemental Compositions of Spanish and Spanish-Colonial Majolica Ceramics in the Identification of Provenience. In *Archaeological Chemistry*, Vol. 2, edited by Giles F. Carter, pp. 200-229. American Chemical Society, Washington, DC.

Olsen, Stanley J., 1963, Dating Early Plain Buttons by Their Form. *American Antiquity* 28(4):551-554.

Pablos, Hernando, 1965 [1582], Relación que envió a mandar Su Magestad se hiziese desta ciudad de Cuenca y de toda su provincia. In *Relaciones Geográficas de Indias: Perú*, Vol. 2, edited by Marcos Jiménez de la Espada, pp. 265-270. Biblioteca de Autores Españoles, Madrid.

Palomeque, Silvia, 1980, Historia economica de Cuenca y sus relaciones regionales. *Revista del Archiva Nacional de Historica, Sección del Azuay* (Cuenca) 1:105-251.

Palomeque, Silvia, 1982, Historia Económica de Cuenca y de sus relaciones regionales. In *Ensayos sobre historia regional: la región centro sur*, edited by Claudio Cordero E., pp.

117-177. Instituto de Investigaciones Sociales de la Universidad de Cuenca, Cuenca, Ecuador.

Palomeque, Silvia, 1990, *Cuenca en el siglo XIX: La Articulación de una Región*. Ediciones Abya-Yala, Quito.

Paniagua Pérez, Jesús, 1989, *La plata labrada en la Audiencia de Quito (la provincia del Azuay), Siglos XVI-XIX*. Universidad de León, León, Spain.

Parker Pearson, Michael, and Colin Richards, 1994, Ordering the World: Perceptions of Architecture, Space and Time. In *Architecture and Order: Approaches to Social Space*, edited by Michael Parker Pearson and Colin Richards, pp. 1-37. Routledge, New York.

Parry, John H., and Robert G. Keith, 1984, *New Iberian World: A Documentary History of the Discovery and Settlement of Latin America to the Early Seventeenth Century*. Vol. 4: *The Andes*. Times Books, New York.

Parsons, E. C., 1933, *Mitla: Town of the Souls*. University of Chicago Press, Chicago.

Paynter, Robert, and Randall H. McGuire, 1991, The Archaeology of Inequality: Material Culture, Domination and Resistance. In *The Archaeology of Inequality*, edited by Randall H. McGuire and Robert Paynter, pp. 1-27. Blackwell, Oxford, UK.

Paz Flores, Percy, 1983, Trabajos de Arqueología en la casa del Almirante, Cuzco. Manuscript on file, Instituto Naciónal de Cultura, Lima, Peru.

Perry, Mary Elizabeth, 1990, *Gender and Disorder in Early Modern Seville*. Princeton University Press, Princeton, NJ.

Phelan, John Leddy, 1967, *The Kingdom of Quito in the Seventeenth Century: Bureaucratic Politics in the Spanish Empire*. University of Wisconsin Press, Madison.

Pizarro, Pedro, 1986 [1571], *Relación del descubrimiento y conquista de los reinos del Perú*. 2nd ed. Edited by Guillermo Lohmann Villena. Pontificia Universidad Católica del Perú, Lima, Peru.

Poloni, Jacques, 1992, Achats et ventes de terres par les Indiens de Cuenca au XVII[E] siècle: éléments de conjoncture économique et de stratification sociale. *Bull. Inst. fr. études andines* 21(1):279-310.

Porro, Nelly R., Juana E. Artiz, and María M. Rospide, 1982, *Aspectos de la vida cotidiana en el Buenos Aires virreinal*. Universidad de Buenos Aires, Buenos Aires, Argentina.

Porro Girardi, Nelly R., 1995, Arqueología e historia. Páginas sobre Hispanoamérica colonial. *Sociedad y cultura* (PRHISCO, Buenos Aires) 2:81-97.

Pounds, Norman J. G., 1989, *Hearth and Home: A History of Material Culture*. Indiana University Press, Bloomington.

Powers, Karen, 1990, Indian Migrations in the *Audiencia* of Quito: Crown Manipulation and Local Co-optation. In *Migration in Colonial Spanish America*, edited by David J. Robinson, pp. 313-323. Cambridge University Press, New York.

Powers, Karen, 1995, *Andean Journeys: Migration, Ethnogenesis, and the State in Colonial Quito*. University of New Mexico Press, Albuquerque.

Prakash, Gyan, 1995, Introduction: After Colonialism. In *After Colonialism: Imperial Histories and Postcolonial Displacements*, edited by Gyan Prakash, pp. 3-17. Princeton University Press, Princeton, NJ.

Ranum, Orest, 1989, The Refuges of Intimacy. In *A History of Private Life*, Vol. 3: *Passions of the Renaissance*, edited by Roger Chartier, pp. 207-263. Belknap Press, Cambridge, MA.

Rabinow, Paul, 1989, *French Modern*. MIT Press, Cambridge, MA.

Ramos, Gabriela, 1989, Las manufacturas en el Perú colonial: 100 abrajes de vidrios en los siglos XVII y XVIII. *Historica* (Lima) 13(1):67-106.

Rapoport, A., 1969, *House Form and Culture*. Prentice-Hall, Englewood Cliffs, NJ.

Rappaport, Joanne, 1990a, Cultura material a lo largo de la frontera septentrional Inca: los Pastos y sus testamentos. *Revista de Antropología y Arqueología* (Universidad de los Andes, Bogotá) 6(2):11–25.

Rappaport, Joanne, 1990b *The Politics of Memory: Native Historical Interpretation in the Colombian Andes.* Cambridge University Press, Cambridge, UK.

Redfield, Robert, 1929, The Material Culture of Spanish-Indian Mexico. *American Anthropologist* 31:602–618.

Redfield, Robert, Ralph Linton, and Melville J. Herskovitz, 1936, A Memorandum for the Study of Acculturation. *American Anthropologist* 38:149–152.

Redfield, Robert, and M. S. Singer, 1954, The Cultural Role of Cities. *Economic Development and Cultural Change* 3:53–73.

Reitz, Elizabeth J., and Stephen J. Cumbaa, 1983, Diet and Foodways of Eighteenth-Century Spanish St. Augustine. In *Spanish St. Augustine: The Archaeology of a Colonial Creole Community,* edited by Kathleen Deagan, pp. 151–185. Academic Press, New York.

Reitz, Elizabeth J., and Bonnie G. McEwan, 1995, Animals, Environment, and the Spanish Diet at Puerto Real. In *Puerto Real: The Archaeology of a Sixteenth-Century Spanish Town in Hispaniola,* edited by Kathleen Deagan, pp. 287–334. University Press of Florida, Gainesville.

Reitz, Elizabeth J., and C. Margaret Scarry, 1985, *Reconstructing Historic Subsistence With an Example from Sixteenth-Century Spanish Florida.* Society for Historical Archaeology Special Publication Series, No. 3. Society for Historical Archaeology.

Reps, John, 1965, *The Making of Urban America.* Princeton University Press, Princeton, NJ.

Requena y Herrera, Francisco, 1992 [1774], Descripción Histórica y Geográfica de la Provincia de Guayaquil, en el Virreinato de Santa Fe. In *Relaciones Histórico-Geográficas de la Audiencia de Quito, Tomo II.,* edited by Pilar Ponce Leiva, pp. 502–651. Consejo Superior de Estudios Historicos, Madrid, Spain.

Rice, Prudence M., 1988, *Pottery Analysis: A Sourcebook.* University of Chicago Press, Chicago.

Rice, Prudence M., 1994, The Kilns of Moquegua, Peru. *Journal of Field Archaeology* 21(3):325–344.

Rice, Prudence M., and Donna L. Ruhl, 1989, Archaeological Survey of the Moquegua Bodegas. In *Ecology, Settlement, and History in the Osmore Drainage, Peru,* edited by Don S. Rice, Charles Stanish, and Phillip R. Scarr, pp. 479–501. BAR International Series No. 545 (ii), Oxford, UK.

Rice, Prudence M., and Greg C. Smith, 1989, The Spanish Colonial Wine Industry of Moquegua, Peru. *Historical Archaeology* 23(2):41–49.

Rice, Prudence M., and Sara L. Van Beck, 1993, The Spanish Colonial Kiln Tradition of Moquegua, Peru. *Historical Archaeology* 27:65–81.

Richardson, Miles, 1982, Being-in-the-market versus Being-in-the-plaza: Material Culture and the Construction of Social Reality in Spanish America. *American Ethnologist* 9:421–436.

Rippy, J. Fred, 1944, *Latin America and the Industrial Age.* Putnam, New York.

Ronan, Charles E., 1978, *Francisco Javier Clavijero, S.J. (1731–1787), Figure of the Mexican Enlightenment: His Life and Works.* Loyola University Press, Chicago.

Roseberry, William, 1989, *Anthropologies and Histories: Essays in Culture, History and Political Economy.* Rutgers University Press, New Brunswick, NJ.

Rostworowski de Diez Canseco, María, 1988, *Historia del Tahuantinsuyu.* Instituto de Estudios Peruanos, Lima, Peru.

Rousseau, A., 1989, *Excavaciones arqueológicas en el Hospital San Juan de Dios, Quito.* Informe Técnico, Instituto Ecuatoriano de Obras Sanitarias, Quito, Ecuador.

Rousseau, A., 1990, *Proyecto Arqueológico Plaza Santo Domingo.* Folleto Informativo: Investigación Arqueológica. I. Municipio de Quito, Quito, Ecuador.

Rovira, Beatriz E., 1984, La cerámica histórica en la Ciudad de Panamá: Tres contextos estratigráficos. In *Recent Developments in Isthmian Archaeology,* edited by Frederick W. Lange, pp. 283–315. BAR International Series 212, Oxford, UK.

Rowe, John Howland, 1945, Absolute Chronology in the Andean Area. *American Antiquity* 10:265–284.

Rowe, John Howland, 1946, Inca Culture at the Time of the Spanish Conquest. In *Handbook of South American Indians,* Vol. 2: *The Andean Civilizations,* edited by Julian H. Steward, pp. 183–330. Bureau of American Ethnology, Bulletin 143, Smithsonian Institution, Washington, DC.

Rydén, Stig, 1947, *Archaeological Researches in the Highlands of Bolivia.* Elanders Boktryckeri Aktiebolog, Göteborg, Sweden.

Safford, Frank, 1987, Politics, Ideology and Society. In *Spanish America after Independence, c. 1820–c. 1870,* edited by Leslie Bethell, pp. 48–122. Cambridge University Press, Cambridge, UK.

Salomon, Frank, 1983 Crisis y transformación de la sociedad aborigen invadida (1528–1573). *In Nueva Historia del Ecuador,* vol. 3, edited by Enrique Ayala Mora, pp. 91–122. Corporación Editora Nacional, Quito.

Salomon, Frank, 1986a, Vertical Politics on the Inka Frontier. In *Anthropological History of Andean Polities,* edited by John V. Murra, Nathan Wachtel, and Jacques Revel, pp. 89–117. Cambridge University Press, New York.

Salomon, Frank, 1986b, *Native Lords of Quito in the Age of the Incas: The Political Economy of North Andean chiefdoms.* Cambridge University Press, Cambridge, UK.

Salomon, Frank, 1988, Indian Women of Early Colonial Quito as Seen Through Their Testaments. *The Americas* 44 (3):325–341.

Sarmiento de Gamboa, Pedro, 1947 [1572], *Historia de los Incas.* 3rd ed. Edited by Angel Rosenblat, Emecé Editores, Buenos Aires, Argentina.

Schaedel, Richard P., 1992, The Archaeology of the Spanish Colonial Experience in South America. *Antiquity* 66 (250):217–242.

Sabastián, Santiago, 1979, Dos programs simbólicos del siglo XVII on Hispanoamérica. *Actes du XLIIE congrès International des Américanistes* (Paris) 10:37–47.

Service, Elman, 1975, *Origins of the State and Civilization.* Norton), New York.

Shackel, Paul A., 1992, Probate Inventories in Historical Archaeology: A Review and Alternatives. In *Text-Aided Archaeology,* edited by Barbara J. Little, pp. 205–215. CRC Press, Boca Raton, FL.

Shammas, Carole, 1990, *The Pre-Industrial Consumer in England and America.* Clarendon Press, Oxford, UK.

Silverblatt, Irene, 1995, Becoming Indian in the Central Andes of Seventeenth-Century Peru. In *After Colonialism: Imperial Histories and Postcolonial Displacements,* edited by Gyan Prakash, pp. 279–298. Princeton University Press, Princeton, NJ.

Skar, Sarah, 1981, Andean Women and the Concept of Space/Time. In *Women and Space: Ground Rules and Social Maps,* edited by Shirley Ardener, pp. 35–49. Croom Helm, London.

Smith, Greg C., 1991, *Heard It through the Grapevine: Andean and European Contributions to Spanish Colonial Culture and Viticulture in Moquegua, Peru.* Ph.D. dissertation, University of Florida. University Microfilms, Ann Arbor, Michigan.

Smith, Greg C., 1995, Indians and Africans at Puerto Real: The Ceramic Evidence. In

*Puerto Real: The Archaeology of a Sixteenth-Century Spanish Town in Hispaniola*, edited by Kathleen Deagan, pp. 335–374. University Press of Florida, Gainesville.

South, Stanley, 1977, *Method and Theory in Historical Archaeology*. Academic Press, New York.

South, Stanley, 1988, Santa Elena: Threshold of Conquest. In *The Recovery of Meaning: Historical Archaeology in the Eastern United States*, edited by Mark P. Leone and Parker B. Potter Jr., pp. 27–71. Smithsonian Institution Press, Washington, DC.

Stanish, Charles, and Don S. Rice, 1989, The Osmore Drainage, Peru: An Introduction to the Work of the Programa Contisuyu. In *Ecology, Settlement, and History in the Osmore Drainage, Peru*, edited by Don S. Rice, Charles Stanish, and Phillip R. Scarr, pp. 1–14. BAR International Series, No 545 (i), Oxford, UK.

Stanislawski, Dan, 1946, The Origin and Spread of the Grid-Plan Town. *Geographical Review* 36 (1):105–120.

Stern, Steve J., 1982, *Peru's Indian Peoples and the Challenge of Spanish Conquest, Huamanga to 1640*. University of Wisconsin Press, Madison.

Stern, Steve J., 1988, Feudalism, Capitalism and the World-System in the Perspective of Latin America and the Caribbean. *American Historical Review* 93(4):829–872.

Stone, Gary W., 1988 [1977], Artifacts Are Not Enough. In *Documentary Archaeology in the New World*, edited by Mary C. Beaudry, pp. 68–77. Cambridge University Press, Cambridge, UK.

Téllez, Germán, and Ernesto Moure, 1982, Repertorio Formal de Arquitectura Doméstica: Cartagena de Indias, época Colonial. Corporación Nacional de Turismo, Bogotá, Colombia.

Terán, Paulina, 1989, *Arqueología Histórica en el Convento de San Francisco de Quito.* "Licenciada" thesis, Escuela Superior Politécnica del Litoral, Guayaquil, Ecuador.

Thébert, Yvon, 1987, Private Life and Domestic Architecture in Roman Africa. In *A History of Private Life: Vol. 1, From Pagan Rome to Byzantium*, edited by Paul Veyne, pp. 313–410. Harvard University Press, Cambridge, MA.

Thomas, Keith, 1971, *Religion and the Decline of Magic: Studies in popular beliefs in sixteenth- and seventeenth-century England.* Weidenfeld and Nicolson, London.

Torre Revello, José, 1945, La casa y el mobiliario en el Buenos Aires colonial. *Revista de la Universidad de Buenos Aires* 3 (4):285–300.

Trimborn, Hermann, 1981, *Sama.* Haus Völker und Kulturen, Anthropos-Institut, Collectanea Instituti Anthropos, Vol. 25, Bonn (?), Germany.

Truhan, Deborah L., 1991, "Mi ultimada y postrimera boluntad," Trayectorias de tres mujeres Andinas: Cuenca, 1599–1610. *Historica* 15(1):121–155.

Tschopik, Harry, 1950, An Andean Ceramic Tradition in Historical Perspective. *American Antiquity* 15:196–218.

Turner, Victor, 1974, *Dramas, Fields, and Metaphors: Symbolic Action in Human Society.* Cornell University Press, Ithaca, NY.

Uhle, Max, 1983 [1923], Las Ruinas de Tomebamba. In *Compilación de Crónicas, Relatos y Descripciones de Cuenca y su Provincia*, Vol. 1, edited by Luis A. León, pp. 157–197. Banco Central del Ecuador, Cuenca, Ecuador.

Upton, Dell, and John Michael Vlach, 1986, *Common Places: Readings in American Vernacular Architecture.* University of Georgia Press, Athens.

Van Buren, Mary, 1993, *Community and Empire in Southern Peru: The Site of Torata Alta under Spanish Rule.* Ph.D. dissertation, Department of Anthropology, University of Arizona. University Microfilms, Ann Arbor, Michigan.

Van Buren, Mary, 1996, Rethinking the Vertical Archipelago: Ethnicity, Exchange and History in the South Central Andes. *American Anthropologist* 98 (2):338–351.

Van Buren, Mary, 1996, Preliminary Investigation of Colonial Potosí, Bolivia. Paper Presented at the 29th Annual Meeting, Society for Historical Archaeology, Cincinnati, OH.

Van Buren, Mary, Peter Burgi, and Prudence Rice, 1993, Torata Alta: A Late Highland Settlement in the Osmore Drainage. In *Domestic Architecture, Ethnicity and Complementarity in the South Central Andes*, edited by M. Aldenderfer, pp. 136-146. University of Iowa Press, Iowa City.

Vansina, Jan, 1985, *Oral Tradition as History*. University of Wisconsin Press, Madison.

Vaz, J. Eduardo, and Jose M. Cruxent, 1978, Majolica Pottery: Determination of Its Provenience Using Thermoluminescence. In *Advances in Andean Archaeology*, edited by David L. Browman, pp. 277-290. Mouton Publishers, The Hague, Netherlands.

Vázquez de Expinosa, Antonio, 1969 [1630], *Compendio y Descripción de las Indias Occidentales*. Edited by B. Velasco Bayón. Biblioteca de Autores Españoles, Atlas, Madrid, Spain.

Vega, Garcilaso de la, el Inca, 1966 [1609], *Royal Commentaries of the Incas and General History of Peru*, edited by Harold V. Livermore, University of Texas Press, Austin.

Vega Ugalde, Silvia, 1986, Cuenca en los movimientos independentistas. *Revista del Archivo Nacional de Historia, Sección del Azuay* (Cuenca) 6:9-48.

Velasco, Juan de, 1981 [1789], *Historia del Reino de Quito en la América Meridional*, edited by Alfredo Pareja Diezcanseco. Biblioteca Ayacucho, Caracas, Venezuela.

Veyne, Paul, 1987, The Roman Empire. In *A History of Private Life: Vol. 1, From Pagan Rome to Byzantium*, edited by Paul Veyne, pp. 5-234. Harvard University Press, Cambridge, MA.

Vicente, Marta V., 1996, Images and Realities of Work: Women and Guilds in Early Modern Barcelona. In *Spanish Women in the Golden Age: Images and Realities*, edited by Magdalena S. Sánchez and Alain Saint-Saëns, pp. 127-139. Greenwood Press, Westport, CT.

Villasante, Salazar de, 1965 [1573], Relación general de las poblaciones españolas del Perú. In *Relaciones Geográficas de Indias: Perú*, Vol. 1, edited by Marcos Jiménez de la Espada, pp. 121-146. Biblioteca de Autores Españoles, Madrid.

Villavicencio, Manuel, 1858, *Geografía de la república del Ecuador.* R. Craighead, New York.

Vintimilla, María A., 1981, Las formas de resistencia campesina en la sierra sur del Ecuador (Gran Colombia-primeros años de la República). *Revista del IDIS* (Instituto de Investigaciones Sociales).

Violich, Francis, 1962, Evolution of the Spanish City: Issues Basic to Planning Today. *Journal of the American Institute of Planners* 28 (3):170-179.

Vogt, Evon Z., 1969, Structural and conceptual replication in Zinacantan culture. *American Anthropologist* 67(2):342-353.

Wallerstein, Immanuel, 1979, *The Capitalist World Economy*. Cambridge University Press, Cambridge, UK.

Weber, Max, 1964, *The Theory of Social and Economic Organization.* Free Press, New York.

Whymper, Edward, 1892, *Travels amongst the Great Andes of the Equator.* London.

Wilson, Fiona, 1984, Marriage, Property and the Position of Women in the Peruvian Central Andes. In *Kinship Ideology and Practice in Latin America*, edited by Raymond T. Smith, pp. 297-325. University of North Carolina Press, Chapel Hill.

Wolf, Eric, 1982, *Europe and the People without History.* University of California Press, Berkeley.

Yentsch, Anne, 1991, The Symbolic Divisions of Pottery: Sex-Related Attributes of English and Anglo-American Household Pots. In *The Archaeology of Inequality*, edited by Randall H. McGuire and Robert Paynter, pp. 192-230. Blackwell, Cambridge, MA.

# Index